The Next Generation

The Next Generation

Lives of
Third World Children

Judith Ennew
Brian Milne

New Society Publishers

Philadelphia, PA   Santa Cruz, CA

The Next Generation was published simultaneously in the United Kingdom by
Zed Books, Ltd. 57 Caledonian Road, London N1 9BU, UK and in the United
States of America by New Society Publishers. 4527 Springfield Avenue,
Philadelphia, PA 19143.

Cover design by Andrew Corbett.
Cover photograph © Mark Edwards.
Typeset by EMS Photosetters, Rochford, Essex, UK.
Printed in the United States of America on partially recycled paper by
BookCrafters, Fredericksburg, VA.

To order directly from the publisher, add $1.75 for the first copy, $.50 for each
additional. Send check or money order to:
New Society Publishers
PO Box 582
Santa Cruz, CA 95061

New Society Publishers is a project of the New Society Educational Foundation,
a nonprofit, tax-exempt, public foundation. Opinions expressed in this book do
not necessarily represent positions of the New Society Educational Foundation.

Contents

Tables

Maps

A map with demographic and social indicators accompanies each case study

Preface

It is often stated that most people in the Western world can tell you exactly what they were doing when they heard that John Kennedy had been assassinated. Likewise most people under 50 can tell you how they first heard of the death of John Lennon. It is our guess that the images we now have of Third World children also have common starting points. International communications systems help to produce what might be called communal history, and the fact that images of events appear within our own homes, at the centre of our personal lives, gives them an acutely intimate flavour. Kennedy and Lennon died in *our* living rooms. So did the Biafra Babies.

We are all now accustomed to viewing sickly, starving children expiring, over and over again as films are repeated in newscast after newscast. But, looking back to the time before Biafra, there seems to have been a curious innocence about Western views of the Third World. It was an innocence built on ignorance, a naivety based on school-books with pictures of Children from Other Lands: smiling in different costumes and settings, but smiling none the less the eternal happiness of 'childhood'. Of course we also heard that some poor children were starving, often as part of an injunction to eat up our supper. But we didn't *see* them starve, and if told that starving children would be grateful for our hated carrots we were likely to answer 'they can have them'.

The main point about the images of Biafran children which filled news broadcasts at the end of 1967 was that they brought home to us the impotence of wanting them to have the carrots, or any other food we felt able to offer. The brutal Nigerian civil war dragged on for four years, but the media gave it special treatment at the end of that year. There was regular and shocking news of Biafran children starving and dying while we prepared to enjoy our own Christmas feast. What made this particularly worthy of media attention and produced a special irony was that, although the religious significance is now muted, Christmas remains a social celebration of childhood and birth. The impulse was to invite these children to share the feast. The reality was that in most cases this was impossible, although some rescue programmes did airlift children to the West, away from the war zones. A further irony for people who were young in the 1960s was that the summer was spent in the celebration of a new age, of love and flowers, brotherhood and peace. Self-consciously wearing beads and blossoms, humming the tunes that symbolized freedom from old ideas and restrictions, we of the sixties' generation believed that love alone could build a better world. But if we had given more serious thought to the starving babies about whom we expressed such emotional concern, we should have been aware that the Age of Aquarius had dawned differently on other parts of the world.

It also dawned on other wars. Particularly important for 1960s idealism was the imperialist war in Vietnam, which joined Biafra in the communal imagery of our time. And there were children there also: orphaned urban children, abandoned victims of war. Once again the impulse was to rescue them, to bring them to the safety of the West. The airlifts from Vietnam were on a far larger scale than those from Biafra; adoptive homes were found for many children, in the USA, in Canada and Australia for example. But time has shown these publicized rescue operations to have been largely misconceived. Children found alone were not necessarily orphans. Problems arose years later when parents traced them to their adoptive homes in other countries. And the difficulties of cultural transition, even for quite small children, were often underrated.

These two images of Biafra and Vietnam seem to be the basis of our preconceptions about Third World children. In fact they first define the Third World itself as a place of danger from which people need to be rescued, a place of helplessness to which charity must be given, for which solutions must be sought. Within this danger zone children are victims: they starve, they are abandoned, they are powerless. It is their needs that are emphasized in Western media. We see them naked and thin, lacking shelter, food, health care, parents and childhood itself. These are potent images in the 1980s, but images which tell only half, or perhaps even less than half, of the truth. What is omitted from the narrative is knowledge of how the situation arose, of the ancient cultures to which these children are heirs, of the social background of the states in which they live. Lacking this knowledge we remain impotent, able to respond only through occasional limited acts of charity, unable to provide more than short-term palliative help, even in the face of worldwide acts of goodwill such as the response to Band Aid and Sport Aid.

Even those who stop watching the news and start trying to take direct action remain feeling impotent. Perhaps we can illustrate the frustrations best with an anecdote from our own experience in South America. We had returned there in 1986, just after the fund-raising efforts of Sport Aid, during which sponsored runners from many countries had collected money for children in Africa, and while the *USA Africa* long-playing record was still accumulating charity funds by worldwide sales. We found that *USA Africa* T-shirts were high fashion garments in the Peruvian capital of Lima. Unfortunately many of these were commercially produced by pirate companies, cashing in on the trend but having no connection with charity. Most of our time was spent in Lima's shanty towns, where shelter is poor, food limited and money scarce. But people in shanty towns are proud, they like to appear modern and Western and try to acquire prestigious goods like radios, televisions and Western clothes. It was not until we returned to England that we were able to discuss with each other the way we had felt when we met barefoot, hungry children, whose parents cannot afford to send them to school, wearing *USA Africa* T-shirts, which they knew were fashionable without knowing why, and which they were unable to wash because the water supply was deficient.

Sometimes when we are talking about children in the Third World, people ask us if there is really anything that can be done and suggest that the problem is too huge to be tackled realistically. Others are quicker to give solutions. The Third World now, they state, is in the same condition as Europe and North America during the nineteenth century. Modernization will solve the problem in time. Or population control is said to be the answer: these people are poor because they are irresponsibly having too many children. They need to be taught and controlled. We have even been told categorically that such natural disasters as flood and famine are nature's way of providing a solution to over-population. Like most people involved in development we have also heard the confident opinion that there is no point in providing money for aid charities because it 'all goes on administration' or 'you can't be sure it gets to the people who need it'. Yet these are not uncaring responses and the people saying such things are humanitarian and genuinely concerned about the situation.

The problem is that they know so little about it. There are so many misconceptions and preconceptions about Third World societies, particularly children, that we have sometimes been tempted to agree with the half-serious remark of a charity fundraiser that the best way to spend money given by the public would be to educate people in the West. If we unpack the taken-for-granted ideas that underlie the sort of statements we have just quoted, we find many other ideas about our own society which do not bear too close a scrutiny: ideas like 'childhood', 'health', 'aid' and the 'Third World' itself. So, in a sense, that is what this book is about. We want to unpack a few ideas and dispel a few misconceptions, about children in the Third World and, ultimately, about ourselves.

We are writing this as a very personal exploration of the reality behind popular images of the lives lived by Third World children. The book takes three approaches. First we look at ideas of childhood and the way they are constructed in Western ways of thinking about children in rich and poor nations. This leads us to look at what international bodies have to say about Children's Rights and at the multiple ways these are violated throughout the world. Finally we look at twelve countries in more detail. We have chosen the countries according to two criteria. One was that each case study should be interesting either because of a special problem experienced by its children or for a particular child-centred social policy. Thus we chose Brazil because of its street children and China for the one-child family policy. The second criterion was personal knowledge, based on our own experience or that of close friends, so that we could, as far as possible, use the stories of individual children, their words or drawings. In addition to the fact that statistics tend not to be child-centred, the voices of children themselves are very rarely heard in the clamour of opinions about what action should be taken in their best interests.

Our intention here is to try to redress the balance.

Thus, although this is a personal book, it would not have been possible without the ready co-operation of many other people. Among organizations to which we have had reason to be grateful over the years, the Save the Children Fund has been particularly helpful both in the United Kingdom and in the field and also through the Swedish (Radda Barnen) and Canadian (Cansave) branches of the Federation. We have had consistent help from UNICEF, in the United Kingdom, Geneva and New York. The African National Congress, Amnesty International, the Anti-Slavery Society, the Catholic Institute for International Relations, the Centre of Concern for Child Labour (Bangkok), Children in Development, Defence for Children International, the International Catholic Child Bureau, MANTHOC (Lima), Minority Rights Group, TIPACOM (Lima) and the Tata Institute (Bombay) have been supportive and helpful. Among the individuals who have made the book possible we are especially grateful to Tara Ali Baig, Neera Burra, Nigel Cantwell, Alec Fyfe, Leah Levin, Usha Naidu, Sue Reading, Pamela Reynolds, Jane Ross, Beatriz Rojas, Danny de Silva and Stefan Vanistendael. Rosie sat patiently at our feet but made sure we got air and exercise whenever she needed a walk. Ginny Morrow supplied us with cheer, coffee, research assistance and a goodly part of the section on India, but refused to take credit as a third author. Perhaps she didn't want to take any of the responsibility for the many mistakes we have undoubtedly made. But as they were made in good faith, we hope they will be forgiven.

One final point concerns the style in which we have chosen to write. We tried to think how 'Third World' children appear to white, Western, middle-class people, like ourselves, and what sort of preconceptions and misconceptions this entails. All the case study materials and anecdotes are written in ways that we hope will alter this perspective and provide new insights. Our experience of developing countries has led us to conclude that the picture painted of them in our media is often mistaken and even exploitative. Throughout the book we write as if all the personal anecdotes happened to both of us and we hope that this fiction is excusable. Some is indeed drawn from joint experience, the rest is individual but, because we have subsequently discussed all of it intensively, it is now part of a shared reality. In any case, it is easier to write that way!

Judith Ennew
Brian Milne

Part 1

1.   Paved with Good Intentions

Concern with the needs of children is a very twentieth-century phenomenon and, because this century is also characterized by the growth of a world society, this is also a global concern. Children used to be viewed as a means of family or lineage survival into the future. With the rise of nationalism in the nineteenth century they began to represent the future of nations, which meant that policies had to be devised for ensuring a nation's survival through its children. The next generation should be healthy, in mind and body: physically fit, useful for the economy and for maintaining the continuity of national culture. When we attend conferences and debates about child welfare throughout the world, we often hear the catch-phrase 'children are our future'. That is the way many societies view the next generation, as belonging not to itself and a new society, but to the adult present as a means of conserving the values of the status quo. Yet 10 million of the first generation of the twentieth century died in the First World War attempting to preserve the values of the late nineteenth century.

And what can we say of subsequent generations? What kind of future do we have in store for our children now? And what kind of future do they have in store for us? There is no doubt that these are global as well as national questions. Not long after the Second World War had destroyed the future of 60 million people who died before their time, the international community established the United Nations Emergency Fund for Children (UNICEF). Initially UNICEF was envisaged as a short-term organization to deal with the problems of children in Europe who ended the war as homeless refugees. It was itself the child of the United Nations Relief and Rehabilitation Administration (UNRRA), which had been established in 1943, when the term 'United Nations' still referred to the Allied nations fighting in Europe against the Axis powers. UNRRA was faced with tackling a relief effort of unprecedented size and complexity, which the conquering allied armies had left in their wake. In the two years after peace in Europe was declared, UNRRA spent $4.5 billion in food and technical aid. Its operations ceased in 1946 once it became clear that 'impartial' United Nations' aid could not be continued in view of the widening rift between those nations which had previously been allied in the European war. Nevertheless, there was also a very strong feeling that children remained, in some way, an international concern that overrides political differences between nations.

It was this that gave birth to UNICEF. At the request of President Truman, former United States President Herbert Hoover undertook a survey mission to advise on relief needs, and called for a global campaign against famine, in which children should be given top priority. In Europe, he stated

> From the Russian frontier to the Channel there are today 20 millions of children not only badly undernourished but steadily developing tuberculosis, rickets, anaemia, and other diseases of subnormal feeding. If Europe is to have a future, something must be done about these children (quoted in UNICEF 1986 p. 3.).

So, between 1947 and 1950, UNICEF provided aid of $87.6 million to 13 European countries, until the emergency in Europe was obviously on the wane. Attention then shifted to less developed countries and UNICEF's remit widened almost out of recognition.

Forty years after it was founded, UNICEF is engaged in a major reassessment of its work. By now it is almost exclusively concerned with developing countries and with what has come to be called the Child Survival Revolution. Like the World Health Organization and most non-governmental aid agencies, UNICEF now regards preventive medicine as the best way to tackle the problems of children in poor countries. The goal and the slogan is that of the Alma-Ata Conference of 1977: 'Health for all by the Year 2000'. As the 1986 UNICEF Report *The State of the World's Children* states, if the opportunities needed to reach this goal are not met,

> then the 1980s and 1990s will be rightly stigmatized as the generation which . . . presided over the co-existence of unprecedented financial and technical capacity with the continued malnutrition, stunting and death of millions of its most vulnerable citizens. (UNICEF 1986(b) p. 1)

The most important factors of all in preventing the unnecessary 15 million infant and child deaths in the world each year are not money and high technology, but simple, cheap methods: growth charts, oral rehydration therapy, breast feeding, immunization, food supplements, female education and family spacing. The initials of this programme add up to what UNICEF calls the GOBI FFF formula.

Later we shall look at what 'Health for All' has achieved for children now, but here let us examine what that enormous figure of 15 million really means, because global campaigns for children are full of figures of millions and billions, so often repeated that they become numbingly meaningless. Fifteen million became a reality for us because we were trying to come to grips with it ourselves. In 1986 we were discussing the possibility of marking the Bread Not Bombs campaign week in the large Cambridgeshire village where we live, attempting to find a way that would bring home the reality of global child mortality figures to people for whom child death is a tragic rarity. We hit on the idea of using the play meadow, which stretches from the infants' school to the river, to plant a cross for every child who died needlessly that day from a curable disease such as gastro-enteritis. The number of crosses we would have needed over a 24 hour period was 41,096. This meant we would have needed to make that many small, cardboard crosses and plant 660 every hour — 11 every minute. We gave up the idea reluctantly because, when we set about trying to get people to help, it seemed not to be feasible and, in any case, we were told that it was not a good idea because it might 'frighten the children'.

Perhaps we were weak not to press the project. After all, children outside Western countries have to come to terms with the death of relatives and friends. Or perhaps our neighbours were right and these deaths belong in a different category. Should we regard them as a form of natural population control, like the people we quoted earlier (see Preface p. xi). Is it true, as we often hear stated, that people who have large families do not suffer the same grief as those who lose a precious planned child? We think not. We think of one Peruvian friend of ours, mother of many children, who lives in desperate urban poverty. Her ninth child, a little girl, died of gastro-enteritis when still a baby, a death which could have been prevented by simple remedies, had advice been available. Five years later our friend still spoke of her grief. 'For months I could not stop crying, day and night. I thought of her all the time. Then suddenly one day I realized that I had to get on with life — for my other children. So I stopped crying.' A year later, she gave birth to her tenth child, a little girl whom she called Celia, after the child she had lost.

So the quality of grief is not different. But there is one fundamental difference between these 15 million deaths and those we mourn in a more personal sense in our own society. For there are three reasons why people die. First, they die of incurable diseases or conditions, of illnesses we do not understand, like AIDS, or because of the ageing process. Second, they die from curable or preventable diseases because they cannot obtain the right treatment or are unable to prevent the condition — from gastro-enteritis like baby Celia, from TB like many of the children in her neighbourhood, from illnesses made worse by malnutrition, or from lack of food itself. Finally, they are killed by drugs that are supposed to cure disease, either because these are badly prescribed or used (or both), or because they spend more on buying drugs than they do on buying food. The difference is that the last two, *preventable*, reasons for death are more common, overwhelmingly more common, in the Third World.

Let us give another example; this time it concerns Celia's brother. Manuel, who was then six years old, is nearly always ailing. He is one of those children who always seems to have a runny nose. He is small for his age and usually has some kind of skin disease: both typical indications of malnutrition. His parents are illiterate and very poor. The family lives without running water or sewerage in a shack in central Lima, half an hour away from the city centre, the Presidential Palace, the financial centre and expensive private clinics. When we visited the family one day a couple of years ago we found that Manuel had suffered from fever and earache for two days. His mother had taken him to the out-patient department of a large public hospital, where the doctor told her Manuel had stones in his ear and needed an operation, but that there was no equipment for this kind of treatment. They were sent home without even an aspirin. Naturally, the family was very worried and Manuel was crying, his nose running more than usual. We talked it over with them and decided that we should all take him to a nearby children's hospital. Even though children of his age often poke stones in their ears, we did not think it an impossible task to get them out.

By the time we arrived at the hospital night was falling and we had to wait in the emergency out-patients department for some time, crowded into a single room where other children were receiving treatment. When we were finally allowed to talk to the middle-aged doctor he dismissed us without looking at Manuel, saying that the boy obviously had stones in his ears. We suggested that he could at least look and insisted that he found an auriscope, even though he first stated that there was no such instrument in the hospital. A junior doctor finally found one, and then there was a further delay while a battery was located.

By this time it was clear that only the fact that we said one of us was a doctor (omitting to mention that the degree is in social anthropology!) had forced this course of action. The older doctor gave Manuel's ear a cursory look with the auriscope, pronouncing that stones were there as he had told us and then dismissing us. As we started to protest that stones should be removed, the embarrassed junior doctor looked into Manuel's ear himself. Very respectfully he asked his superior to look again — there were no stones, but he saw evidence of a 'fierce infection'. Reluctantly the older man agreed and wrote out a prescription for penicillin syrup and a note to attend out-patients the next day.

But the story doesn't end there. The cost of penicillin, prescribed for a week, was more than a week's normal income for the whole family. Moreover, the parents had no idea how to administer it, for they could not read the instructions. We managed to persuade them not to use the entire bottle at once.

Next day Manuel was a little better. The morning spent at the out-patient department meant that his mother lost income from selling in the market, and both she and Manuel had to get up at 5 a.m. in order to be attended to in the queue. The next doctor told her to throw away the costly penicillin syrup and prescribed antibiotic injections, which were available for purchase at the hospital pharmacy at reduced cost. Unfortunately the pharmacy had run out some weeks before. Or fortunately as it turned out, because the chemist's shop from which she tried to buy the antibiotics refused the fill the prescription. The pharmacist had noticed Manuel's age — the dose prescribed was for adults; it might have killed this small boy. It was mid-afternoon when they returned to the hospital to find the out-patients' department closed. No one would alter the prescription. Manuel's father had to take time from his own market-selling the next day to go back to the hospital. Once again the cost of the drugs far exceeded a week's income and, because 'modern' injectible antibiotics had been prescribed, the family also had to pay a registered local injection expert to give the drug to Manuel. Meanwhile both he and the rest of his family would have gone without food if we had not been able to provide the money for the medicine.

It is small wonder that UNICEF talks of a Child Survival Revolution. In order to surmount a common childhood infection, Manuel had to survive his own bodily weakness, caused by poverty, lack of money, lack of knowledge, illiteracy, poor doctoring and bad prescribing, to say nothing of the lack of water and sewerage in his own home. He could not even lie in bed with his fever for, at that time, there was no bed in his home and the whole family slept on the earth floor.

So the problem of child health in the Third World is not just difficult to 'take in' in terms of the gross numbers of unnecessary deaths every year. The conditions faced by individual children are also very difficult for Western parents to understand. If a six-year-old boy in England has a fever and earache, his parents worry like our friends in Lima. But there the comparison ends. His mother takes him to the surgery, or calls the doctor to the house. She may complain that the surgery queue is long, but she does not have to leave home at 5 a.m. in order to get in the queue at all. The doctors may be brusque, but they are well trained and have the right equipment. They are unlikely to make a mistake in prescribing and the pharmacist will telephone the surgery to check if there has been an error. Medicine is free for children and, even if it were not, the cost would seldom amount to more than a week's wages. In terms of child survival the West is in a post-revolutionary stage, but how many Western parents know this?

As was the case with Europe in 1946, child health is clearly a priority for developing countries. But the UNICEF campaign is largely directed at survival to the age of five. It has often been commented that the most dangerous days of life are the first and the last. For a pitiful number of Third World children, birth and death fall on the same day. The first five years are the most vulnerable in any life. In 1986, according to UNICEF statistics, in Afghanistan, Mali and Sierra Leone the mortality rate for children under five was around 300 per thousand. Put in human terms this means that, of every three children born, only two will reach the age of five: which means immeasurable childhood suffering, and millions of mothers crying day and night for months.

Yet health is only one way of looking at the situation. Health figures give an objective definition of poverty because it can be shown to be a fact that the poor in any country have the highest illness rates. Nevertheless, the state of the world's children cannot be shown just in medical models. Indeed, one can argue that 'physical survival is the easy part' (*International Children's Rights Monitor* 1984 p. 3). Education, health services and food supplements are relatively simple to supply, compared with preventing the exploitation, torture, killing, abduction and imprisonment of children. Children are victims of war in Lebanon and Iran, of civil strife in South Africa and Northern Ireland, of poverty in India, Thailand, Brazil and nearly every other country in the world. If they survive to the age of five, what sort of society, what sort of life can they expect?

Children born in 1985, still struggling now to achieve the magic statistical fifth birthday, will be 15 years old in the year 2000: old enough to work in most tasks, according to international conventions, but not old enough to vote, marry or fight, according to most national legislations. The adults of the next century are already with us and, if the future is to be viable, today's adults must meet the challenge not only of ensuring their physical survival but also of preventing that survival being a mockery of human dignity because of exploitation, poverty and violence. Although we have called this book *The Next Generation* a better title might be *The Present Generation*, because the responsibility is ours and it is now that we must act. It is essential at this time to see children's rights as a crucial issue for everyone. It is also important that the question is stripped of the sentimentality that so often reduces children to objects which must be filled with medicine, food and good intentions.

Childhood

Children are individuals, but childhood is a social institution and the way we think of it is peculiar to the West. Children are immature human animals but cultures determine the different ways they should act and the things they are supposed to do. When we were children we did not question the smiling faces of children from other lands which we saw in our school-books, for children were expected to be happy. Our parents often told us that these were the happiest years of our lives, and we were forced to accept this even when periods of unhappiness caused us to wonder silently how bad the adult years were going to be. In fact if we were unhappy there might be a lingering feeling of guilt — perhaps we were unnatural children? Certainly an unhappy child can raise feelings of guilt and anger in parents at the thought that they might have failed to provide happiness. It is, after all, an axiom of international declarations that 'the child, for the full and harmonious development of his personality, should grow up in a family environment, in an atmosphere of happiness, love and understanding' (1983 Draft Convention on the Rights of the Child).

That of course is an ideal world. But, because these are the global definitions of childhood, it is important to know how they came about and what they actually mean in the countries where these ideas, which now dominate the international community, originated. There are many arguments among historians in the present growth industry of the history of childhood, but it seems that there was a fundamental change in attitudes to children about two centuries ago in Europe. Until then, the institution of childhood did not exist in the form we would recognize now. In our world, children are separated from adults: they go to school rather than work; they are not expected to take on responsibility; they have special activities called play and special things called toys to play with.

Childhood in the West means a great deal of expenditure on scaled down equipment, clothes and entertainments. Parents taking their new baby on a Sunday visit to grandmother in Third World cities get on the bus with the child in a shawl in their arms or on the mother's back. If the baby is hungry it is breast fed with no fuss. At grandma's it will be handed from person to person and will always find some accommodating lap to sleep on. In the West it is a different performance. The carry-cot will be placed in the back seat of the car, the boot filled with disposable nappies and special seats and bouncing frames and toys to 'keep the baby happy'. Feeding time will be fraught with clashes between grandma's specially cooked lunch and the baby's breast or bottle-feeds, together with 'solid' supplements — all three of which also need special equipment. There is almost bound to be a problem 'getting the baby to sleep'. Both parents and grandma will probably be secretly relieved when the visit is over (the baby's feelings are not known).

This special status of childhood is also marked by the necessity for experts in child welfare, health and psychology. Childhood has become a problem area in which small human beings are segregated from adults: 'quarantined' as the French social historian Philippe Aries put it (Aries 1973). It is the most rigidly enforced division in our age-segregated society. In fact the word 'generation' has taken on a new meaning. Child, youth, middle-aged, elderly are major divisions, each with a separate culture and consumer goods to match. Mutual misunderstanding, even hostility, is expected. Mixing on a social scale is becoming less common, even in such family celebrations as birthdays and weddings.

Within the culture expected of childhood we can detect a normalization process. By this we mean that children are supposed to conform to standards of physical and mental performance, graded according to age. The process begins before birth, sometimes even before conception. Not long ago an article in an English Sunday magazine instructed couples intending to conceive a child how to control their own lives in order to have a bright, attractive baby (*Observer Magazine*, June 1987). This may not, in principle, be a bad idea, except that it implies that less intelligent or beautiful young human beings are less desirable. Life in the womb is usually monitored in the West for 'normal' growth and rigorous attempts are made to avoid abnormality. Once again, this can be seen as a praiseworthy activity, as long as the definitions of normality are also monitored. There is a 'good' birthweight, neither too low nor too high and, after birth, a battery of tests to monitor growth, personality and intelligence. The ideal or normal child can be seen smiling happily in advertisements for the same equipment with which their happiness can be ensured: almost without exception they are white, blonde, plump and bursting with innocent, smiling energy. Forty years ago, we were both small, dark, morose children, uncomfortably aware of the stereotype. Yet think of Manuel: of Indian extraction, undersized, no toys and little energy to play, no chance to go to school, runny nose, flaking skin. By the standards of 'normal' Western childhood he can hardly be called a child. Unfortunately he often goes to watch his neighbour's television which screens many North American drama serials, so he too knows what a 'normal' child is.

Thus malnourished, non-white Third World children are not just a cause for concern because of their suffering. The shock we feel at media coverage of Biafran, Vietnamese or, more recently, Ethiopian children is not simply because we revolt at their dreadful misery. It is also that they are an affront to the ideal of childhood. That is why we tend not to notice the way the media so often treat them as objects; if there is one thing certain about the children who die so publicly on our television screens, it is that they are not granted identity. As if their suffering were not undignified enough, no one seems to bother to ask their names. A BBC documentary on famine in Somalia, screened a few weeks before we began to write this book, illustrated this. The analysis was good, the information well researched but, when it came to showing a starving child, the journalist simply took a baby from its mother's arms and bared its bottom to the camera, pinching the skin to reveal the level of dehydration and malnutrition. He barely asked the mother's permission, he did not otherwise speak to her. Perhaps he had asked her permission beforehand. But if his viewers do not know this how can they help seeing people of the Third World as passive objects of charity, with no history or individuality? It is not that we doubt the integrity of documentary film makers who take the trouble to bring these situations to our notice, but we are asking something more of them: to have respect as well as compassion.

Aid agencies also sometimes make the same mistake, as Nigel Cantwell discovered, when he found two charity advertisements using the same photograph of a dying child. He shows two versions of the same photograph, in which a pitifully thin child appears to be struggling to raise itself from a patch of barren earth.

> The child on the left figured in a UNICEF UK Committee ad to raise funds for Ethiopia. . . . The very same child became 'Mozambican' a few years later when the photo, turned around, was used in a UNA UK advertisement. . . . A blatant illustration of the way in which exploitation of pictures of starving children can lead to obscenity. (*International Children's Rights Monitor*, Vol. 4, No. 2, 1987, p. 10)

Images of Western children are also occasionally used to shock contributions out of potential givers, but they are usually posed by a model or at least have their faces partially masked. Where Third World children are concerned the recourse is all to often to a pornography of misery.

The Third World

Up to this point we have used the term 'Third World' without discussion, indeed it is part of the title of this book. But it is not an uncontroversial term. It arose largely as a response by newly independent countries to the rival claims upon their allegiance from Western and Eastern bloc countries. The idea behind it was that somehow there could be a third way to development, which would be neither capitalist nor communist in its ideology. For some it also represents the possibility of a third power block in the world, one which could be increasingly relevant as these emergent countries became members of the United Nations. The literature of development has, however, pointed to important differences *between* Third World nations, in terms of their rate of industrialization, their resources or resource use, for instance. Thus new terms have been used, such as Developing Countries and Less Developed Countries, North and South and so on.

We ourselves would actually prefer something like the distinction described by the veteran child welfare campaigner, Mrs Tara Ali Baig. At a conference on childhood in Canada in 1987, it became very clear that, at least when one is discussing children, the divisions within nations, between rich and poor and between dominant and oppressed groups, are similar in all parts of the world. What is necessary is some terminology that gives expression to this and acknowledges the validity of cultures that wish to accept 'development' only on their own terms. In the final discussions of the conference, Mrs Baig suggested that the most appropriate terms to use would be 'ancient' and 'modern' cultures. This allows one to think about ancient cultures within developed nations, such as the Inuit of Canada and the Aborigines of Australia as well as about the modern, transnational-oriented sectors of such countries as Brazil and India.

We want to look at both types of culture in this book, but we chose to use the term 'Third World' because of its resonance in communal imagery. The difference between rich and poor children within Third World countries is seldom, if ever, acknowledged by the media. For the purposes of journalism, and often of development literature also, Third World children are all non-white, malnourished and lacking in identity. The sole exceptions are children who are offered by some agencies for sponsorship by people in the West; they are given individuality in the advertisements.

But, in fact, they remain symbols because they stand for a nameless mass of other children needing the same help. The virtue of such schemes is that they emphasize the need for individual commitment by the privileged. The disadvantage is that they limit that commitment to a small number of children and to a small gift by the privileged. They require nothing else of the giver but the gift. No further economic or political action is required and the child, invited, so to speak, to the Christmas feast, is still kept at the foot of the table.

The child of the First World, on the other hand, is essentially an individual. He (still usually 'he') is encouraged to 'a full and harmonious development of his personality . . . in an atmosphere of happiness, love and understanding'. That is what the advertisements selling equipment for a normal childhood are all about. Individuals in the First World are raised to be individuals, independent of community. The way most people think about human rights has to do with the rights of individuals to develop their potential, independently of the needs of others. Instead of fulfilling their potential through love and service to others they may purchase what they need on the consumer market or, indirectly, by buying social services through taxation. Individual desire is raised to the level of right, while duty is relegated to the status of malformed need. This is the message of those pictures of blonde, white, innocent children, smiling with happiness.

Children's rights

Universal concern about childhood throughout this century has thus grown alongside notions of human rights. The way human rights are now understood has more to do with the individual's civil rights within a nation state than with the universal truths of brotherhood and humanity ('natural' rights) which were proposed in the French Revolution and enshrined in the United States Declaration of Independence. What is peculiar to this century, particularly since the United Nations Organization (UNO) was established in 1945, is the notion that 'how a sovereign state treats its own citizens is no longer a matter for its own exclusive determination, but a matter of *legitimate* concern for all other states and for their inhabitants' (Sieghart 1985 p. vii). The UN Charter established an international community which sets out ideal standards to be aspired to in many matters, including the treatment of children. The problem is that as far as childhood is concerned, the suggested ideal standards tend to be appropriate to what we are calling here 'modern' society: to liberal-democratic, industrial societies.

Children have not always been on the human rights agenda as a separate group. The question of children's rights was not an issue for the French Declaration of the Rights of Man in 1780. Children were regarded as a residual category of persons, lacking full human rights. At that time European societies simply thought of children as the property of their parents. According to legal commentaries in England, for instance, child stealing was not theft unless the child were wearing clothes. Otherwise child theft was like theft of a corpse. The body was not inhabited by a legal person in either case.

Early ideas of children's rights emphasized their need for special protection. Although these notions were current throughout the nineteenth century, many authorities trace the proposal that children have particular kinds of rights to the work of Eglantyne Jebb. As a result of her experiences working with the Macedonian Relief Fund in the Balkan War, this rather splendid lady, on the outbreak of the First World War, declared herself a pacifist. This stand was not always popular with the British public, but she withstood persecution with the claim that 'all wars are waged against children' (Wilson 1976 p. 5). Miss Jebb was the prime mover in setting up the Save the Children Movement in 1919, dedicated to child protection and operating under a Declaration of Child Rights which was taken over, almost without alteration, by the Geneva Declaration of the Rights of the Child of the League of Nations in 1924 and by the United Nations in 1959.

Children were mentioned in the UN Universal Declaration of Human Rights, which established the principle of interference in the affairs of other sovereign states in 1948. Article 25, Paragraph 2 states that 'Motherhood and children are entitled to special care and assistance. All children, whether born in or out of wedlock, shall enjoy the same social protection.' Other Declarations and Covenants have echoed this concern with protection, both the United Nations' and statements of other international bodies, such as the European Social Charter. The perceived need of children for protection is based on their physical and mental immaturity. The 1959 Declaration states in its preamble that 'mankind owes to the child the best it has to give' and interprets this in a series of protections, benefits and priorities. But the twentieth century has also been marked by another agenda for children, represented most notably in the work of educationalists like A. S. Neill, which recognizes the rights of children to be actors and givers, rather than just passive receivers. It has a longer history than one might imagine: children have led armies and kingdoms, gone independently on crusades and taken political action — like the boy who presented to the English Parliament in 1669 a 'Modest Remonstrance of that intolerable grievance our Youth lie under in the accustomed severities of the school discipline of this nation' (quoted in Hoyles 1979 p. 214).

It is paradoxical that these rights to independent action are most likely to be granted to the ideal children of the First World, whose status is defined by their need for protection. This is a point of conflict between two Western ideas: the development of individual personality, and the quarantine of childhood. But this is no more of a paradox than the situation of Third World children, most of whom take on a large burden of responsibility from an early age and yet are defined by the media as exceptionally passive and in need of protection. There can be no greater example of the paternalism of the West than this difference between the independent, acting, Western child and the receiving, passive, Third World child. It is even taught in schools. Development education tends to emphasize the needs of Third World children, and attaches importance to giving them aid. If one of the good results of the publicity surrounding the Ethiopian famine in 1985–86 was that thousands of primary school children learned something about this African country through school projects, one of the bad results was that, because of the emphasis on present disaster, few learned anything about the long cultural history of this complex nation.

The other agenda for Children's Rights became part of the deliberations of the international community in 1979, the International Year of the Child, following which the UN Commission on Human Rights began to consider a proposal of the Polish government for a Convention of the Rights of the Child. Perhaps we should explain that a UN Declaration has no more than symbolic force. When a Declaration is accepted by the United Nations General Assembly it is no more than an agreement between member nations that this is a 'good thing'. Nothing need be done about it and very little usually is. A Convention, on the other hand, is a statement of intent that member states sign and later ratify, when they have brought their own legislation into line. After this, other member states have the right to treat the provisions of the Convention as a 'matter of *legitimate* concern' for intervention.

Deliberations about the Convention have taken place over the past decade. These things take time to resolve because of social and legal differences between nation states. A paragraph on legitimacy, for example, becomes complicated because of different marriage laws; a statement about sexual exploitation may not be acceptable to states that deny the existence of sexual exploitation of children in their society and thus refuse to make provisions for it within their own laws. But it seems likely that the final draft of the Convention will be put before the General Assembly in 1989. One feature of these discussions has been the extraordinary involvement of non-governmental organizations, such as Defence for Children International. Another has been the extent to which enabling rights of children, which allow them to have a voice in decisions made for their protection and welfare, have been taken into consideration. The 1959 Declaration contained no hint whatsoever of the sort of thinking which lies behind Article 7 of the draft Convention:

> The States Parties to the present Convention shall assure to the child who is capable of forming his own views the right to express his opinion freely in all matters, the wishes of the child being given due weight in accordance with his age and maturity. (1983 Draft: the texts of Declaration and draft Convention are given in Appendices 1 and 2)

A further notable feature of the deliberations, however, has been the virtual absence of Third World states.

The best it has to give

Three decades separate the Declaration of the Rights of the Child and the date when the Convention is expected to be put to the UN General Assembly. One might ask 'Why the delay?' But one might also suggest that, because children are such a universal subject of concern and because the General Assembly adopted the Declaration unanimously, there should be no need for a Convention. In a world in which it is universally recognized that 'mankind owes to the child the best it has to give' surely the only reason why children lack rights must be lack of the means to provide them with rights. By this token, the starvation of Biafran babies is due simply to them being unfortunately caught up in a war which does not involve them; the starvation of Ethiopian children must be caused by natural disasters over which states have no control. But these are fallacies. Biafran babies suffered because they were Biafran and, although famines may be related to environmental factors, they can be both made and continued by human agencies.

One important point to remember about child suffering is that it is *human* suffering. The reason why it arouses special concern is because of the mental and physical immaturity of children: because they are seen as needing more care and protection than adults and particularly if they suffer because of the acts of adults over which they have no control and for which they have no responsibility. But there is a further question which was brought out strongly in the Minority Rights Group publication on children's rights (Boyden and Hudson 1986). Children suffer from a double disadvantage precisely because they are children. The situation of children in society has actually changed little since the eighteenth century, when they were legally compared with the dead. It isn't pushing the comparison too far to say that just like a corpse, which lacks the ability to act because it has no biological life, a child lacks the ability to act because it has no legal life.

Children cannot choose, but have to accept the choices made for them by adults, usually with the best intentions. Unfortunately, as the proverb states, good intentions may pave the road to hell. If we take a look at each of the ten Principles of the Declaration of the Rights of the Child, agreed unanimously by United Nations member states in 1959, in the light of the way children have actually been treated in this concerned and caring world over the past decades, then we shall unfortunately see that for many children, life is indeed a living hell.

2. The Declaration of the Rights of the Child

Principle 1: The child shall enjoy all the rights set forth in this Declaration. Every child, without any exception whatsoever, shall be entitled to these rights, without distinction or discrimination on account of race, colour, sex, language, religion, political or other opinion, national or social origin, property, birth or other status whether of himself or of his family.

If you have read this Principle through without noticing the contradiction, we suggest that you read it again. It uses one of the very discriminations which it sets out to combat, for it implies that children deserving of rights are all male. Of course we understand that this was not the intention of the drafters and that the masculine pronouns 'himself' and 'his' are supposed to encompass little girls. But, as many feminists have pointed out in the past two decades, even the assumption that male 'encompasses' female gives some implicit priority to one sex. In English language childcare manuals, babies are usually written about as if they were all male. This is an even more acute problem in gendered languages, where the very word for child is different according to sex, as in the Spanish *niño* (boy child) and *niña* (girl child) for example. Moreover, the evidence is very clear that just about every society we know about does make a social distinction on grounds of gender.

Social anthropologist Meyer Fortes once teasingly berated a student for her interest in economic anthropology. 'What is interesting in societies', he said, 'is why men wear trousers and women wear skirts.' What he was referring to was not merely fashion, but rather the way in which human cultures make a point of emphasizing some very noticeable biological differences. From the moment they are born, boys and girls are obviously not physically the same. One of the first things which is remarked about a child is its sex. With modern technology it is possible to discover this even before birth. But, even without this foreknowledge, parents and families have often decided which sex they would prefer — almost always the preferred firstborn is a boy. Women who produce only girls may be treated with less respect. Sometimes only a male name is chosen and, when a girl arrives, there is difficulty thinking of a name for this unwelcome new family member. Some societies have practised female infanticide in order to save scarce resources for a desired future male child. Even in the absence of such drastic measures, the birth of male and female children is welcomed differently. The Chinese call the birth of a boy a 'great happiness' while that of a girl is a 'small happiness'. The food writer, Claudia Roden, describes the Arab custom of preparing a Ceremonial Rice Pudding to celebrate the birth of a boy, which will be made to welcome the birth of a girl only after several sons have appeared. She also records these contrasting songs:

Lullaby for a Son

After the heat and after the bitterness, and after the sixth of the
   month,
After our enemies had rejoiced at her pain and said, 'There is a
   stone in her tummy!'
The stone is in their heads! And this overwhelms them.
Go! Oh bearer of the news! Kiss them and tell them, 'She has borne a
   son!'

Lullaby for a New-Born Girl

When they said, 'It's a girl!' — that was a horrible moment
The honey pudding turned to ashes and the dates became scorpions.
When they said, 'It's a girl!', the corner stone of the house
   crumbled,
And they brought me eggs in their shells and instead of butter,
   water.

The midwife who receives a son deserves a gold coin to make
   earrings.
The midwife who receives a son deserves a gold coin to make a ring
   for her nose.

But you! Oh midwife! Deserve thirty strokes of the stick!
Oh! You who announce a little girl when the censorious are here!

(quoted from Maspéro, *Chansons populaire* in Roden 1968 p. 398).

There are many theories put forward to explain the social superiority accorded
to males, but they do not concern us here. What *is* important is that boys and
girls are treated differently from the outset and that this reflects status and
power relations throughout life. It isn't just clothes which are different.
Behaviour towards boys and girls and behaviour expected from them differ

Table 1
Adult female and male literacy figures, 1985
(per cent)

	Male	Female
Sierra Leone	23	11
Somalia	18	6
Mozambique	55	22
India	57	29
Peru	91	78
Brazil	79	76
Lebanon	86	69
Thailand	94	88
China	87	56

Note: Figures for 1985 not available for South Africa and Nicaragua. Cuban figures not
supplied by sex.

Source: UNICEF *State of the World's Children 1988.*

also and, in general, this leads to limited opportunities for girls. Although 'mankind' owes the best it can give to the child, what is best for a girl is not usually what is best for a boy. Instead what happens is that, even though in some cases girls may get the best, boys tend to get it better. Educational opportunities reflect this in all societies, as illustrated by adult literacy rates (see Table 1).

Even in those rare situations where educational opportunities are the same, work and power opportunities in adult life discriminate along lines of sexual difference. The more usual picture is that girls, like women, find themselves with limited opportunities to live an independent life or to make decisions for themselves. Research in both Africa and the Caribbean has shown educationally gifted girls taking this into consideration and dropping out of school to become early achievers in the alternative female status ladder as young mothers. Schoolteachers in Jamaica have noted that some schoolgirls seem to choose to become single mothers as a form of economic strategy, even though they are well aware of the problems of insecurity and poverty they will encounter. This appears more attractive than trying to get qualifications which will not help them get a job in competition with young men. Although nearly one-third of young men do not get a job, about two-thirds of girls under 24 remain without employment. So teachers reported that 'brilliant girls', 'the cream of the school' become teenage mothers. One Work Experience teacher even commented bitterly that Child Care classes intended for training nursery nurses should be 'wiped out completely' because they encouraged girls to take up motherhood as a career (Ennew 1982 pp. 200–201).

For many girls, motherhood is still the only possible career and, for millions of others, any alternative career is seen as merely an interim period before motherhood claims them. This affects not only school attendance but also the type of curriculum available for both sexes. In most societies, technical and scientific skills are taught to boys, while practical subjects for girls are limited to cooking, sewing and childcare. Even if the intention is non-discriminatory, unconscious acknowledgement of sexual status creeps in. We well remember the early planning stages of one rehabilitation scheme for street children. Moments after a bold statement about the equal status to be accorded to girls and boys the discussion shifted to more practical details. In order to save on overheads, the planners agreed, the girls in the scheme could do the washing!

The International Labour Organization has calculated that on a global basis women comprise over half the population, do two-thirds of the work but own half of the property and have far less access to power than men. The oppressed situation of women is well known. Many women do not yet have a vote in democratic countries and the status of women is often similar, if not identical, to that of children. They are legal minors. Even international bodies make this link through claims such as: 'Motherhood and children are entitled to special care and assistance'. Yet there is another group which suffers even greater oppression — children themselves. One-third of the world's population is now under 15 years old; an even greater proportion are legal minors, unable to take any decisions that affect the sort of society in which they live and the way they are treated. For, despite all the sentimentality surrounding definitions of childhood, the category 'child' is a legal one. A child is a legal minor in any society. Children are powerless.

That is the other noticeable feature of Principle 1 of the Declaration of the Rights of the Child. It fails to define the type of human being to which it refers and whose rights it is asserting. The Convention does spell this out by defining a child as 'every human being to the age of 18 years unless, under the law of his State, he has attained his age of majority earlier'. But the Declaration does not refer in any way to the political status of children, being content merely to mention 'physical and mental immaturity' in the Preamble. So, despite the aims of the first Principle to combat discrimination in any form, there is no attempt to stop the discrimination that children suffer simply because they are children.

Over half the world's population are children. They do a considerable amount of the world's work, as we shall show later. They own far less property even than women and they nowhere have the ability to affect fundamental decisions about their lives: 'over 50% of the world's population is completely excluded from the reporting, evaluating and policy-making processes of every society'. (Mendel 1972).

If only the ideal situation envisaged by the Declaration were reality, loved and protected children would not need political power. They would have 'happy', 'normal childhoods' leading to the 'full and harmonious development' of their personalities. But even in countries where these ideals were formulated, this is not the case. In any country, one of the most shocking aspects of this adult misuse of power is that it is so often also a misuse of trust. Most child abusers are members of the child's own family. Parents who are guilty of assaulting their children are treated with horror, contempt and a savage sense of retribution. Popular newspapers refer to them as 'monsters', implying that their behaviour is not that of human beings. But we are sure that they are only the visible face of an overall adult domination of children. Much sexual abuse of children has gone unpunished because adults simply did not listen to children or refused to believe they were telling the truth. It is still difficult to bring many abusers to court in any country, because evidence given by very young children cannot usually be admitted in court unless it is confirmed by an adult. As most sexual abuse takes place in secret there is little likelihood that an adult witness will be found. There are, however, other, less spectacular, ways in which children are automatically discounted, given lower priority than adults, not listened to or not permitted to make quite simple decisions. We are all guilty of doing this and we were all victims when we were children.

Adult power over children arises from authority relations within the family, on which most legal systems are based. Much has been written recently by feminists about the way family relationships affect male power over women, but the situation for children is even worse. In an earlier section we discussed the historical idea that children were not full legal persons and could be compared in this sense to dead persons. In the same period children were also regarded as parental property, like any other item that could be bought and sold or otherwise disposed of. This is by no means rare in our own time.

Throughout the world children are pledged in return for debt. The debt may be owed to a moneylender or to a landlord, and the child is handed over to pay off the money by working. The system is illegal but widespread, particularly among the peasantry of such countries as India. One reason why it persists is that poor people often require considerable sums of money, to pay taxes or to celebrate obligatory festivals or to pay medical expenses. Perhaps advances of seed and tools may be made to small farmers to tide them over a bad season. Any poor family lives on the margins of successful subsistence where even a small setback can lead to hopeless and unending debt. Most parents in these families are also unable to read and write or to do simple arithmetic. They are completely at the mercy of their creditors who manipulate interest rates and contracts to keep the children working permanently in their service. Parents can also pledge themselves in this way. Some men 'retire' from debt in middle age by pledging a child in their place, so parental power still makes it possible for a child to be sold, even if the father himself is a semi-slave.

Authority relations within the family are based on the idea that parents (or more usually fathers) have absolute power over their children, just as sovereigns had at one time absolute power over their subjects. This power has been eroded in most nations by legislation which gives the state the right to intervene between parent and child or even to assume the parental role, by removing children to orphanages, or foster or adoptive homes. But fathers and mothers still have considerable power over children, and many cultural ideas echo this, even more strongly than it is stated in laws. Why else, for example, would a newspaper headline read 'PARENTAL AGONY IN CHILD RAPE CASE'? Of course most parents would suffer if their child were raped, but is this really the *primary* consideration?

What this brings us to is the realization that, although children are the largest single category of human beings, they are also the most powerless. Only one other group suffers greater discrimination and this is not distinguished by sex, race, religion or politics but by the more insidious and less easily defined category of the poor.

Poverty, *pobreza*, *armut*, *pauvreté*: the most ill-used word in any language. However we use 'poverty' it is bound to be relative. We all use it in an intuitive way, to discuss different levels of ownership, for it is impossible to think of poverty without at the same time thinking of wealth. Poverty implies having less than other people and also wanting and needing more than one has. This also means defining needs, which is usually a social or cultural matter. The eighteenth-century political economist Adam Smith was aware of this when he pointd out in a much-quoted passage of *The Wealth of Nations* that the urban poor of Europe were 'as rich as an African king', and the twentieth-century social anthropologist Marshall Sahlins has made a similar point with respect to people of hunting and gathering societies. He suggests that, because these people have simple needs which can be fulfilled easily within their economic way of life, they should be regarded as 'The Original Affluent Society' (Smith 1970; Sahlins 1974).

Such ideas appear to be mere academic nitpicking if one considers the case of an abandoned baby dying on a garbage heap, or refugees from a famine zone who have lost all their belongings and have no access to food. It could be argued that these cases of absolute poverty must constitute some kind of base-line definition. But we would argue differently, simply because all people who suffer such extremes of deprivation are part of a wider social whole. If a baby dies on a garbage heap, this is because it has been left there by an adult, probably a desperate mother who can find no way to feed and care for it. And this usually happens in an urban area in which the social structure is such that it forces the mother to this terrible act, a city in which she has no access to help from society and in which there are many rich and privileged people who have more than enough for their own needs. Similarly, refugees from famine live in countries where not everyone is dying of hunger and where many people are extremely well fed. Moreover they are known to be dying, by people from other countries, like our own, in which death from hunger would most probably be the result of a deliberate wish to die in this way. It is impossible to escape from knowledge of relative wealth or privilege whenever one thinks of poverty. However it is defined it always refers to having more or less than other people: more or less goods, better health, more access to power or services. Marshall Sahlins may be right in suggesting that hunting and gathering people are 'affluent' within their own frame of reference. But even they do not live in isolation from wider societies and one of the main things they lack is access to medical services. Thus their expectation of life at birth may be half that of urban elites with the same nationality, and half the babies born to them may die before the age of 12 months. Perhaps it would not be too far-fetched to suggest that, though they may have an affluent way of life, what they lack is access to life itself.

Ideas of health and ideas of poverty are closely linked in social policy. The rights assumed by the rich and privileged to interfere in the lives of the 'poor' are often based on the need to improve health, through the provision of health services, the imposition of rules of sanitation and of household management. In this way we could almost argue that 'poverty' is more of a problem for the rich than for the poor. It is a problem which 'must' be solved by 'good' government, and child survival is often the main reason for intervention in the lives of the poor. Welfare systems are justified by the need for child health care, which would be all well and good if such systems did not usually entail some means of control and if the generosity of the rich (whether in charitable donations or through taxation) did not so often have limited objectives. The idea is not usually that the poor should become rich, but that they should become less absolutely poor. Moreover, welfare systems tend to discriminate between the undeserving poor, who are poor because of their 'own fault', and the deserving poor, who respond to generosity by behaving in ways acceptable to the givers. Most programmes that aim to 'eliminate poverty' aim only to improve the lot of the relatively poor and not to eliminate the social structures which maintain differences in wealth. Thus a permanent system of reciprocity is set up, in which rich people and rich nations are givers and poor people and poor nations are fixed in the position of receivers, always obliged to accept what is offered and the control this implies. If poverty were really to be eliminated it could only be by the 'true generosity' described by the Brazilian educationalist Paulo Freire:

> True generosity consists precisely in fighting to destroy the causes which nourish false charity. False charity constrains the fearful and subdued, the 'rejects of life', to extend their trembling hands. Real generosity lies in striving so that those hands — whether of individuals or entire peoples — need to be extended less and less in supplication, so that more and more they become human hands which work and, by working, transform the world. (Freire 1972 pp. 21–2)

The way we understand poverty is as a type of powerlessness, not only the relative lack of food, shelter, material goods and amenities compared to other people or societies, but also the inability to affect the situation. What it amounts to in the last instance is being denied human rights, in the most basic sense.

As far as children are concerned, their especial powerlessness intensifies the problem. Children are particularly vulnerable to the effects of poverty; food, shelter, health care and sanitation are crucial aspects of their physical survival, and lack of education severely affects their adult lives. Yet children are not just poor on their own, they experience poverty in the context of familial or societal poverty. Their access to any of the rights they may be supposed to have because they are children will be governed by the overall situation of poverty or wealth into which they are born. The discriminations against which they are 'protected' by Principle 1 of the Declaration of the Rights of the Child do not even mention this, yet surely it is the most crucial and profound discrimination of all. There is also no doubt that poverty is the ruling, but unmentioned, factor in all the Principles of the Declaration. Yet a Principle to protect the child against poverty, or which declares that all children have equal rights to material wealth, seems impossible, almost ridiculous. Unless, of course, one did set out to transform the world.

* * *

Principle 2: The child shall enjoy special protection, and shall be given opportunities and facilities, by law and by other means, to enable him to develop physically, mentally, morally, spiritually and socially in a healthy and normal manner and in conditions of freedom and dignity. In the enactment of laws for this purpose, the best interests of the child shall be the paramount considerations.

What special protection do poor children, 'Third World' children, need in order to develop in a healthy and normal manner? We will set aside for a moment the whole question of what is normal because, as we have already shown, 'normal' children are white, Western and wealthy and their development must be assumed to be the implicit standard by which underprivileged development is judged and found wanting. The main questions raised by this Principle are, therefore, how to protect poor children against poverty, how to secure conditions of freedom and dignity and what are the best interests of the child.

Let us begin with the last question first, because it affects all children, whether rich or poor, and takes us back to the issue of parental rights and legislation. Even though there are differences between legal systems they all distinguish only. two categories of person by age: adults and children. There may be differences for various purposes between babies, toddlers or teenagers, just as there can be differences between working and retired adults at the other end of the age scale. But the main legal distinction is between adult persons who have reached the age of majority and are full citizens and children who are not quite legal persons. Adults, particularly parents, have a duty to make sure that everything that happens to a child happens in its best interests.

Instructions for child nutrition, for example, have one thing in common, despite the obvious differences of culture and class. They are all written in the best interests of the child. Childcare experts may differ in their views of what are actually the best means of feeding, clothing, caring for a child but they do not doubt that whatever *is* best, adults know what it is better than children. Although manuals are written about diet, and religious affiliation may have major effects upon what people are 'allowed' to eat, food is usually a matter of culture rather than legislation. If there are such huge variations in cultural ideas about which diet ensures the best interests of the child, the more rigid provisions of legislation will show even greater variations, with more profound social effects for the next generation. Yet every modern society makes some kind of legal provision for children simply because they *are* the next generation. The form this takes depends partly on the resources available, but mostly on ideas about how society should function. 'Children are our future' is the phrase that sums this up. Most modern governments base their policies for children less on the needs of children and more on what the future society of adults should be. Sentimental treatment of the topic of childhood simply masks the fact that childhood is the time when future citizens and workers are socialized.

Legislation for children may take the form of a special Children's Code but this does not always account for all the needs children may have or all the situations in which they find themselves. Other legal provisions affecting children are incorporated in family law, welfare legislation, health and educational law, laws affecting women (such as abortion law or maternity leave), labour law (the minimum age for work, for instance), criminal law (the age of legal responsibility) and penal law. Because these laws are designed for different purposes and are implemented by different government agencies, there is frequently a conflict or contradiction between them, which rarely results in serving the best interests of the child.

One of the clearest conflicts, hotly debated in most countries, is the contradiction of interests between different categories of human being implied by legislation on abortion. The way this is debated tends to divide between a woman's right to make decisions about her own body, about whether to bear a child, and the opposing view which asserts that a foetus has a right to life. Some people also add that a child should have the right to be a wanted child, or a child for whom social and welfare provisions can be ensured. So social factors can be taken into consideration as well as the psychological state of the woman involved or simply her wish not to be a mother at that time. Whatever the case there is bound to be an impasse in abortion debates if it is rights alone that are discussed and if absolute moral positions are taken.

Even the laws specifically made with children in mind can conflict dramatically. To take a historical example of a law quickly passed in the wake of a national scandal: after public uproar about child prostitutes in the 1880s, the age of sexual consent in England and Wales was raised to 16 (for girls) while for the next 25 years the age of marriage remained at 12. Penal law, also, often creates problems for children especially if there are insufficient means to implement the provisions. For it is one thing to pass a law to cater for the best interests of the child and quite another to carry those provisions through. For example, legislation frequently expresses societal concern about children being kept in detention on criminal charges in the same institutions as adult prisoners. Their physical, psychological and educational needs are not met and adult inmates may present further dangers or bad influences. But what if there are no resources available to detain children in separate institutions?

In Turkey many poor children are arrested for such minor offences as petty theft or vagrancy. Often these are children from very poor backgrounds, runaways or street children. Thousands, some as young as seven years old, are detained in Turkish adult prisons. The regulations about child offenders state that they cannot be detained with adults, but there are few provisions made for children on remand, who are kept with adults. As the pre-trial period is often prolonged, many children spend most of their formative years in adult prisons. The five juvenile penal establishments in Turkey are able to offer very few places and, in any case, those available for children on remand tend to be given to the offspring of wealthy or powerful families. Poor children may have offended in the first place because of their poverty — street children who are pickpockets, for example, often have little or no contact with their parents and no other means of survival besides theft. So they suffer a double disadvantage and pay dearly for it.

Sentences for those under 18 at the time of the offence are half that of an adult convicted of the same crime. Theoretically, children under 11 cannot be arrested, but they may still be detained in adult prisons while identity checks are made, especially in the provinces. Children over 11 years of age may be kept in custody until they can be charged. Detention on criminal charges often drags on for years, so that when sentence is eventually passed the child may be due for release in any case, thus having passed the entire period of detention in an adult gaol. Where part of the sentence remains to be served, the law states that, for humanitarian reasons, children should be transferred to prisons in their home towns. But the process of transfer usually takes so long that the sentence is completed where it began. Such cases often involve runaway children, which compounds the problem.

Turkish authorities are not unaware of the problem or indifferent to these children's plight. There has been a lot of publicity about children in prison and, at governmental level, successive Ministers of Justice have stated their dissatisfaction with procedures. Legislation intended to provide a solution has been passed but not yet implemented, nor have dates for implementation been given. Thus officials are in the paradoxical position of having to deny the existence of children within adult prisons in order to comply with the law. The children have been officially abandoned, forced out of existence: we are tempted to argue that this is precisely because 'In the enactment of laws . . . the best interests of the child . . . [have been] the paramount considerations'.

What are the effects for individual children? Within the prisons a further paradox is that children who are kept in mixed blocks with adults may suffer less than those in separate juvenile blocks. In any case, the prison regimes are arranged to suit the needs of adults, and child prisoners are a secondary consideration. Thus juvenile blocks are often those which have been deemed unsuitable for adults: dilapidated or damaged as the result of inmate riots, for instance. Repairs to prisons are usually paid for by inmates, but children have no economic resources of their own so their physical surroundings are frequently far worse than those of adult prisoners. Because they have no income they also find it difficult to pay for the other essentials of life, such as food, clothing, even plates and spoons, let alone such luxuries as soap or toothpaste.

So these children form a sub-class within the prison population. Even if they are housed in separate blocks (which is the exception rather than the rule) they come into contact with adult prisoners when they go to court, when they have visits, when they go for health treatment or if they attend the prison schools, which are designed for adult prisoners anyway, and where they have to buy pencils and books. Far from being separated from adults they are an indispensable feature of prison life, especially as workers. Children are used to collect rubbish, distribute food, and for kitchen work, cleaning, running messages, even building and decorating. As far as both warders and adult prisoners are concerned they are welcome workers because they are easily disciplined and need not be paid.

Between 1976 and 1987, Danny de Souza was a prisoner in Turkey in various prisons where boys were interned with adults. Danny kept a diary throughout his imprisonment and wrote numerous letters to friends outside, detailing prison life and especially the lives of child prisoners, about whom he became increasingly concerned. Extracts from his voluminous writings speak for themselves:

There's some kind of epidemic in the kid's block and we've all been ordered to keep well clear from them. Vomiting and diarrhoea plus fever, the doctor came quickly enough but none of the kids have the money to pay for the prescriptions he's written. We're going to have a whip-round to try to raise the money here. The real miracle is that the epidemic isn't more serious, how the kids survive on just the totally inadequate prison fare is beyond me. Add to that unhygienic conditions as none of them are bothering to wash properly in this freezing weather, yet somehow they survive!

A story Danny tells in more detail is that of Turan, the illegitimate son of a black United States soldier, whose mother left him in the care of an uncle. Danny met Turan when he had just entered prison, aged 11, for his first offence — stealing two oranges. In their first conversation Turan showed Danny a precious Polaroid photograph of the father who left when Turan was six. Turan fervently believed that his father would soon come to take him to the States, where he would enjoy education and all the aspects of a 'normal' childhood which he had never had in Turkey. Danny befriended Turan and managed to get him protected from the brutal initiation rites which begin a boy's prison career. After a while Turan was released but, two weeks later, he was arrested for a new offence and returned to prison. The last time Danny saw Turan was some five years later, 17 years old and awaiting trial for mugging on his last 'reduced length' sentence as a juvenile. By then the boy's dream of being collected by his father and taken 'home' to the USA was like a half-forgotten fairy tale.

Going back to the questions we posed about Principle 2, we can see that children like Turan do not live in conditions of either freedom or dignity, despite legislation which aims to secure their best interests. And the main reason why they suffer incarceration and indignity is poverty. If they are petty thieves in the first place it is likely to be out of individual need, and if they are then subjected to grossly inadequate or harmful treatment when they are caught it is likely to be because of societal poverty. Children's Legal Codes, Declarations and Conventions of the Rights of the Child or any other legislation made specifically for the welfare of children and in their best interests cannot have any real effects, any real meaning, unless both the means and the will exist to implement them. The most effective means of securing children's rights must not be legislation directed narrowly to this end but legislation that attacks the structural causes of poverty itself. Child labour legislation, for example, has never been effective in any country in the world without also being accompanied by welfare measures which remove the need to work.

But this is not the whole story. There is a tendency in many reports and discussions of street children, child labour, prostitution and theft to attribute all these social ills to poverty, and this is manifestly not the case. Many poor families do not send their children out to work, many destitute girls do not become prostitutes and there are people who would rather die then steal, even when they are starving. It is easy to understand why these alternatives are chosen but there is little understanding about why some people do not choose them. Many of the families we have worked and lived with show an extraordinary resilience in the face of the drudgery of surviving in desperate physical and economic conditions. Lacking adequate food, clothing and shelter they still interact with affection, co-operation and happiness. The magic ingredients that enable these small human miracles to take place, which we would characterize by the words love and duty, are never taken into account by either economic or political planners; they certainly cannot be accounted for in legislation. Whoever heard of legislating for love? And yet this seems to be what the drafters of the Declaration and the Convention must have had in mind — remember the Preamble to the Convention? The 'atmosphere of happiness, love and understanding'?

The danger of following this line of thought is that it often leads to a romanticization of poverty and misery. This is akin to all the platitudes about suffering making you a better person or insanity being the price you pay for creativity. Make no mistake about it, poverty is no less dispiriting for being borne with fortitude, suffering is no less painful for the lessons it may teach, and insanity is no less sordid for all the expensive paintings of sunflowers in the world. If a poor family does create a loving atmosphere it is in spite of the days of despair; the lessons learned through physical or mental anguish may be small in comparison to the agony itself and, for every Van Gogh, there are mental hospitals full of people who find it impossible to lift a spoon to their mouths, let alone a paintbrush to a canvas.

The key to making some sense of these problems is probably contained in one word in Principle 2: children need to develop 'spiritually'. But just as one cannot legislate for love so there is no way that spiritual growth could be the basis for any kind of modern Western legal provision. International Human Rights Law contains many references to such ideas but it can make actual provision only for more mundane aspects of existence, like the physical conditions under which children may be incarcerated. Declarations and Conventions are particularly meaningless and empty when they use terms like 'love' and 'spirit'. This is because what are now referred to as 'Human Rights' are really best understood as 'Civil Rights' — those that an individual has a right to expect will be secured by modern government. Such words as 'love', 'spirit', 'understanding' belong to an older discourse of ancient cultures, the 'Natural Rights' which eighteenth-century thinkers like Tom Paine suggested should be expected by all human beings. Although modern society uses these words as slogans, it can no longer discuss them without embarrassment, for there is nothing to account for them in scientific explanation and no way legislation can be framed to include them so that they can be implemented. Yet they remain the best that mankind has to give — if only the means to do so can be rediscovered.

*   *   *

Principle 3: The child shall be entitled from his birth to a name and a nationality.

If ever there was a Principle derived from the Western cultural context it is this one, based as it is on notions of individuality and nationalism which are appropriate to industrialized Christian societies. What's in a name?, as the old saying goes. In our social world, gender-appropriate names are usually prepared well in advance of a baby's birth and give some indication of the type of position it is expected to fill in the future. This may be explicit parental intention. One of our friends called his son George; 'because it's a reasonable name to hear in a pub: "Will you have a pint, George?"' According to their attitude to the position of women in society, other parents chose a particularly feminine name for a girl baby, such as Julie or Karen, or names with a certain gender-ambiguity, like Lesley, or which can be shortened to a masculine-sounding form, Josephine (Jo) or Teresa (Terry). The individuality of the child can be highlighted by using a word which is not in the accustomed class of names, thus a number of Jades and Stars are now reaching their teenage years. Alternatively the child's place within a family group can be emphasized by naming it after a grandparent, aunt, uncle or even a dead sibling. Family names are less mutable and nearly always reflect the paternal interest in the baby. Many couples marry before or just after the birth of their child 'In order to give the baby a name', meaning the name of the father. And for modern states, it is (paternal) family names which are of the greatest importance in the registration, counting, taxing and control of their populations.

These types of considerations are not human universals, particularly in societies in which individualism receives less stress. Babies are not always given a name from birth and the naming process can be delayed until they have reached a state of social awareness. Some groups think that appropriate names cannot be given until other members of society have been able to decide on the most suitable name for this new person. Sometimes new names are given at initiation ceremonies and people may have more than one name according to the circumstances; one name may even be a closely guarded secret.

David Maybury-Lewis has spent many years researching the Akwe-Shavante group in the Amazon basin, for whom inheritance is matrilineal, passing from a brother to his sister's son. Thus the name of the father is irrelevant to the child. Naming is marked by a gift of a necklet from uncle to nephew. But this does not happen at birth. Maybury-Lewis tells us that,

> the lack of a name in his early years is of no particular inconvenience to a Savante since he is, during this period, addressed either by a kinship term or as 'boy' or 'girl' as the case may be. Even in later life his name will only be used to address him on very rare occasions . . . Girls, on the other hand, are named in a public ceremony by the representatives of the community as a whole. (Maybury-Lewis 1967 pp. 73–4)

Delays in naming are also described among the Ilongot people who live in the forests of Northern Luzon in the Philippines. Illongot children are distinguished only by gender during their early years, and the question that Westerners are accustomed to put to new parents — 'What is it's name?' will receive the answer 'A boy' or 'A girl' (Rosaldo 1980 p. 64). Michelle Zimbalist Rosaldo, who lived with the Ilongot for almost three years, explains this in terms of the way these people think of infants:

> a child who cannot speak or recognize a name should not have one . . . I imagine that the custom is rooted in a sense that a 'named' but not yet conscious heart can be called away by spirits or controlled by forces it can neither recognize or ignore . . . The infant, unable to 'know' or reflect on the forces — like naming — that move it, is too much their subject. Only when

the child acquires understanding (usually in the second or third year) will a name, made up in play or the more serious reflections of senior kinfolk, enter habitual usage, becoming uniquely his or her own. (Rosaldo 1980 pp. 65–6)

So, even in a less individualistic society, the uniqueness of human beings is recognized. Certainly it is necessary that a child should have an identity and that this should be recognized by the civil society into which it is born. This is the intention behind Principle 3. It is designed to prevent situations in which children do not know who they are, or where they belong. There are too many stories like that of the little girl rescued by the National Society for Prevention of Cruelty to Children in the UK who thought that her name was 'Oi', because that was the only way her parents ever addressed her, or the small boy found wandering the streets of a South American capital who believed his name was Sucio (dirty) because he was always being chased away by respectable householders with the words 'Get out, dirty boy!'

Principle 3 also addresses the need for the type of identity conferred by knowing the name of one's 'real' (meaning biological) parents. Children who have been abandoned or handed over into adoption or separated from their parents by war or natural disaster often spend considerable time and money in later life tracing their roots in an attempt to find out 'Who they really are'. Such people are usually relatively lucky, however, because at some stage they have been given a civil identity by state authorities. They do have an official existence, even though this lacks the emotional certainty they desire. This is not the case for the large numbers of babies who are not registered with the authorities at birth, or whose documents cannot be located, because the state in which they live may refuse to acknowledge their existence and give them access to citizenship. They cannot go to school, gain access to state health care, obtain employment documents, vote or hold a passport. Ironically, it is not simply that the state chooses to withhold benefits, for they are also subject to being imprisoned or maltreated by state agents, like the police, with impunity — because they do not exist.

Argentina provides the best known example of children whose natal identity has been lost or removed. But, in this case, the searchers are adults rather than the children themselves. After the military coup d'etat in March 1976, Argentinians of all social classes and ages disappeared, among them very young children and others who were born to imprisoned mothers. The Association of Grandmothers of the Plaza de Mayo was created in October 1977 to look for those children, to return them to their natal families and to ask for justice for their parents. One complication they have to contend with is that the children have been adopted, usually by military families, and registered as the biological offspring of their adoptive parents.

The Grandmothers claim that identity is an inherited characteristic and that this is one of the reasons why the children should be returned to them.

Each person is born with their own biological, cultural and social heritage, which is transmitted through previous generations and makes up that person's characteristics. These factors make each human being different, even if his traditional roots bind him to his own social group. Further experiences acquired in his mature years go together with this identity to make him into a complete and balanced human being. All this makes up a person's identity.

It is not humanly possible to change, supplant or suppress someone's identity without doing that person a great deal of damage. Without roots, family, social history or a name with which to identify himself, he ceases to have an identity and has no power to transform into someone else. (Barnes de Carlotto 1987, p. 4)

Their search is aided by a battery of modern blood and genetic tests, which aim to establish their relationship to children who have been adopted, often without knowing their own parents or at an age when they would have little memory of them. Nevertheless, the psychologists attached to the group claim that:

Out of all the words that a child hears the one that has fundamental importance is his name. From the moment of birth a name contributes in a decisive manner to the way a person structures an image of himself. A name is the first and last word in a person's life. That is why it is so serious to deny a person the right to his real name and to substitute another for it. (Barnes de Carlotto, p. 8)

What is difficult to establish is whether the biological or fictive identity has the greatest reality for the children in question. The grandmothers' anguish and dedication are unmistakeable. For the children, anguish will surely be prolonged, whether or not they ever knew their biological parents.

'It's a wise child that knows its own father', as another old saying goes, but a sense of self in adult life is based on more than knowing the name of your father, even if Western literature, and especially soap opera, often assumes that this is the fundamental question of existence. Part of identity is also constructed on feelings of belonging to a community and, as Principle 3 recognizes, modern society assumes that this equates with nationality. Certainly citizenship entails certain rights with respect to the nation state in which one lives, but nationality often conflicts with other, more ancient, communities.

Our ideas of nationality are derived from the sometimes romantic ideas of nineteenth- and twentieth-century Europe. Colonialism, especially in Africa, created artificial entities according to international politics rather than the pre-existing, local political order. In Western European countries, with their long experience of state power and national consciousness, citizenship determines nationality. But other nationalities are based on political experience of shorter duration, built on a common, but not necessarily native, language, and a national self-image which may conflict with ethnic diversity. Some are specifically founded on anti-colonial ideology, and identity of this kind can transcend artificial national boundaries, as does Arab nationalism. New identities of this kind use myths of ancient unity, which can be as diverse as the Aryan 'origins' of the German nation or the 'Ethiopian' origins of Rastafarianism. The most important feature of this for the study of disadvantaged children is the existence of ancient cultures or ethnic minorities within dominant national cultures: gypsies, Inuits, Aboriginals, Amazonian Indians and other threatened or dispossessed peoples.

The terms often used to describe these groups — aboriginal and indigene — imply that the close historical relationship with the place where they live is their common feature, 'a world view which incorporates as its dearest principle a custodial concept of the land and natural resources' (Burger 1987 p. 10). They form about four per cent of the world's population (World Bank 1982 p. 11) and can be found on all five continents. Sometimes they are a numerical majority but remain dominated by their 'civilized' rulers,

> powerless, by and large unheard, misunderstood or simply ignored . . . Their past history is disdained; their way of life scorned; their situation of subjugation unrecognised; their social and economic system unvalued. (Burger 1987 p. xvii)

The communal nature of their social and political organization, which is not based on our ideas of individualism, force and leadership, together with an economic life which is not geared to profit, make them particularly vulnerable to encroaching forms of capitalist exploitation. Their intimate relationship with the environment, which is held in trust for future generations, is incomprehensible to those national and international interests for whom land is a resource and a commodity to be expropriated for short-term gain and development. Mutual misunderstanding has contributed to a history of racism and outright genocide; present reality reveals that an insidious, hidden genocide continues.

Indigenous peoples suffer poor health compared with that of dominant cultures, and this is most marked in infant mortality rates, meaning that it is children who bear the brunt of the suffering. This is just as true of rich countries as it is of the Third World. In the United States, malnutrition is higher for Indians than for any other group, including blacks, and Indians also have a higher incidence of tuberculosis. In Australia also, the average life span of an Aboriginal is 20 years less than that of a white Australian, and it is infant mortality that largely accounts for the difference. In the United States and Canada the infant mortality rate is twice as high for Indians as for any other North Americans (Burger 1987 p. 17).

One obvious answer for the dominant culture is to 'assimilate' or 'integrate', the modern euphemisms for 'civilize' the aboriginals. Clearly, the most powerful tool for this is schooling, which takes the next generation and teaches it to despise the language and ideas of its forebears. The agencies that engage in this 'ethnocide' are not always those of the state or international powers.

> In 1976 a French anthropologist accused missionaries in Venezuela of ethnocide against the Yanomami Indians. Like Pied Pipers, the missionaries were arriving by motor launch and luring the children away with sweets, cakes and presents. Once on the boat, the children were kidnapped and

taken to a boarding school where they were subjected to intensive deculturisation. 'Everything Indian is devalued, scorned, set aside . . . Children cried for their parents. Only busy adults speaking an incomprehensible tongue came to console them'. (Burger 1987, p. 86)

Children born into minority groups within a dominant national culture are thus particularly disadvantaged. But crossing national borders also creates problems, for the United Nations High Commission for Refugees (UNHCR) estimated that of the 12,393,300 refugees in 1986, more than half were children. The UNHCR recognizes people as refugees if they leave their home country and cross the border to another country 'because they fear persecution for reasons of their race, religion, nationality, membership of a particular social group, or political opinion'. But, if people who have been internally displaced, by civil strife, famine or disaster, are taken into account, the total number of refugees could be as high as 25–30 million.

Field reports from Africa indicate an alarming rise in levels of displaced persons due to droughts, violence and armed conflict. As with so many other social and economic problems, the world distribution of refugees is uneven. According to UNHCR, more than 80 per cent of refugees are in non-industrial, underdeveloped countries, which have little in the way of resources for their own population, let alone for an influx of distressed strangers (UNHCR 'Current Problems in International Protection', *Refugees*, No. 22, October 1985, Geneva, p. 5). It is often the poorest countries which are forced to play host to the largest refugee population. Pakistan, which in 1983 had an annual per capita income of only US\$400 and a population of 18.9 million, became host to nearly one million refugees. In 1980, Somalia, one of the poorest countries in the world, was inundated by 1.5 million refugees, equal to one-third of the country's population. By contrast, the rich nations of Western Europe find themselves able to 'afford' to assimilate refugees in ratios of less than 1:3,000, for fear of being overwhelmed by the needs and influences of foreigners.

Television news and documentaries have given us some images of the impersonality and squalor of refugee camps. What is seldom realized is that, in many cases, over 80 per cent of displaced persons in settlements and refugee camps are women and children. It is not that they have been abandoned by men, but rather that husbands and fathers prefer to leave their dependants behind in the relative security of the camps while they return to try to rebuild their lives and provide an income once more. Both parents sometimes leave children behind as a temporary measure. But they are usually illiterate and live in areas where communications, censuses and administration were sketchy before the crisis which disrupted their lives. Messages are unlikely to arrive and relief workers are left wondering what to do with thousands of 'abandoned' children, many of whom are too young to remember such details as their parents' names or their village of origin.

The needs and problems of refugee children are more acute than those of adults in the same position. It is not simply a matter of identity and citizenship, although these may become more crucial factors as they grow older. It is childhood itself that makes them more vulnerable to hunger and disease, both during the flight and in the crowded and often insanitary camps. Emotionally too, their needs are greater. Much is made of the apparent 'resilience' of childhood, but psychologists are now beginning to realize that this is better understood as 'frozen response', an inability to react to trouble and misery because of an unbearable burden of unresolved pain. Apparently impassive children do not respond to further problems through the simple remedy of telling themselves 'this isn't happening to me' (Baskar 1985). Nevertheless, children in refugee camps do show higher than usual rates of disorientation and mental health problems as well as the physical disturbances, like bed-wetting, which are the language of childhood misery (Berry 1987, p. 14; Barudy 1987, p. 28). This is often the only way in which children can express their feelings in the face of the tensions and anxieties expressed more openly by their parents, and their puzzlement at the change which has overtaken their lives.

> Prior to flight the refugee child has experienced the disruption and anxiety within his family and the larger community. The family network may have changed radically and the child may have been forced to assume new roles or ways of behaving for which he/she was not prepared. (McCallin 1987, pp. 5–6)

Exile is a bereavement process in itself and may be accompanied by actual mourning for family members and friends who have died. Worst of all, perhaps, is to lose a sense of belonging to a community. Refugees are not always welcomed by their hosts and they may face years of living in cramped institutions which are virtual prisons. The refugee camp in Hong Kong, for instance, is a closed institution surrounded by wire and guards, in which welfare and education are managed by the Correctional Services. Sri Lankan Tamils face similar conditions in India, where they began to arrive in 1985, their numbers increasing to about 26,000 by the summer of 1987. About half are under 15 years of age but it is those in the 16–30-year-old age group who have fled the most immediate danger, because the security forces of Sri Lanka assume that they must be Tamil Tiger guerrillas. Younger children had already had their education disrupted before their flight and many have left their parents behind.

An Indian newspaper relates one story, which illustrates the military nature of relief camps.

> Padmavathy, a widow with six children, narrates her grievances. After a short stay at Manatpam [reception centre], her family was sent to a cyclone shelter camp . . . 'where there is no school, no church, no hospital, and we had to walk three miles to town'.
>
> She and her children went back to Manatpam and registered themselves as refugees again. But some other refugees 'betrayed' her. She was shunted to Koodal Nagar and her family's cash dole was cut . . . The same is true of Rani her neighbour, who has four children. She too committed the mistake of going back to Manatpam and paid for it. Indeed 'Radial house block No.

27' is called a punishment block. Fourteen 'punished families' are herded there (*The Hindu*, August 1987).

In this situation, unable to get work, men suffer depression and some turn to alcohol for comfort, but women and children are in a worse condition. They are anaemic because of iron and protein deficiencies in their diet. Many children have sore tongues due to vitamin-B deficiency and the corners of their mouths are permanently cracked and sore. The children also suffer from night blindness, spots in the eyes and skin changes because of vitamin-A deficiency. Malnutrition is very common among infants, especially those whose mothers do not have enough to eat: 'We have 18-month-old children who are unable to sit up,' says a doctor. These nutritional problems mean that all the camp dwellers, but especially the children, are vulnerable to infectious diseases, including measles and cholera (*The Hindu*, August 1987).

For some of the world's children, the right to a name and a nationality confers the blessings of being born in the right place, with full enjoyment of citizens' rights in a rich nation. But, even within those rich nations, there are nationalities and nationalities, conferring differential citizens' rights, even in terms of access to health or the right to be educated in your own language about your own culture. The very nature of nationality also entails an inexpressible irony for the six million children who are refugees outside 'their own' countries. They do not have the correct nationality to be able to enjoy any of the citizens' rights of the country in which they are living and in which, indeed, they may have been born. Given the nature of many refugee camps, they are condemned, by their nationality, to lifelong imprisonment in this and also probably the next generation.

*   *   *

Principle 4: The child shall enjoy the benefits of social security. He shall be entitled to grow and develop in health; to this end, special care and protection shall be provided both to him and his mother, including adequate pre-natal and post-natal care. The child shall have the right to adequate nutrition, housing, recreation and medical services.

In the broadest sense, social security for children means either that society will care for a child whose parents cannot do so, or that society will aid the parents to care for their offspring if they have insufficient resources. Clearly ideology makes for differences in the way in which this is translated into policy. Although food, shelter and health are rights, there are societies which visualize these rights as the right to purchase from the open market and make a choice between different health practitioners, for example; other societies in which free access to welfare is a right for all citizens; and still others which designate citizens' obligations to society at the same time as they set out the right to obtain basic necessities. The differences in provision are dependent not only upon political ideology but also upon the resources available to the state and the structures of inequality within it. Some of these distinctions will become clearer in our case studies. Here we simply wish to examine the general field in which the child's right to 'grow and develop in health' might be secured.

UNICEF's *State of the World's Children 1988* was launched with a press pack which contained some large glossy photographs. One shows a child apparently saying 'I want to be a statistic': a statistic in the success of the Child Survival Revolution. We have several problems with this. The Child Survival Revolution, you will remember, is a major strut in the UNICEF programme, allied to the Health-for-All-by-the-Year-2000 policy of other United Nations agencies. It is a programme which constantly sets targets, the year 2000 for preventive medicine for the whole world, 1990 for universal infant immunization and 1990 also for a 'radical change' in infant mortality figures (*Development*, 1983). These targets had to be set because, in most countries, health care provision for the poor is still seen as a concession by the state, rather than as a right.

Despite all the publicity, the targets will not be met. It is not that science lacks the knowledge or the technology or the medicines to combat most known diseases, nor that there is insufficient wealth in the world to pay for medicine and health care, but rather that the world has other priorities. Take universal immunization, for example. By the end of 1987 only half the children in the developing world had been fully immunized against preventable but killing diseases, and these children have been the easy ones to reach. The task is likely to be harder from now on . . .

> In the 1980s, vaccine preventable diseases have killed over 25 million young children, more than the entire under-five population of the United States or Western Europe. The lives saved by immunisation each year are still only 36% of the deaths caused by the same diseases. (UNICEF 1988)

The problem no longer lies in technology. At one time refrigeration was necessary for all vaccines, but modern versions deteriorate less rapidly. It is not just the cost, for the annual cost of full, worldwide, infant immunization is about $500 million — the cost of ten advanced F14 fighters, of which the USA has hundreds.

The first difficulty is simply one of priorities. The proportion of public money spent on welfare always lags well behind the cost of 'defence'. The figures make painful reading. In Nigeria in 1986, US$1,807 million was spent on the military, and military expenditure was US$22 a head. By contrast, a total of US$463 million was spent on health, amounting to US$6 a head. How much health care would that supply in a country in which life expectancy is 49 years, over half the population has no access to safe drinking water and 178 children in every 1,000 do not reach their fifth birthdays? Fewer than one-quarter of Nigerian children are fully immunized.

The second difficulty is also a matter of priority. Fieldworkers find it difficult to get the vaccines to the children. This is not just a matter of education, although persuading parents to come for a single appointment, much less to return for a course of vaccines, is difficult. We take immunization for granted, but it is a relatively new idea even in the West. We are not only used to it as a routine part of early childcare, it also fits in with our ideas of preventing disease and having a positive attitude to health. We expect to be healthy rather than sick and know that we can do this by combating germs, bacteria and viruses. We believe we can take positive action to maintain health as a normal condition. This all seems logical to us but in fact we are simply believing what our local experts, the doctors, tell us. It is doubtful that many of us could actually explain what germs, bacteria and viruses are, much less how they work or precisely how immunization functions. So it is not surprising that people who believe in other sources of disease, such as spirits or the evil eye, take a little longer to believe our story that a needle scratch on a baby's arm will stop it getting smallpox throughout its life. Such an unlikely tale may not convince a mother that it is worth her while to give up a day in the fields and walk several miles in the heat to a crowded clinic.

Even when people are convinced of the importance of immunization, it may be impossible for them to get to the clinics because of civil strife. Some of the 50 per cent of the world's children who *have* been immunized owe this opportunity to UNICEF field staff who have managed to stop the hostilities for a brief period so that children can come for this preventive treatment. In 1987, when a cease-fire could not be arranged in Beirut, the idea was altered with some subtle arrangement to 'three days of tranquillity', which enabled thousands of children to be immunized. It is a question of priorities. But, like many other people, we ask: 'If it is possible to stop the fighting, why isn't it possible to stop the war?' There are fieldworkers in Nicaragua who say that it is a waste of time immunizing children now, because they will only grow up to die as teenage soldiers. Better that they should die earlier from childhood diseases.

The third question regarding priorities is that of cost-effectiveness. If the total defence budget of Nigeria is only enough to buy, for example, three F14 fighters, whereas the United States has a large complement of these and much more besides, increased spending on defence for Nigeria would bring only minimal returns in terms of fighting power. Health services, on the other hand, could benefit to a very large extent from relatively small inputs of money, especially if primary health care is targeted in preference to expensive, hospital-based medicine.

The technological sophistication of Western medicine often bamboozles people into thinking that the hospital-based, curative health systems of urban, industrial nations must be regarded as the only model. Inadequacies in health care for the poor are still explained away in some quarters in terms of 'inadequate infrastructure'. As the former Deputy Executive Director of UNICEF, Tarzie Vittachi, says, this is 'like a doctor telling a patient that he is too sick to receive medical attention, since the absence of infrastructures is underdevelopment, the very disease itself' (Vittachi 1986 p. 5). It also stops the development of cheap, preventive medical systems. One obstacle is the medical profession itself, which is unwilling to turn over some aspects of medical care to paramedical personnel, or even to the patients themselves.

The essential health services for young children are not expensive. They consist of ante-natal check-ups for women and regular check-ups for children in the 0–5 age group, with the addition of the provisions of Child Survival Revolution. These services need to be available from trained medical workers, who need not be doctors or nurses, at places that can easily be reached by local means of transport within an hour. This is the front line of medical care, which picks up problems at an early stage and refers them to the technology of trained doctors, ideally before they become serious. In industrialized countries, all pregnant women and all children under 12 months can go for regular check-ups. But this is not yet the case in developing countries. In Africa only 59 per cent can do this, in Central and South America such care is available to only 69 per cent of women and 78 per cent of children while the situation in Asia is even worse because only 54 per cent of children are able to receive health care in the first 12 months of life (UNICEF 1988, p. 50).

The greatest childhood killer in these vulnerable first months is diarrhoea, which kills an estimated five million children a year, most of whom die not from the actual diarrhoeal disease but from dehydration. Diarrhoea itself causes body fluid to be lost, but sometimes local beliefs mean that mothers stop breast-feeding or giving drinks during an attack, or the water that is given, or in which bottle milk is mixed, is contaminated. Most of these deaths could be prevented by the use of Oral Rehydration Therapy, which uses a mixture of sugar, salt and (boiled) water to replace vital body fluid.

The main point about Oral Rehydration Therapy is that it is a cheap and simple remedy. It replaces expensive drug therapies, which may be unsuitable and can kill babies, as well as being unnecessary, and rehydration by intravenous drip, which requires both trained personnel and expensive equipment. Cartoons showing women how to mix the spoonful of sugar and pinch of salt in the right quantities are now used in health education schemes throughout the developing world. UNICEF's Director, James Grant, is reputed to be so enthusiastic about Oral Rehydration Therapy that he carries packets of the special, foil-wrapped UNICEF ready-mixed salts in his pocket and spreads them out on the table before anyone who will listen. These bright packages can give the illusion of being Western medicine and thus satisfy people's desire for high-technology drugs at a very low cost. But they are still outside the spending capacity of many poor families and even some health workers will not mix their own salts because the packages are the 'real thing'. Thus Oral Rehydration Therapy is not without its critics and problems. It was reported to us that when packets of Oral Rehydration Therapy arrive in a certain East African capital, cakes suddenly appear on the streets soon afterwards, even though sugar is still in short supply. The cakes are called rehydration cakes. And a nurse with many years of development work experience almost snarls when she hears of James Grant's enthusiasm, saying 'I'd like to see him sit up all night spooning Oral Rehydration Salts into a vomiting child, give me an intravenous drip any day!'

There are never any totally simple or blanket solutions. If there were, then the process of modernization, which relies heavily upon technological problem-solving, would have improved the lot of Third World children by now. Instead, it seems to have caused more problems than it has solved. For the first two decades after the Second World War it seemed as if a technological leap, aided by capital investment, would lead to planned and self-sustaining growth in all 'backward' countries. The main obstacle to this, as is now recognized, was not the traditional attitudes of the people, but the fact that their situation of relative poverty was not the result of being left behind by history but rather the dependent state in which colonial expansion had left them. Large-scale, planned economic development, which advocated industrial growth as the solution to wealth differentials, has had two effects. The first is environmental pollution and the second is the increased poverty of the already poor nations and of the poor sectors of all nations.

Environmental concerns about untrammelled industrial development were already being mooted in the 1970s. There was concern about the rapid depletion of non-renewable energy sources such as coal and oil, about the disposal of nuclear waste, about the level of such chemicals as DDT in the air, about the shrinking acres of arable land and the increasing world population. By 1989, further disquiet was being voiced, particularly about the effects of the destruction of the forest areas of the world, not just because of the dire effects of this on minority groups, but also because of the erosion and desertification this causes, and the long-term effects on the global atmosphere and climate. The wisdom of ancient cultures, which retained a balanced relationship with the environment and held the land in trust for future generations, is becoming clear. Because their heritage is being virtually destroyed, children of all countries and social groups are more affected by this process than any other part of the world's population. If present trends continue they will not have health for all by the year 2000 but an environment which is itself mortally sick: more crowded, more polluted, less environmentally stable and more vulnerable to 'natural' disaster than we can even begin to imagine. In the face of that, Oral Rehydration Therapy seems like whistling down the wind.

Already the children of Third World cities are beginning to feel the effects of this. Recent incidents of gas pollution in India (Bhopal) and radiation pollution in Brazil (Goiânia) bear this out. But these are just the specific effects of uncontrolled development processes. A more widespread effect has been accelerated urbanization in the Third World, where urban growth has been faster over the past decade than anywhere at any time in history. Third World cities are ringed by many square miles of shanty towns and riddled with slums, full of street and pavement dwellers and people who live, not in concrete jungles, but in tangled constructions of tin, cardboard, asbestos and mud. A 1987 UNICEF report from 32 countries showed unprecedented drops in living standards of as much as 15 per cent throughout Latin America and Africa, affecting child nutrition, schooling and health provision (Jolly *et al* 1987). These problems have been produced by the 1980–83 recession, which was the most severe since the Great Depression of the 1930s. The worst hit are the poor, and especially poor children because children are the majority of the population in the poorest countries (see Table 2).

Malnutrition is not a disease, but it produces the weakness which is the basis for disease, helps disease take the worst possible course and fails to build up

Table 2
Relationship between national wealth and proportion of children

Country	GNP per capita (US$ 1982)	Population under 15 (per cent)
Brazil	2,240	45
China	310	38
Ethiopia	140	48
India	260	43
Kenya	390	51
Nigeria	860	50
Sri Lanka	320	40
United Kingdom	9,660	23
United States	13,160	23

Source: World Development Report 1984.

strength afterwards. It is this, rather than starvation, that is the greatest killer of hungry children. Starvation is not a health problem, it is a nutrition problem and an economic problem. If parents have money, children do not usually go hungry. When the West thinks of death from hunger it is with an image of bulging bellies and wrinkled limbs, but how many of us realize, as Tarzie Vittachi says,

> that this is only the pornography of poverty — the perverse excrescence of reality? Most malnutrition, perhaps 95% of it, is invisible. It is a vampire disease, a furtive thief that eats a child away from inside (Vittachi 1986, p. 3).

Within all countries, even the wealthiest, there are distinct differences between the health and nutritional status of rich and poor children. In New York City in 1983, for instance, one low-income, minority-group area had an infant mortality rate of 25.1, compared with the city average of 15.5. Equality of access to health care, clean water and food is not ensured by relatively high national incomes alone. That is why Brazil, with a relatively high income per head, still has an IMR of 89 while China, with a much lower per capita income, boasts 47. Differences between different groups in the same country may be very wide indeed. The Peruvian paediatrician Dr Meza Cuadra pointed this out at a conference in 1983. He claimed that the 'Peruvian child' of statistics does not exist. According to the figures he used, the Peruvian IMR was 120 but this was only an average figure. In the rich suburbs of Lima, where children live a luxurious, Western-type lifestyle, the IMR was eight, which, at that time, was the same as the lowest-scoring country, Sweden. Meanwhile, in the slums of the same city, where children live in huts lacking water or electricity, the figure is closer to 200 and, in remote areas of the Andes and the Amazon basin, where health services are non-existent, one child in two dies before it reaches its first birthday, an infant mortality rate of 500 (Meza Cuadra 1983).

The problem is that the poor are getting poorer, which means that these disparities will increase rather than decrease. In Latin America as a whole, income per head fell between 1980 and 1985 by 9 per cent, while the price of basic commodities, especially food, rose inexorably. Unemployment rose in the same period (see Table 3).

Table 3
Unemployment in the 1980s
(per cent)

	1980	1985
Turkey	15	20
Chile	15	24
Bolivia	7	13

Source: Jolly at al 1987.

Meanwhile, even those in urban areas who are lucky enough to have jobs are not bringing home a family wage.

National incomes are also decreasing, because of the overall debt-repayment situation which means that the net outflow from the Third to the First World exceeds by many times the amount received in aid or trade. Thus government expenditure on any kind of social security or such basic services as sanitation, health and education has to decrease too.

Between 1979 and 1983 expenditure per head on health at constant prices decreased in nearly half the African countries for which data exist, and in 60% of the countries in Latin America. Education expenditure per head declined in a third of African countries and 59% of Latin American countries.

Real expenditure per head on the health services fell by 80% in Ghana from 1974 to 1982; by 78% in Bolivia from 1980–1982; and by 32% in El Salvador from 1980 to 1984. In Liberia, the allocation for drugs fell by 35% from fiscal year 1981/2 to 1982/3. In Jamaica, expenditure per head on education fell by 40% and on health by 33% between 1981 and 1985. (Jolly et al 1987, p. 32)

With such a strain already on health services, the effects of the AIDS pandemic can scarcely be gauged. The World Health Organization estimates that the HIV virus will have affected 50–100 million by the year 1991 and that the majority of those affected will develop AIDS and die. Given the rate of spread of the virus, these estimates may well seem minuscule by the year 2000. The virus mostly affects people in the 15–40 age group, in other words the economically active and parental generation. What this means for children already born is not easy to predict. At the very least it means that the economic and personnel resources of badly-affected countries will be reduced, with dire effects for both family-based and state-based welfare and health provision. In many African countries, AIDS is already placing a further burden on overstretched health services. Children themselves are affected, mostly through the placenta before birth.

One disease which causes malnutrition in children which is not restricted to the poor is, of course, AIDS. It is estimated, as a result of surveys at the University Teaching Hospital, that 6–8 per cent of mothers giving birth in Lusaka are HIV+. Their babies, if they develop AIDS (which they have a high risk of doing) are particularly susceptible to pneumonia, diarrhoea, and tuberculosis. Although tuberculosis cases had been falling steadily in Lusaka, last year the number of cases began to rise; this the medical staff believe is directly related to AIDS. On my visits to the hospital wards the tuberculosis wards were overflowing, a sharp contrast to the measles ward which contained many empty beds. There are special cubicles reserved for HIV+ babies in the malnutrition wards. They are perhaps the most distressing of the cases to be found there because death within 4 or so months is inevitable. (Seeley 1988, pp. 14–15)

Nevertheless, even AIDS raises questions of priorities. At one level, panic over the actual number of cases and deaths in First World countries is completely out of proportion, considering the absence of panic induced by the preventable deaths of 15 million Third World children a year. At another level, the amount of resources being pumped into AIDS-related programmes by development agencies is likely to exceed by many times the aid given to primary health care. The tables are being turned once again, not only in favour of the perceived needs of the First World but also to its emphasis on curative, high-technology medicine.

* * *

Principle 5: The child who is physically, mentally or socially handicapped shall be given the special treatment, education and care required by his particular condition.

'Fidel' was perhaps about 18 months old, and looked like any other child of that age except that he was slightly overweight. By half way through their second year, most children have lost their original milk fat because of their constant activity, the effort of learning to walk and run and the excitement of exploring the world. Fidel's world was a cot in a room crowded with similar barred worlds, each containing an overgrown, inactive child. The windows let in little light so his cheeks were unnaturally pale. He looked at us with no interest on his unsmiling face and did not respond to the tickles and hugs of the teenager who visited him most days.

Patty had asked us to visit the home, run by a group of nuns from the order founded by Mother Teresa of Calcutta, particularly to see this little boy. The Sisters thought that, with constant stimulation and the sort of expertise developed in the West, he might grow up to live a near normal life. Like several other handicapped children, he had been abandoned on the doorstep of their convent, putting immense pressure on the caring capacity of a home intended for the indigent old and dying. Patty and the nuns asked us if we could adopt him, but 'Fidel' had no birth certificate or identity documents and we knew that the bureaucracy would be insurmountable.

Two years earlier we had been in a remote village that had no medical facilities, where the harvest had failed for three years running. Everyone was malnourished and the children showed the effects more than anyone else: listless and small for their ages, with thin lifeless hair and dry, scaly skin on which the small cuts and scrapes of childhood failed to heal. Walking wearily away from a long meeting with the village council, breathing heavily in the thin atmosphere, we came across a knot of children sitting in the sun outside their house. Taking advantage of the opportunity for a moment's breather we stopped to chat. They told us that they were all brothers and sisters apart from the tiny scrap of humanity who sat in the centre of the group. 'Salvador' was 'given', they said, a child whose parents did not have the resources to care for him, and who had been left with this slightly better-off family. The children treated him with affection, but his response was little more than that of the boy in the convent. He was painfully thin, but he had a swollen belly and, although he could sit up, it was clear that his tiny legs would not support his weight. He was about three years old and had never been able to run or to talk. His nose and ears were running with mucous and his eyes stared unseeingly out of crusted rims.

The children offered to 'gift' him to us. As in the case of Fidel, we declined. Yet, in both cases, we did not refuse without much discussion about the possibilities and difficulties. Lack of identity documents was only one of the hurdles involved. In each case we decided that our efforts would be better employed working with local people on behalf of the whole community. Yet we still feel we have failed those two small boys and, of all the images of children we have met in the developing world, 'Fidel' and 'Salvador' are the two which come back to haunt us most regularly.

It is one of the pleasures and pains of this kind of work that individual cases often transcend the numbing numbers of children who suffer, but there seems no apparent logic as to why a particular child should have this effect. Dr Pauline Cutting describes the process vividly in the prologue to her book on the siege of Bourj el Barajneh, a Palestinian refugee camp in Southern Beirut.

> I was in the emergency room of Haifa Hospital in the centre of the camp when Bilal was brought in on a stretcher. The bullet had passed through his right arm, both sides of his chest and out through the other arm. My first sight of that child I will carry in my mind till the day I die. He was a beautiful dark curly-haired boy of seven years, with a cherubic face and dark brown eyes. Both his arms and both sides of his chest were bleeding through his T-shirt. He was not crying or struggling, but his lips were blue and he was gulping for air like a fish out of water . . . The bullet had cut his spinal cord. He would be paralysed from the waist down for the rest of his life.
>
> I had been working in Bourj el Barajneh for 13 months by then, and I had seen many injured children. But for some reason Bilal's case moved me like none of the others. What had this little boy done to deserve such a fate? What part had he played in the struggle that was raging around me? (Cutting 1988, pp. 1–2)

The following year, Dr Cutting was able to arrange for Bilal and another paraplegic boy to receive treatment at Stoke Mandeville Hospital in England, thanks to the intervention of radio and television personality Jimmy Savile. The boys will never walk unaided but they are now mobile and relatively independent. These small victories show that, with determination, publicity and large cash inputs, individual disabled children can be helped. But what of the rest? It is estimated that 500 million human beings suffer from disabilities which prevent them from taking a full part in ordinary daily life and that at least a quarter of these are children (Hammerman and Tishman, 1983 p. 57). Within the Third World, disabled children and their families exist as a particularly disadvantaged group. Their quality of life is lower than that of able-bodied persons, mortality rates among disabled children are higher than among the unimpaired and the stigma attached to disability is a further obstacle to their advancement. When the quality of life of the majority is so low that they need emergency aid and resources, many agencies take the same despairing decision we took about Fidel and Salvador. It gives a new and terrible meaning to 'the survival of the fittest'.

Even among the disabled a hierarchy of help exists. An Australian couple who work in a small Indian project recently discussed this problem with us. Where resources are slim it is necessary to choose those children who can show the greatest improvement, in their case polio victims who, like Bilal, can be given the chance of relatively independent existence. Their improvement can be swift and dramatic and this is also the best type of proposition for attracting charitable funding. People like to know that their money has shown results. Not so the profoundly disabled; like Fidel they require long-term costly care, which may not in the end show any 'successful' result. And Fidel had been lucky to encounter the Sisters who will give him not only care but also unfailing love, out of their own deep commitment to the wretched of the earth. As one Sister said to us, 'Jesus is good, he gives us these little ones to care for and he always also gives us the resources'.

One of the most terrible facts about many disabled children in the Third World is not that they are born handicapped but that, like Bilal, their handicap is preventable. Hundreds of thousands of children are maimed because of armed struggles in which they have played no part. But poverty, lack of health care and malnutrition not only kill children, they also leave them permanently impaired. There is no need for children to be disabled by a disease such as polio. When we were children every summer seemed to bring the fear of 'infantile paralysis' to haunt our cosy world. Everyone knew someone who had been struck down. Now a few drops of vaccine on a sugar lump have brought freedom from this disease to developed countries. Polio vaccine can now be given to about half the children of developing countries also. Yet UNICEF estimates that 175,000 children are permanently disabled by paralytic polio each year and, as long as this happens, aid will be needed to deal with these preventable disabilities.

Although we could not be sure about the causes of Salvador's handicaps our hunch is that they were caused by malnutrition. Dozens of studies have shown that lack of food, or incorrect feeding, in the early stages of life or in the prenatal period impairs intelligence. A malnourished child is also less able to fight the infectious diseases that lead to disability. Manuel, the boy with earache, who we described earlier, has an older sister, Nancy, who contracted both polio and meningitis before she was two years old. It says much for her ebullient nature that she survived, although she has one leg paralysed and considerable mental handicap. Even the help available at a charitable hospital for children was beyond her parents' slim resources until they were given some cash aid. A day at the hospital meant that her mother could not sell in the market and the whole family would have even less food to eat. In any case, how do parents who are illiterate find out about the help available?

Acquired disability from preventable disease, inadequate nutrition and accidents are far more likely to affect children of the very poor. It is difficult to protect your child from burning or scalding when you live in an overcrowded dark room and cook with battered saucepans on a rickety kerosene stove. Wounds cannot be kept clean, neither can they be treated by doctors whom you cannot afford, nor do they heal quickly in malnourished children. If, as a single mother, you have to go out to work and leave three small children locked up (for safety) in the room, you consider yourself lucky if the five-year-old manages to cook, clean and care for the baby without accidents. But the long-term effects of this can also be disabling.

Violeta was five years old and attended a pre-school playgroup in the dusty slum. She mixed very little with the other children, and had almost no language development. When given the opportunity to draw she always repeated the same small scrawl in purple on the centre of the page. She described it with one of her few words — 'dog'. Her mother was an infirm beggar with two daughters by different fathers. Every day she left the girls locked alone in the one room they shared, while she went to beg in the city centre. Violeta had been brought up by her sister, only three years older than she was and similarly lacking linguistic development. The dog was their only companion and source of affection during the long days alone. It seemed unlikely that either girl would recover fully from the effects of this early deprivation (Ennew 1985, p. 78).

Long-term research in developing countries shows that, despite falling rates of infant mortality, there is a sharp increase in severe developmental disabilities among the children who do survive (Fryers, 1981).

A United Nations Expert Group estimated that 25 per cent of any population is either directly or indirectly affected by the consequences of disability. The implications are serious. The very nations which now have the least reserve of rehabilitation resources are the nations which must confront the most severe disability burdens. The mix of young population growth, under-development and prevailing causes of disability, is producing an accelerating pattern of impairment among children of the developing world of a severity unlike any with which the rehabilitation systems of the developed world have been accustomed to deal (Hammerman and Tishman 1983, p. 58).

*   *   *

Principle 6: The child for the full and harmonious development of his personality, needs love and understanding. He shall, wherever possible, grow up in the care and under the responsibility of his parents, and, in any case, in an atmosphere of affection and of moral and material security; a child of tender years shall not, save in exceptional circumstances, be separated from his mother. Society and the public authorities shall have the duty to extend particular care to children without a family and to those without adequate means of support. Payment of State and other assistance towards the maintenance of children of large families is desirable.

If it were only possible to legislate for love and understanding! Even the most consumer-oriented societies do not pretend that either can be bought. And yet here we have a Principle in the Declaration of the Rights of the Child that attempts to set out the conditions in which they can be secured, when after a century of study, neither sociological theories of the family nor anthropological theories of kinship have managed to produce a social theory of familial affection. True, there are psychological theories about family dynamics, but these hardly provide sufficient information upon which to base social policies for whole societies. Hidden within the wording of this Principle are so many assumptions about childhood and family life that we make no apologies for taking time to consider its implications, before going on to look at what happens to Third World children who are separated from their families.

An atmosphere of affection

When a child is born it is not simply introduced into a world of light and air with which it will become physically able to cope, from the confusion of which it will learn to perceive sights and sounds and within which it will move and grow. It is also born into a social position. As the physical world pre-exists the child, so does the social world. But the physical world is more impersonal — in itself it prepares no place for the child. The social world, on the other hand, has already situated the child in such a way that access to, use of and ability to partake of the physical world are predetermined. Moreover, within certain economic systems, the less the child can learn in the course of its life to understand and manipulate the social world, the more prepared that world is to receive it, the more immutable is the initial predetermined position. The main institution mediating between the child and social and economic realities is the biological family. But, although sociological theories seem to suggest that 'the family' is a relatively unchanging institution, or that it varies only between cultures, the variations between the actual family experiences of individual children are enormous. The harmonious development of personality is an acutely difficult and finely balanced process. As we have already said, love and affection are unlikely topics for legislation, and yet this Principle tries to make them so.

The elements of social determination of childhood as it is individually experienced can be separated analytically into three main aspects: political, economic and domestic. A child is born into a particular state formation, within a part of the total economic structure and also situated within a particular family context in relation to adults and other children. Most academic studies of childhood stress this obvious, familial aspect. Children are defined and given a primary identity according to real or fictive kinship bonds, as our discussion of Principle 3 pointed out. Childhood and socialization are defined and described in kinship terms, and academic works refer to political or economic aspects as mere descriptive background. The family will be described as more or less 'poor', more or less 'traditional', attached to a particular class or race, belonging to a religious group and speaking a particular language or languages. But these backdrops do more than determine the scenery of childhood: they also determine the people who take part in the family drama, the words and actions in the script and even the length of the play.

Differences in socialization and family form tend to be described in the social sciences as cultural variations which are the product of relationships between biology and environment. Thus the anthropologist Margaret Mead claimed that human childhood universals could be found through cross-cultural comparison. 'Because of . . . recurrent biological similarities — of growth, of parent–child relationships, of needs and fears, and resonances — it is possible to compare childhood in one society with childhood in another' (Mead 1955, p. 7). She suggested that adults regard children as weak, helpless and in need of protection, supervision and training. Children are,

> pygmies among giants, ignorant among the knowledgeable, wordless among the articulate, with incomprehensible urgencies and desires and fears among adults who appear to have such matters reduced to a system — a system which must be mastered. (Mead 1955, p. 7)

But this seems to us a very Western notion. Socialization is more than material for psychoanalytic anecdotes, and the system which has to be mastered consists of more than a set of emotional reactions. Childhood is a social event, perhaps the most important of all social events, and political and economic structures condition the way individual children grow into adulthood. Literature and anthropology are steeped in adult reminiscence of childhood, but how different these times remembered can be! Working childhood at the turn of the century is recorded by Oscar Lewis in the words of a Mexican peasant:

> I can say I had no childhood. I was born in a poor little village in the state of Veracruz, very lonely and sad is what it was. In the provinces a child does not have the same opportunities children have in the capital. My father didn't allow us to play with anybody, he never bought us toys, we were always alone. I went to school for only one year when I was about eight or nine years old . . . Usually I would take a *machete* and rope and would go into the countryside to look for dry wood. I came back carrying a huge bundle on my back. That was my work when I lived at home. I worked since I was very small. I knew nothing of games. (Lewis 1964, p. 3)

The Edwardian childhood of Vera Brittain in England at the same time knew no such labour.

I must have been about eighteen months old when my family moved to Macclesfield, which was a reasonable though none too convenient railway journey from the Potteries. Here, in the small garden and field belonging to our house, and in the smooth, pretty Cheshire lanes with their kindly hedges and benign wild flowers, I and my brother Edward, less than two years my junior, passed through a childhood which was, to all appearances, as serene and uneventful as any childhood could be. (Brittain 1979, p. 21)

For the future social reformer, time spent as a dependent child was extended through the provision of more than one year of education. 'When I was eleven our adored governess departed and my family moved . . . to a tall grey stone house in Buxton, the Derbyshire "mountain spa", in order that Edward and I might be sent to "good" day schools' (p. 27).

But for children of other classes in that same England, adult roles and responsibilities were acquired earlier. Laurie Lee remembers his mother:

She was the pride . . . of the village schoolmaster, who did his utmost to protect and develop her . . . [he] found this solemn child and her ravenous questioning both rare and irresistible . . . When she was about thirteen years old her mother became ill, so the girl had to leave school for good. She had her five young brothers and her father to look after, and there was no one else to help. So she put away her books and her modest ambitions as she was naturally expected to do . . . There was probably no one less capable of bringing up five husky brothers than this scatter-brained, half-grown girl. But she did what she could at least. Meanwhile she grew into tumble-haired adolescence, slap-dashing the housework in fits of abstraction and sliding into trances over the vegetables. (Lee 1959, pp. 112–13)

When her brothers had grown, this girl went into domestic service in the 'world of great houses which in those days absorbed most of her kind' (p. 114), rather than becoming a teacher as her talents and earlier ambitions indicated. The range of choices that shape or distort childish hopes is dictated by more than culture, chance or inclination. Then, as now, the economy determined the physical circumstances of childhood, the relative degree of ease and comfort in which it was experienced from 'very lonely and sad' to 'kindly and benign'. But the economic also tempers the psychological experience of childhood, the harmony and affection to which Principle 6 refers. Thus, when the girl who day-dreamed over the vegetables was herself a mother, she brought up a large family of children and step-children on the erratic income provided by her absent husband. Her novelist son describes his childhood in affectionate terms. Despite the lack of wealth

. . . our waking life, and our growing years were for the most part spent in the kitchen, and until we married, or ran away, it was the common room we shared, here we lived and fed in a family fug, not minding the little space, trod on each other like birds in a hide, elbowed our ways without spite, all talking at once or silent at once, or crying against each other, but never I think feeling overcrowded, being as separate as notes on a scale. (Lee 1959, p. 66)

Such a pleasant picture is often taken to be the norm for the domestic existence of the pre-industrial family and this is often presumed to be a nuclear or extended family ideal. Yet Laurie Lee's family was not nuclear — it was mother-headed and included children who did not share both parents. This type of family is usually regarded as 'irregular', or even 'malfunctioning', by social workers, yet Lee describes it as profoundly functional in the affective sense. Moreover, traditional extended families do not always provide an 'atmosphere of affection and moral material security' even when economic circumstances are more stable. Maxim Gorky wrote of his early years in Russia thus:

> That dreary life was so full of violence . . . and in fact I am not writing about myself alone, but about that close-knit suffocating little world of pain and suffering where the ordinary Russian man in the street used to live . . . Grandfather's house was filled with a choking fog of mutual hostility. It poisoned the grown-ups and even affected the children. Later on, Grandmother told me that Mother had arrived just at the time her brothers were continually pestering her father to divide up the estate. Mother's unexpected return only sharpened their desire to get what they thought was their rightful share. They were afraid that Mother would ask for a dowry . . .
>
> Soon after our arrival a fierce quarrel started in the kitchen. The uncles, without warning, suddenly leaped to their feet, leaned across the table, and started howling and roaring at Grandfather, shaking themselves and baring their teeth like dogs. Grandfather retaliated by banging his soup-spoon on the table. Then he went red in the face and screeched like a cock; 'I'll cut you all off without a penny!'. (Gorky 1966, p. 25)

States and parents

Both Laurie Lee and Maxim Gorky spent their childhoods largely outside the influence of their fathers, in what modern Western sociology regards as irregular families. Nuclear families, consisting of a married couple and legitimate children of both parents, are implicitly the norm. Yet there is a vagueness about international legislation on the family. It is not specified what is meant in the Universal Declaration of Human Rights by the statement 'The family is the natural and fundamental group unit of society and is entitled to protection by society and the State' (Article 16, para. 3). Katarina Tomashevski, a lawyer with Defence for Children International, claims that this is because 'excessive individualism' prevails in international human rights policies. 'A child is treated as a solitary individual, not as a member of his/her family. A father is treated as a breadwinner. A woman is treated as a mother, less frequently as a wife, almost never as a daughter, sister or niece' (Tomashevski 1987, p. 12).

Although family unity is affirmed by all human rights documents, it is never explicitly stated that the nuclear family — described cynically by some sociologists as a man, a woman and one wage packet — is regarded as the norm. Nevertheless, social work practices, first elaborated in Western societies, tend to assume this even though there is no proof that nuclear families are a universal human norm, nor that they provide the most successful form of child rearing. Likewise the idea that the traditional 'extended' family is particularly warm and affectionate is a sociological myth; until warmth and affection can be meaningfully or accurately measured, it will remain so. In the meantime, different States and different social work practices protect the nuclear family form and criticize, regulate or dismantle other 'unsuccessful' forms.

The example of the 'matrifocal' family, which sociology usually treats as typical of the Caribbean, illustrates what we mean. The existence of mother-headed families among the black populations of the Caribbean islands and Southern United States has taken on a meaning which it does not have in fact, except through the imposition of legislative and administrative attempts to deal with it as a social problem. Some writers have described these families in derogatory terms, using words like 'concubinage' (Clark, 1957), and all start from the observation of the number of births taking place outside wedlock in these areas. The two- or three-generation mother- or grandmother-headed household that contains children of the same mother but more than one father is regarded as intrinsically weak and a problem for the State. Agents of the State, like social workers, are empowered to intervene in the best interests of the children, who are thus used as ideological hostages of State power.

Even though mother-headed families are more frequent than nuclear families in these areas, sociological studies still persist in regarding them as anomalous. The fact is that nuclear families are more usual among the lighter skinned and wealthier elite groups. Mother-headed families are always described in terms of what they lack — a husband or father figure. Evidence of the economic and affective strengths of women (like Laurie Lee's mother) to rear children successfully on their own is ignored in favour of a pathological approach. In the First World, this reached its height in a United States Government Report in 1965 which claimed the negro family was breaking down because husband/father figures were statistically absent and this apparently correlated with delinquency and the poor school performance of children. Without using either control groups or historical evidence, the Report assumed that nuclear families had existed, 'successfully', beforehand and that the structures they observed were evidence of breakdown and disorganization (Moynihan, 1965). This provided fuel for those political agents who wished to control the black population — easily-combustible fuel, because the reason for intervention is not an overtly racist one but the 'best interests' of the children.

This situation is repeated in Third World countries, where nuclear families may be even less 'traditional', but where it suits the purposes of elite groups to use social work practice to denigrate and control poor populations. Just the fact that a couple is not married is often taken to be proof of an unstable relationship, and myths about the prevalence of single mothers caught in a string of casual relationships are used uncritically as facts by middle-class social workers in poor areas. We lost count of the number of times Peruvian social workers described this as the root cause of poverty in Lima and of the number of reports which concluded that abandoned children were always the offspring of single mothers, in defiance of the actual statistics presented. In fact, according to the 1981 Peruvian census, only 22 per cent of household heads are female, and a national fertility study published in 1979 showed that, of the women studied, the overwhelming majority (80.5 per cent) had only ever had one relationship (*Encuesta Nacional de Fecundidad*, 1979).

Christian and Jewish ideals of monogamous marriage, and the principle of legitimacy, underlie this concern with the nuclear family. In the Caribbean, islands like Jamaica were subject to colonial attempts to legitimate both cohabiting couples and their offspring through mass marriages in the 1940s. Yet consensual unions continued and, after independence, extra-wedlock births still accounted for up to three-quarters of the Jamaican birthrate. In 1976 the Jamaican government abolished illegitimacy by passing the Status of Children Act. This might be seen as an important step in the field of human rights, because discrimination on the basis of the marital status of one's parents would be contrary to several of the Principles of the Declaration of the Rights of the Child. Similar legislation passed after the French Revolution of 1789 makes it clear that this was regarded as an important Natural Right. Laws to secure this as a Civil Right were also passed after the Russian, Chinese and Cuban Revolutions, even though, in all four cases, the laws were rescinded as the constitutions returned to the idea that the nuclear family is the basic unit of state organization. The difference in the Jamaican case is that the Status of Children Act seemed to have abolished the distinction between legitimate and illegitimate children *in order* to strengthen the nuclear family.

One vital aspect of the 1976 Act is that it made it compulsory for fathers to be registered on birth certificates and provided for blood tests to be used to prove paternity. The intention of the law is to return the absent father to the household and thus supply what the mother–child unit lacks. By 1980 it seemed that fathers were voluntarily registering their names on birth certificates and even seeking custody of their out-of-wedlock children, especially in cases where mothers were unable or unwilling to care for them. Thus father-right was being strengthened, but without forming nuclear families.

By 1980, when we were researching in Jamaica, the attention on out-of-wedlock births had turned towards considering parenting in general. Family Life education schemes in schools, and outside, sponsored by international aid agencies, stressed a moral association between illegitimacy, poverty and promiscuity, just as was the case in nineteenth-century Europe, when social work practice began among the desperately poor in urban slums. Working-class mothers then (like poor black mothers in Jamaica now) were thought of as being unable to practise proper household economy and needing to be taught good ways of parenting. Despite the fact that state agencies, like doctors and social workers, discuss motherhood as the natural destiny of women, they no longer regard good mothering as natural. It is a *problem* for women, which can be solved only by heeding the good advice of experts. Women among the poor are also usually regarded as being sexually disorganized, and illegitimate children are 'proof' of this, even if the parents are living in a stable, permanent union.

Nineteenth-century campaigns in Europe, like Family Life campaigns in the Third World now, tried to 'morally re-arm' the poor by persuading them to marry and establish the correct kind of household unit, living according to the principles of good social economy — a man, a woman and one pay packet. Illegitimacy undermines this policy and is equated with immorality; this is unnecessary because the fact that illegitimate children do tend to show higher rates of infant mortality is morally neutral. However, it is also illogical to use state resources to persuade people to marry, rather than to support mother–child units where children are at risk of higher morbidity and mortality.

Even state support to unwed or unsupported mothers takes a moral stance. Family allowances paid to mothers by the state constitute an exchange in which women receive money on condition that they maintain certain standards of hygiene and household economy and do not enter into further sexual relationships. This establishes the state's right to withhold allowances, intervene in family life and even dismember 'unsuccessful' families. Morality becomes part of the state's strategy, but appears in the guise of liberal policies that protect women and children. The nature of the problem of poverty is transformed from a matter of civil rights to a question of moral conduct. Most of these social work practices are directed towards poor populations. When we were translating a book about French social work practice some years ago, the topic of standards of hygiene became a matter of much hilarity between us and our neighbour who was typing the manuscript. It became obvious that no French social worker would have regarded our houses as fit for happy family life, we exhibited so many of the features (like 'overflowing dustbins') which were used to justify removing children from their parents. But, of course, we are middle-class and not poor enough to require state help or attract the intervention of social workers.

Most developing countries do not have extensive social work systems and those that do exist are limited to urban areas, mostly in capital cities. Although Jamaican welfare state resources are weak, they are assisted by international aid to produce Parenting and Family Life education schemes that stress population control above all other aspects, rather than taking especial care of large families as Principle 6 suggests. Instead of tackling the difficulties of economic existence which can put external pressure on the security of families, sexual behaviour is the focus of particular concern. National economic factors, which are responsible for lack of educational and employment possibilities, are not treated as possible causes of breakdown in parenting and abandonment of children. Instead, a number of programmes are aimed at the control of reproduction, particularly among young people. Even some of the researchers employed on these programmes have their doubts. One told us in 1980 that he had difficulties regarding teenage pregnancy as necessarily a social problem: 'My mother and grandmother were both 15 when they had their first pregnancies, and I'm doing all right.'

Separation from parents: the Good Orphan

Principle 6 also tries to lay down criteria for those children whose parents are unable or unwilling to care for them and who thus become the responsibility of the wider community.

> The children vary in age from nine to twelve years, all are Protestants, and nearly all are absolute orphans, are bound (when not adopted) till they are eighteen years old, on the following terms: up to fifteen years old they are to be fed, clothed, and sent to Sunday school. From fifteen to seventeen they are not clothed but paid three dollars a month wages and four dollars a month from seventeen to eighteen. If, through any unforeseen circumstances it is necessary for a child to be returned to the Home, due notice of the same must be given in writing, a full fortnight before the child is removed; and if the child has been away from the Home six months, her clothes must be returned new and whole and in same number as they left the Home . . . (Bagnell 1980, p. 34)

Thus ran a circular written by Maria Rye, who was responsible for settling some 5,000 solitary British children in Canada during the latter part of the nineteenth century. More than 80,000 impoverished children from the British Isles made that journey between 1870 and the Great Depression, they and their descendants now forming as much as one-tenth of the population of Canada. A further large group of British children was sent to Australia by various philanthropic bodies after the Second World War. Now middle-aged, they are beginning to tell the story of their misery and sense of dislocation. Most were already in homes or foster care when the good intentions of adults sent them to a strange country, and many of them are still unable to trace their relatives in this country or even find out the details of their birth certificates.

The image of the orphan child is a sentimental one. Oliver Twist, Rebecca of Sunnybrook Farm, Little Orphan Annie and others in that genre are the Good Orphans, who succeed, are reunited with their (often aristocratic) families or, like Smike in *David Copperfield*, die young and are gathered to their Maker. Yet the history of childhood in Europe shows an unremitting cruelty and harshness towards children who have no parents. The problem has always been that, if the cost of children cannot be borne by parents, it must be a drain on the public purse. Thus English parishes always tried to shift responsibility for orphaned children on to other ratepayers, or to apprentice them as soon as possible to a tradesman. (This, you will remember, was the fate of Oliver Twist.) The cost of the child's upkeep is then borne by the master, although in reality the child works for its keep. This is not simply an historical occurrence, for many formal and informal adoptions in the Third World take this form. Sometimes it is just a matter of using family contacts or 'shuffling children around' as one Jamaican researcher calls it (Phillips 1973, p. 33): 'I am not living with my parents any more. That means that I have more work to do because I am living with my cousin, who is a teacher, and my grand aunt' (Jamaican girl of 16, quoted in Ennew 1982, p. 144).

Girls, especially rural migrants in search of education in the cities, are particularly likely to be drawn into this type of domestic service disguised as family relationships. Sometimes actual family connections are used, formal and informal adoption may be practised, or godparenthood, or fostering. But, whatever the fiction, these children pay for their keep with domestic services. The lack of wages is given in the pseudo family connection, which their new relatives often describe as benevolent interest. But the conditions under which they live are generally far poorer than those of their new 'family' — some sleep under the kitchen table, for instance, and they usually dine of scraps of left-over food. The hours of work are exceptionally long; many are on call 24 hours a day. In a Report to the Sub-Commission on Human Rights, Special Rapporteur Abdelwahab Boudhiba referred to these 'maids of all work' as living in virtual slavery in most parts of the developing world (Boudhiba 1982). Even if they are not orphans they usually lose all contact with their family of origin or are afraid to return to the countryside, where they might be a burden to their parents. School is generally not compatible with their hours of work and they have little chance to improve their lot, exhausted by work and isolated from contact with other 'families'. Many girls are prey to the sexual attentions of males in the household but, if they become pregnant, they and their children are usually ejected from the 'family'.

Because of the lack of social work resources, state-organized fostering and adoption schemes are not usually well administered and the same abuses may take place, even where family placings are supposedly controlled. Some states simply refuse to believe that fostering is a possible solution. When the predominant ideology stresses the importance of blood ties above all others, it is impossible to contemplate non-abusive altruism in foster parents. But even the misery suffered by isolated, overworked maids and apprentices pales into insignificance against the harsh conditions of many Third World orphanages. Both human and financial resources are too low to provide adequate amenities or prevent abuse and corruption. The family is an important source of unpaid labour for the state in the production of future workers and citizens. If the family fails, the state does not have the political will to make the care of unparented children a priority; and this is the case in most countries of the world. Conditions within institutions for orphans vary, but this account, by Indian journalist Sushil Verma of orphanages in Uttar Pradesh, is not untypical:

> There are 85 children in a Bal Sadan [children's home] in Kanpur. Fifty children sleep in three small rooms while the others rough it out on the veranda. A small child told me that they 'manage' during the summer but suffer in winter. In 1982 a small boy named Harishanker Saxena died of cold.
>
> There are three wooden cots in one room; the children sleep on the floor in the other two rooms. According to the children, reptiles crawl out of deep holes in the ground. The rooms are badly lit and the students cannot study in them. The authorities claimed that Rs 529 had just been spent on provisions but the provisions could not be seen anywhere.
>
> Children receive no medical treatment when they are ill. The

superintendent of the home, Shamim Javed Farooqui, was amazed that the children had spoken their minds on the matter. He showed me his muscles and said that he would have set each one of them right if he had been there. He displayed his broken thumbs and said that they were in that condition because he often beat the children. (*Indian Express*, 12 July 1987)

Development workers in Mogadishu paint a similar picture of an orphanage there:

The Lafoole orphanage started in May 1970. The first children to live there were street children who had been collected off the streets of Muqdisho the same year. Since then other boys have come there from Afgooye orphanage, as they grew older, and from families who cannot support their children. The boys living there range from 5 to 18 years of age. Almost all the staff are male. This centre is larger, much more military in its approach to discipline and organisation, and the living facilities are in poor repair. The dormitory ceilings often leak, and again there was little evidence of the fact that people lived in the institution. For a place that accommodates 1,100 children the Somali term *Xarrunta* meaning camp is far more appropriate a description than orphanage. It is a huge institution. (CIIR 1987, p. 275)

Of course there are well-run orphanages and children's villages and boys' and girls' towns, where better treatment is available. But even these, according to our experience, set the sights of the children no higher than the nineteenth-century models of apprenticeship, in which boys were sent out to learn a trade or join the armed forces and girls went into domestic service. Throughout the world it seems that orphaned children who find their way into an institution are usually destined to learn carpentry, if they are boys, or sewing and cooking, if they are girls.

Separation from parents: the Urchin Rascal

In Dickens' story, the opposite of the sentimental image of Oliver Twist is a cheeky pickpocket, the Artful Dodger.

He was a snub-nosed, flat-browed, common-faced boy enough; and as dirty a juvenile as one would wish to see; but he had all the airs and manners of a man . . . He was altogether, as roystering and swaggering a young gentleman as ever stood four feet six, or something less in his blutchers. (Dickens 1838, p. 12)

This character is also romantic, despite the negative criminal connotations. Some writers give children of the street, who live outside family and state control on the urban streets of the world, the free, bandit status of modern Robin Hoods. Certainly the excitement of street life for a successful pickpocket, harassing the population of adults and house-dwellers and freed from the restrictions of paternal authority and schools, holds some attractions. In Colombia, where street children have been an acknowledged social problem for nearly a century and a half, the Bogotá daily newspaper *El Tiempo* has a cartoon character '*Copetín*', who is a streetchild making anarchic comment on the affairs of the day.

Other street children, however, bear more resemblance to the hopeless figure of Joe the crossing-sweeper in *Bleak House*.

> Joe sweeps his crossing all day long . . . He sums up his mental condition, when asked a question, by replying that he 'don't know nothink'. He knows that it's hard to keep the mud off the crossing in dirty weather, and harder still to live by doing it. Nobody taught him, even that much; he found it out.
>
> Joe lives — that is to say Joe has not yet died — in a ruinous place, known to the like of him by the name Tom-all-Alone's. It is a black, dilapidated street, avoided by all decent people; where the crazy houses were seized upon, when their decay was far advanced, by some bold vagrants, who, after establishing their own possession, took to letting them out in lodgings. (Dickens 1853, p. 160)

But why do we use these examples from novels of nineteenth-century London? The Third World now is teeming with street children: *gamines* in Bogotá, street sparrows in Zaire, *Tarzanilis* in Khartoum, *pelones* in Mexico, *canillitas* in La Paz and *pajaros fruteros* in Lima; or, nearer home, pedlar children in Dublin, gypsy children in the Paris Metro and urchin pickpockets in Rome. One reason for our use of Dickens is that his characters are clearly drawn from actual 'street arabs', as can be judged from the real life descriptions in Henry Mayhew's *London Labour and London Poor*, written at the same time. Many present-day journalists and people who work with street children assume that this is a relatively new, or recently increasing, phenomenon. Far from this being true, there are many ancient accounts of street children. Homeless wanderers, including children, have always resulted from periods of social chaos. In this century, the United States had thousands of vagabond boys and girls during the Depression, free youth wandered Germany after the First World War, Italy had its child tramps and Russia its wild boys. The *gamines* of Bogotá were first recognized as a problem in the 1850s.

Our main reason for reverting to Dickens for our first examples, however, is because, like the Good Orphan, the street child is a powerful image in the Western world. If the family is taken to be basic to social life, then children outside families are particularly anomalous and none more so than street children who demonstrate their independence from adults and the anarchy of living outside respectable society. Journalistic representations of street children are usually illustrated with photographs and anecdotes of children in adult activities: smoking cigarettes, taking drugs, carrying weapons, earning money as prostitutes. They are an affront to our ideal of childhood and thus lend themselves to scandal-mongering treatment, which occasionally hinders programmes aimed to help them. Our case study of Brazil will illustrate this further, but here we also wish to bring in yet another aspect of street children, which we usually think of as the Numbers Game.

Nearly all existing numerical estimates of street children apply to, or are derived from, Latin America. A common feature is that the basis on which they are derived is seldom specified, as the following examples show:

It is said that there are 20 million or more, living in the streets [of Brazil] at least during the day and living in some form of abandonment: more conservative estimates claim the existence of half this number. (UNICEF 1983-84, p. 1)

There are 30 million severely deprived children in Brazil today. It is reasonable to assume that the majority of all these children are street children. (Past President of the Association of Children's Court Judges of Brazil, quoted in UNICEF, 1984–85)

While the region [Latin America] represents only 10% of the world's children, it has more than 50% of the world's street children. The numbers involved in this estimate are: 20 million abandoned in Asia, 10 million in Africa and the Middle East and 30–40 million in Latin America. (Interamerican Parliamentary Group on Population in Development, 1984)

None of these sources gives any indication of who has made these estimates, why 'it is reasonable to assume' the statements asserted, what constitutes abandonment, how to define street children, or even the criteria for severe deprivation. Even a 'back of the envelope' guesstimate reveals that the numbers may be severely exaggerated.

Table 4 gives our estimate of the world incidence of street children using data from the 1984 UNICEF Report 'State of the World's Children', together with some easily available world demographic figures. Although it is an *ad hoc* estimate it does employ at least some idea of definition and some of the conceptual structures that should be used in this type of estimate. More accurate figures could be produced more laboriously, by taking each country in turn and using figures which take into account such factors as:

percentage of child population in each age group;
urbanization;
labour force participation of children;
enrolment in education, absenteeism and drop out rates;
known rates for abandonment at birth, to orphanages, fostering or adoption agencies, juveniles taken into care or in the control of the state.

The present estimate starts with the premise that there will be some relationship between infant mortality rate (IMR) and child welfare in general, and thus aggregates the population figures for countries with high, low and medium rates of IMR, according to the schema used in UNICEF 1984. The populations of socialist countries are excluded from this because they seem to have a low reported incidence of children living on the street. Using the figures provided by UNICEF for the mean percentage of population urbanized in each group, the urban population is derived. As street children are usually found in the 5–15 years age group, a total urban child population in this age group is derived, using rather crude percentages (this may be the area of greatest error). The number of economically active children in each group is taken to be about one-third, as this tends to accord with most known studies of child labour. As not all urban children work on the street (many are employed in factories, workshops and private homes) it is estimated that one-third only will be

Table 4
Estimated number of street children (million)

Infant Mortality Rate (per 1000)	Total Population (1981)	% of Population Urbanised (1981)	Urban Population	Urban Child Population aged 5-15 years	Economically Active Urban Children	Children on the Street	Children of the Street
Over 100	1,301.9	21	273.4	90.2 (33%)	29.8	9.8	3.2
60–100	657.1	41	269.4	89.9 (33%)	29.3	9.7	3.2
26–50 (excluding socialist)	322.3	51	164.4	36.2 (22%)	11.9	3.9	1.3
Under 25 (excluding socialist)	741.0	76	563.2	61.9 (11%)	*	*	*
Socialist	1,438.7	*	*	*	*	*	*
Totals	*	*			71.0	23.4	7.7

Source: Based on UNICEF Report. *State of the World's Children.* 1984.

'children on the street' (working, but with families or household ties and relatively permanent dwelling place; this figure may well be higher or lower in different areas, and could be a further source of error). The final estimate that one-third of these will be 'children of the street', heartless children without family or shelter, is taken from the pyramid diagram used by Peter Taçon, the founder and Director of CHILDHOPE, who has many years' experience of working with Latin American street children.

Figure 1

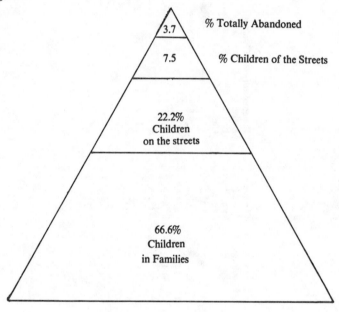

The final figure of 7.7 million abandoned street children does not include the runaway population of the developed world, because the problem of estimation in that case is different. What we are trying to demonstrate with this exercise in instant demography is that some estimates of the extent of children's problems may be wildly inaccurate. And if you are trying to help destitute children, it is important to have some idea of the size of the problem, because planning can be effective only if it has some factual basis. There seems to be a tendency for the publicists of children's difficulties, particularly in the cases of street children and sexually abused children, to deal in huge numbers of thousands and millions which have no basis whatsoever in reality. Moreover, these numbers are seldom questioned and often enter into official documents where they become 'fact'. It is our contention that, just as no child is served by being treated simply as a statistic, so no children are served by being reported in irresponsibly inaccurate 'statistics'.

* * *

Principle 7: The child is entitled to receive education, which shall be free and compulsory, at least in the elementary stages, he shall be given an education which will promote his general culture, and enable him, on a basis of equal opportunity, to develop his individual judgement, and his sense of moral and social responsibility, and to become a useful member of society.

The best interests of the child shall be the guiding principle of those responsible for his education and guidance: that responsibility lies in the first place with his parents.

The child shall have full opportunity for play and recreation, which should be directed to the same purposes as education: society and the public authorities shall endeavour to promote the enjoyment of this right.

'Education, some pants and a shirt' is how a Jamaican street child summed up what he wanted most in the world (Ennew and Young 1982 p. 1). Similarly, more than half the working children interviewed in 1985 in the Paraguayan capital, Asunción, said that their immediate future wish was to continue in school. Yet enrolment and drop-out figures in many developing countries do not reflect this desire, rather they reflect a progressive weeding-out process in which many end up on the rubbish heap. Education seems to head the list of wishes and yet to be out of reach even in countries which, like Jamaica, provide full, free primary and secondary education for the nation's children. The statistics speak for themselves.

In Table 5 we have not followed our usual method of ranking our case study countries according to infant mortality rate. This time we have used relative income, although a further significant factor is the proportion of the national budget spent on education. To give some idea of the variation, and the effects this may have on achievement: in 1985, Sierra Leone spent 16.5 per cent of its national budget on education; Mozambique 16 per cent; India 1.9 per cent; Brazil 3.2 per cent; and Thailand 19.5 per cent. Nevertheless, comparative wealth and economic resources are not the only factors determining educational success for a country nor yet for an individual child. The most important determinants are deeply rooted in the structure of society itself, in the way in which inequalities are experienced by different groups. For it is not intelligence alone that determines which children form the 20 per cent of Peruvians who finish primary school and are able to take up the 'compulsory' secondary school education. Very few rural children in that country will be able to attend any secondary school — unless they migrate to an urban area, probably the capital, where nearly all secondary and higher education institutions are concentrated. It is not simply the level of ability that decides who are the one per cent of children in Somalia, Sierra Leone and China who go

Table 5
School enrolment figures: selected countries

	School enrolment rates 1982[a]			Percentage completing primary 1980-1986	No. of years' compulsory education
	Primary	Secondary	Higher		
Somalia	30	11	1	33	
India	79	30	9	45	5 (age 6-11)
China	110	35	1	66	
Sierra Leone	40	12	1	48[b]	
Mozambique	104	6	—	26	7 (age 6-14)
Thailand	96	29	22	64	7 (age 7-15)
Nicaragua	104	41	13	27	6 (age 7-13)
Peru	114	59	21	51	9 (age 6-15)
Lebanon	118	58	28	66	
Brazil	96	32	12	20	8 (age 7-15)
South Africa[c]	90	15	4		

[a] expressed as percentage of age group: figures over 100 per cent indicate that students outside the appropriate age group have enrolled.
[b] 1976 figure.
[c] 1965 figures.

Sources: UNICEF *State of the World's Children* 1988. World Bank *World Development Report* 1985. pp. 222-3. UNESCO Education Statistics 1981, pp. 13-24.

on to higher education and that means so many of those who enrol in compulsory, free education fail to complete even the primary years.

Why do children fail to enrol, fail to complete or simply fail? In Asunción the working children of the street gave their own replies:

'I had to work.'
'I always got there late.'
'I was bored.'
'I got tired.'
'When I was little they hit me over the head a lot.'
'My mother told me I'm not intelligent.'
'I haven't the head for it.'
'I was short of money for my uniform.'

First there are the hidden costs of education. The following list of the direct costs of free education in Asunción, where the state provides six years of compulsory education, can be repeated with a few variations elsewhere:

Registration
Uniform or overalls
Pens, notebooks, etc.
Bus/train fares
Teachers' wage fund
    (not including tax, service, bribes, etc.)

As if this were not enough, there are indirect and opportunity costs. Many children are important breadwinners in their own right, or contribute to the household income either through giving their labour to family production, particularly in agriculture, or through taking care of younger siblings and doing domestic tasks which free an adult for wage earning. In many cases, their labour is too important to the family for them to be released for a long-term investment of their time in schooling, which may in any case have an uncertain outcome.

> It was on a Friday when I was absent from school, because my mother wasn't going to be at home and I had to stay home. On that particular day, I had to stay with my little baby sister which is approximately two months, above all things I had to tidy the house, and give an eye on the shop, because I was the only person at home, except for my smaller brother and sister. They too help me by staying out front and telling me when someone needs to be served. When I'm not in the shop, I'm in the house tidying or nursing the baby.
>
> After I had finished tidying the house I had another problem, and that was the baby. Although I have given her her bath and had fed her she didn't want to go to sleep so I locked the shop and took her up and sang her a 'rock-a-by' song until she finally went to bed and my problem was solved. Then I opened the shop and as I opened the shop my mother had arrived. She was very tired when she came, and I still had to stay in the shop while she went inside and rested a while. Soon it was nightfall and I went to bed early because I was going out next morning.

This is the way an 11-year-old Jamaican girl described a typical absence from school. With no supervisory adult nearby she was not only missing school, she was also carrying a large weight of responsibility for three younger children. Despite her skills in child care, her three younger siblings were largely reliant on her linguistic and intellectual stimulation, which might mean less capacity to cope with school when they, in their turn, first enter a classroom.

Children like this girl and like Violeta cannot help but fail when they leave the restricted environment of their homes for the unbending school system. They have developed no skills with which to make sense of formal education. In addition, the school may be far away, the hours too long or incompatible with the work they have to do to survive. The knowledge imparted may be irrelevant to their lives, the methods of teaching and even the language unfamiliar to them.

> Like most of the children in our country, the working children of the street come from Guaraní-speaking environments: the language in which they are competent and in which they can express themselves. Even though the cultural environment in which they live is unstable and heterogeneous, it has values, behaviours and images of its own. Its structure, thought and knowledge might be called its 'internal logic', which corresponds to that of Guaraní and has its own indigenous way of being. The culture of these children is, just like the culture of the majority of the population, predominantly oral rather than written and its thought is based largely in

the concrete, not in abstractions. Some of them scarcely speak any Spanish and the majority of those who do, speak it badly, on the basis of a very limited vocabulary and with a rudimentary ability to express themselves. (Espinola et al 1987, p. 95, our translation)

Imagine, if you can, being a six-year-old on your first day in class, in a strange, violent and unwelcoming world where the very language is incomprehensible. That is not so difficult a task for the imagination, for this type of disorientation happened to most of us on our first day at school — it is an effect of the dissonance between the familiar world of home and the routines and structures of schooling. But what if the language really was strange, and you were already tired from your household chores and the long journey to school? What if your stomach ached from an all too familiar hunger and you suffered from constant fevers and illnesses which were consequent upon your malnutrition? What if your perpetual lack of nourishing food had already dulled your mind so that the unfamiliar language never became quite familiar and the whole school day passed in some kind of uncomprehending fog and muddle? So you give the wrong answers, and the teacher shouts at you. You doze off because you are tired and the teacher hits you. Next time she asks you a question you are wide awake and anxious to give the right answer — so tense that you cannot make out what she is saying in that unfamiliar language. Too afraid to ask her what she has said, you give the first answer that comes into your head. She hits you again and shouts at you for being stupid.

At the end of the year you fail your examinations. You have outgrown your uniform which, although very worn, will be passed on to your little brother who starts in the First Grade next year. Your baby sister has bronchitis and the medicine costs your parents more than a week's wages. You start work helping a woman sell fruit in the market, where you enjoy working out the weights and giving change. Anyway, as your mother says, you're not very bright, better to spend the money to see if your little brother is intelligent. You do not bother to re-register for school next year . . .

Given the obstacles, it is amazing that so many children do continue in school, attending crowded shifts after hours of work, walking miles in the blazing sun on an empty stomach, paying for their own uniforms, books and pencils and learning in schools without desks, chairs, books or even simple visual aids.

Finally, there are the problems of misunderstanding between the main groups of people involved in the actual process of schooling: the parents, the children and the teachers.

Children are affected by the parental perception of what a good education consists of, which is frequently associated with the parents' own educational experience (if any). As parents were often schooled under colonial systems to value rote learning and the colonial culture, this may not operate to the child's advantage when newer and more relevant methods and curricula are employed. Teaching about the local culture in the local language may not be regarded as 'proper education' compared with European knowledge and languages.

If parental experience of education has been limited, teachers may be viewed with deference, because of their competence in elite culture, or despised, for their lack of training, poor pay and conditions of work. Parental commitment to education is also dual. It may be very strong — education is the high road to social mobility and the whole family may work so that one child who is successful, according to the criteria of the education system, can make it to professional status and thereby drag the whole family out of poverty. Yet this can lead to unrealistic expectations on the part of parents and children about the relationship between schooling and white-collar jobs. Like most people who have researched educational issues in the developing world, our notebooks are full of 16–18-year-old functional illiterates who still give 'doctor', 'lawyer' and 'teacher' as their career preferences. Perhaps the cruellest aspect of many compulsory education systems is that even successful completion of secondary level often gives no entry to higher education. Entry to university, technical college, nursing and even such trades as electrician is often gained only by obtaining a certificate from a private college. What is remarkable is that some very poor families do manage to send not just one but several children successfully through this expensive and exploitative private sector and on to trades and professions.

At the other end of the scale, parental commitment to education may be very weak. Poor educational performance in rural areas is not simply due to lack of schools or the preference of more highly qualified teachers to remain in urban areas. There is also a prevailing idea that children do not need much education, that three days a week is enough and five excessive, so absenteeism and drop-out rates among rural schoolchildren are high. This attitude can persist in slums and shanty towns also, particularly when economic resources are low. 'High schooling to them may be looked at as a long term plan which may not come within the scope of their values. People living at barely subsistence level are scarcely attracted to years of academic grind' (Thompson 1969, p. 72).

Teacher/pupil relationships are often the least satisfactory aspect of education systems. Because of low staffing ratios and resources in schools, records are often inadequate and cases of absenteeism and drop-out are not followed up. Teachers may be afraid to go into the slum areas surrounding the school, or feel that they would jeopardize their middle-class status by going there, or be too exhausted at the end of a double shift of teaching classes of 50 and long hours of travel between home and two places of work. In any case, remedial or educational social workers are usually overworked, where they exist at all. With little or no welfare state back-up, even if teachers do find out what home factors are keeping children from school, there may be nothing they can do about it. Thus many children with a poor commitment to school receive only minimal provision. This is part of the explanation for the apparently paradoxical fact that most street children claim to be schoolchildren and are always 'going to start back at school next Monday'.

Underlying this there is often an unbridgeable gulf between teachers and pupils inherent in the structure of many education systems. Children report that teachers have no personal interest in them, that they are distant and impersonal, especially in secondary education. Authoritarianism in schools provides the socialization necessary for authoritarian regimes, sometimes through the exercise of direct violence in routine corporal punishment. Even more successful is what a Pink Floyd song of the 1970s so graphically described as 'dark sarcasm in the classroom', which prepares future worker citizens for a life of subjection (Pink Floyd, *The Wall*, 1979).

In countries which were formerly colonies or which are now under the influence of economic and cultural imperialism, such authoritarianism penetrates deep into teachers and pupils alike. Education systems may appear to be a means of developing individual talent, but they are also the means by which economic domination of a colonizing country or an oppressive class is ensured through the systematic denial of local cultural autonomy and imposition of foreign ideas. Thus, in Jamaica, the over-valuation of English culture, with the Englishman as 'the model of Humanity', persists two decades after independence (Brown 1979, p. 83). This is both explicit and implicit in the Jamaican system, partly because those now teaching were themselves educated in a system in which 'Empire Day and other English holidays, some of which were not even remembered in England . . . had to be celebrated here [in Jamaica] with gusto' (Haughton 1979, p. 10).

The exclusion of local culture from education throughout the developing world means that many teachers and pupils have a better knowledge of European culture, nature and literature than they do of the life of their own country. This tends to make them defensive and insecure about curriculum changes. Paolo Freire sums this up in his book *Education: the Practice of Freedom*:

> Our traditional curriculum, disconnected from life, centred on words emptied of the reality they are meant to represent, lacking in concrete activity, could never develop a critical consciousness. Indeed, its own naive dependence on high sounding phrases, reliance on rote, and tendency toward abstractness actually intensified our naiveté. (Freire 1973, p. 37)

In Brazil, as in so much of the developing world, this tendency to inauthenticity of knowledge penetrated deep into all intellectual life.

> The point of reference for the majority of Brazilians was Brazil as an object of North American thought . . . they thought about Brazil from a non-Brazilian point of view . . . The Brazilian intellectual lived in an imaginary world, which he could not transform . . . he suffered because Brazil was not Europe or the United States. Because he adopted the European view of Brazil as a backward country, he negated Brazil; the more he wanted to be a man of culture, the less he wanted to be a Brazilian. (Freire 1973, pp. 39–40)

Why is it that the most sophisticated inhabitants of Buenos Aires refer to their city as 'the Paris of the southern hemisphere', while it is unimaginable to describe Paris as the Buenos Aires of the northern hemisphere? 'How early do we learn to lie to ourselves?' was the question over which our two young Peruvian research assistants agonized in a discussion into the early hours of the morning, after realizing the psychological implications of some infant school pupils who had copied pictures of Western families in preference to drawing their own (see also Ennew 1986, p. 22).

Authoritarianism also places a dead hand on critical awareness and creativity. Because of the elite nature of educational content in the past, knowledge is treated as inert property to be handed down intact and unquestioned. Successful students may simply be those with good memories, excellent motivation and convergent minds. Creative, lateral thinkers who might innovate and criticize tend to be labelled educational failures very early in their careers and either be pushed out or drop out of school. In most countries of the world, education assumes the passivity of pupils, so that teaching becomes what Freire calls an 'act of depositing . . . in which the scope of action allowed to the students extends only as far as receiving, filing and storing the deposits' (Freire 1972, pp. 45–6). The type of teaching that involves both teacher and pupil in an exploration of a real rather than imagined world, in 'problematizing' their own social situation, ends in producing a critical awareness, which is not the aim of most education systems. Even science which, according to the ideology of problem solving, should teach children how to explore the natural world and find out how it works, has a conservative function and preserves social inequalities. For science does not allow criticism from outside its own paradigms. It allows only questions about how nuclear bombs work, for instance, but does not give any legitimacy or frequently show any interest in whether such knowledge should be sought. Scientific thought produces an elite stratum of 'experts' who distance themselves from reality, devise technical and efficient solutions and dictate policies for implementing them. Just as colonialism ruled through the imposition of European culture in the arts, so transnational companies dominate the world by asserting their technological superiority and the overall supremacy of 'science'. Third World cities are today dominated by the elite, international culture of technology, which, rather like the man who 'knows the price of everything and the value of nothing', knows the way things work but does not ask if, or why, or for whose benefit they should work at all.

The scientific, problem-solving answer to the problems of Third World countries include the provision of technical education so that economic growth can be established. But this raises the question of the purpose of education. What is education for? For the labour market or for the child? The answer is related to the problem of the statement, 'Children are our future'. In the case of the boy who wanted 'Education, pants and a shirt', the position of his government when he made his wish in 1980 was unequivocal. According to the Five-Year Development Plan, published two years earlier by the left-wing People's National Party, which was then in power, education and training are two of the basic necessities of life in a 'socially responsive economy' (National Planning Agency, (Jamaica) 1978, p. v). Indeed, equal access to education for all citizens was regarded as a major component in 'the promotion of social justice in the widest and deepest sense' (p. 1). The Ministry of Education likewise stated that the education system should play 'a major role in equipping individuals with knowledge, skills, attitudes, creativity and a cultural milieu which assists in the rounded development of its citizens' (Ministry of Education, (Jamaica) 1977–78, p. 1). Alongside many writers on Caribbean education, however, we have to admit that there is an 'air of unreality' about such statements (see for example Henriques 1953, p. 133; Figueroa 1971, p. 71). The Principal of the main Jamaican Teacher's Training College stated that 'one can find no evidence to support the assertion that there has been a great influx of lower class children in High School' (Miller 1976, p. 60). In stronger terms the National Union of Democratic Teachers, drawing on the official statistics of the Ministry of Education, had this to say:

> thousands of our youth are doomed from birth; . . . in the age group (6–11) years when we would expect full universal education, 10.8% are still out of school; . . . during the crucial years (12–15) when schooling is vital to later performance in life, as many as 31.6% are excluded, and lastly . . . education over 15 years of age is still the right of only a privileged few. (Haughton 1979, pp. 1–2)

This lack of fulfilment of individual potential is even more tellingly revealed in the figures for adult literacy, which are officially estimated at around 50 per cent. Unpublished figures from the adult literacy foundation JAMAL show that, in 1980, 45.7 per cent of JAMAL students were in the age group 15–24, lending credence to the comment frequently heard in Jamaica that 'schools exist to produce JAMAL graduates'.

The secondary, and less philosophical, aim of education systems lies in their relationship to the economy. Thus the same Five-Year Plan refers to 'the need to structure the content of educational programmes so as to relate skills and attitudes to the world of work . . .' (National Planning Agency (Jamaica), 1978 p. 98). This contradiction is not exclusive to either Jamaica or the Third World, as the 1988 England and Wales Education Reform Bill makes clear, by stating in its Preamble that the education system should be brought into line with the economy.

We do not wish to appear unrealistic in this respect. It is obvious that an important component of individual fulfilment is the development of skills that enable children to secure a means of adult subsistence in the future. These aims are not necessarily contradictory as they stand. What is odd is that so many children leave school without basic skills of numeracy and literacy, and that, throughout the world, youth unemployment shows that the labour market can absorb only a very few of those who do leave school with employable skills. We can only conclude that such wastage at an individual level serves a wider economic function: the economy does not need them to be educated to the full enjoyment of their potential.

The development of education systems that provide free, compulsory education to the masses, as opposed to a small elite which has the monopoly over knowledge, is related to the scandalization of child work which effectively bans children from the labour force. It produces a particular kind of *industrial* childhood, in which childhood becomes a period of preparation for the labour force, in which skill-acquisition (of the limited kind needed by the labour market and for the limited numbers which can be absorbed) is only part of the process. Another function of education is a hierarchizing mechanism, which preserves the knowledge territory of elite dominant cultures and nurtures only those from the masses who can be trusted to conform. This is now further served by the problem-solving, scientific, technological culture of transnational enterprises, which intensifies the process of denigration and devaluation of ancient cultures that began in the colonial period.

Perhaps most vital of all, education systems transmit messages about ways of being. Besides establishing what counts as knowledge and intelligence they also reward certain habits and behaviours, appropriate to existing social and economic systems.

> School is not one mode of formation among others, it is directly conceived as the first, the final and the only one. Its timetables occupy the child's whole day, its programmes encourage indirect knowledge to the detriment of experience. Formed there in professional instruction, its discipline defines a way-of-being-a-child, made of passivity of blind obedience to a pedagogy of intimidation. (Meyer 1983, p. 11)

In order to improve schools there is no need to wait for new books or buildings or even more teachers, any more than children should have to have uniforms and shoes before they are allowed to learn. (We are not yet aware of any child development theory that correlates intelligence with clothing.) Progressive education systems which could equip the world's children with the skills and information they really need now could to a very large extent be produced through reform of the existing schools, and of teaching methods which, at present, simply impart inappropriate knowledge, creating and deepening social divisions and simultaneously dampening and deadening the creativity and potential of individual children.

This brings us to the last paragraph of Principle 7. When Freire discusses recreation, he means precisely this re-creation of society and people through the process of discovery. But what Principle 7 evokes for us is yet another Western concept which may be inappropriate to the Third World. In theories of child development and education that have emerged in the West over the past century, play has gradually assumed a major part in understanding the processes by which children acquire concepts and ways of manipulating them. Western pre-school, nursery school and infant school provision is now armed with a plethora of materials and techniques through which children can be made to grasp culturally important ideas of colour, shape, size and movement. Play is the means by which children, like all immature mammals, come to understand their environment. There is no doubt that Violeta would have benefited from more external stimulus than was available to her in the windowless prison which was her home. But the nature of play, as produced in the artificial teaching atmosphere of early childhood education, is as artificial as the nature of Western childhood itself. It is a commoditized play, using bought items to produce consumers. When play means toys that have to be bought, it no longer has much relationship to being playful.

One of the delights of working with children is the rediscovery of playfulness, and the best teachers and child workers are those who have never lost this creative ability to savour all experience as if it were for the first time. Commodities shut down this capacity. The ultimate commoditization of play produces Activity Centres in which there are stars for star-shaped holes and circles for circle-shaped holes and which need teacher/parents who only reward fitting in shapes correctly into like-shaped apertures, rather than lying down beside you to see what amazing shadows the wooden star makes in the sunlight.

Children whose ideas are not stunted by the acquisition of toys are to be counted lucky in this sense. For us the symbol of the future is in the kites that fly above shanty towns, made of scraps of paper, string, sticks and offcuts, floating on breezes which scarcely freshen the foetid air below. But children like Violeta who do not glimpse this freedom are not lucky. Nor are children who are weak and stunted from malnutrition or preventable disease, who cannot play or enjoy sport. Nor are children who have no access to open space for kicking and throwing balls. Nor are children whose burden of responsibility to the household is so great that, once they have fulfilled this and done their homework, there is neither time nor energy for their own pursuits.

*   *   *

Principle 8: The child shall in all circumstances be among the first to receive protection and relief.

No one who reads newspapers or watches television news can be unaware of the fact that children are more often defenceless than protected, often need relief because of lack of protection and usually need both protection and relief because of inhumanity in the first place.

When people use the phrase 'women and children first', they are usually thinking of emergencies, crises and wars. The image is something like that of self-sacrificing men helping mothers and small children on to lifeboats from the sinking *Titanic*. The image also includes some idea that men fight to protect their families and it is, therefore, not surprising that Eglantyne Jebb should have raised public anger with her statement that 'all wars are waged against children'. There have been more than 120 wars and armed conflicts since the Second World War, a figure that excludes terrorism and organized violence 'which has disabled, killed, maimed, traumatised and driven tens of thousands of children and their parents into the hell of a refugee existence' (Vittachi 1986).

We doubt if there has been any war in which children have not suffered, directly and indirectly, but no modern war can exclude children. This is because of the nature of modern warfare, which is no longer confined to the battlefield. Of the First World War it can be argued that relatively few casualties were civilians. Technological advances in the manner of killing entailed that half the casualties in the Second World War were civilians, who suffered from shell and bomb damage to their homes. Only two decades later, the Vietnam War counted 80 per cent of its victims as civilians. In the civil strife in Lebanon, over 90 per cent of deaths are civilians to say nothing of those maimed, like Bilal. The number of deaths from war over the past 40 years of 'world peace' is staggering. According to the United Nations Department for Disarmament Affairs, 20 million have died and, although no one counts the deaths of children separately, it is worth remembering that most of the violence since 1945 has taken place in the Third World, where children are 40–50 per cent of the population.

The irony is that, while over 500 million people in the world go hungry, the rich nations export arms to them rather than food: almost US$24 billion worth in 1986. While children still die of preventable diseases, there is now one doctor for every 2,044 Third World people but one soldier for every 250. The ironies do not stop there, however, because the arms trade is so lucrative that countries like Brazil and India are manufacturing and even exporting arms on their own account. Arms manufacture has become one of the acknowledged paths to economic development. Yet this can mean the concentration of power in the hands of the military forces and even a military government. This tendency is on the increase. In 1960, 22 of the world's independent states had military governments but, by 1985, the figure had risen to 58 out of 114, an increase of 22 per cent. What this entails for children is not only an increased threat of becoming victims of conflict but that they become victims before hostilities occur. When militarism begins to dominate the structure and nature of government it also begins to dominate the allocation of public money. What this means is that guns and soldiers come to take priority over food and medicine. War kills many children directly, but indirectly the preparation for war kills an even greater number.

There are further implications of the technological advances of modern warfare, of which few people can be unaware. Both conventional and nuclear weapons are capable of massive and indiscriminate destruction. The 200,000 killed by the first atomic bombs in Hiroshima and Nagasaki are matched only by the lives still ruined as a result. The children of Hiroshima are still suffering over forty years later and yet there are now more than 50,000 nuclear weapons in the world, many of which are 1,000 times as powerful as those dropped in Japan in 1945. The danger to the next generation of actual destruction wrought by these weapons, to say nothing of neutron bombs and chemical and biological warfare, is joined to the projected problems of radiation and nuclear winter.

In times of crisis, and in the preparation for crises, the watchword really is 'women and children first' — first to suffer, because basic resources and services on which they depend are disrupted or not provided. This is so not only in warfare. Disasters of all kinds have a long-term, knock-on effect for vulnerable sectors of any population. Besides being victims of the disaster itself, they are more likely to suffer from the lack of service provision caused by the disaster. Usually there is little information quantifying this. Data collection systems also suffer in crises and the only evidence is the qualitative information of relief workers. It has, however, been possible to compare pre-war and post-war age-specific mortality in the Matlab Bazar district of Bangladesh. The data show a 47 per cent increase in deaths over births in this rural area of Bangladesh during the war period (1971–72). These data document significant excess mortality in children up to the age of nine. An additional cost of the Bangladesh war was the reintroduction of smallpox (transmission had been stopped in 1971) resulting in an estimated 224,000 cases and 42,000 deaths; 18,000 of these deaths were children under the age of five (Curlin, Chen and Hussein, 1976).

Statistics may document accurately the way in which societies fail to provide even the spirit of protection to children in conflict situations but they do not show how the particular powerlessness of children is involved. For that it is necessary to turn to anecdotal evidence.

On 25 May 1986, we had an uneventful day. It was the Spring Bank Holiday weekend and we spent most of the time gardening. In the Negros Oriental area of the Philippines, seven-year-old Pablo Hilardes had an encounter with the paramilitary ICHDF:

> At dusk . . . Pablo and his twelve-year-old brother, Santos, were walking home with their mother when they were accosted by ten armed men led by Berenos Campos, an ICHDF member. The men took their mother away and the two boys were left behind with two armed men to guard them.
>
> The men returned after a few hours without their mother, neither boy knew the men had killed their parents and had returned to give them the same fate.
>
> Both children were slapped and Santos made a futile attempt to fight back but he and Pablo fell to the ground amidst kicks and blows. Then the armed men continuously hit the innocent children with bolo knives. Pablo tried to evade the sharp edge but it continued to batter his body. He covered his head with his hands, an action which he did not know would save his life. He lost consciousness and when he awakened the men had already left.
>
> It was pitch black when he crawled to where Santos was sprawled. The boy tried to shake him awake but Santos did not respond. He continued to urge his brother to wake up but the latter remained silent. Pablo stood up and said weakly, '*Okay, I'll go ahead since you don't want to come with me*'.
>
> A few metres away, Pablo turned back to give Santos one last chance. But when he touched Santos, Pablo felt that his brother was no longer breathing. It was then that his young mind grasped that his brother was already dead.
>
> Very weak from loss of blood, he arrived home and there he saw his 16-year-old brother, Macario, trembling with fear. Macario narrated the brutal way his parents were killed. In one single day, Pablo's world crumbled apart. (From *Philippines Human Rights Update*, June 1986)

The story of Bayo took place in Biafra, in the year with which we began this book. It is narrated by Simon Dring, who later left behind his 20 years' experience as a war correspondent to work for children with Sport Aid. Bayo is for Simon what Bilal is for Pauline Cutting: the child one does not forget.

> Bayo had always wanted to paint. As far back as he could remember, so the villagers said, he had dabbled with colours — splashing water and smearing clays across bits of board, scraps of paper, and even rocks.

He was 12 when civil war engulfed the eastern town of Enugu and separated him from his family. To survive, he fled into the jungles of Biafra.

It was in the week before Christmas that same year that he and his friend were captured by the soldiers. They were shown no mercy. The boys were obviously spies — obviously thieves — obviously in the wrong whatever the truth.

Bayo was forced to watch as they tortured his friend. At one point they made him hold the bayonet as it was plunged into the boy's stomach — the wound that finally killed him.

But Bayo still refused to talk. And he knew that he must escape if he were to live. He could only have one chance. It came when they were burning him with their cigarettes and threatening to cut off the fingers of his right hand. But he didn't remember if he had run or not. When the villagers found him he was alone, unconscious, lying face down in the dirt beside a jungle path — only two of the fingers of his right hand remaining.

There was little the village doctor could do about the infections, the fever, the pain. But the boy never cried. In the end all he did was ask for a piece of board and some coloured dyes and clays.

He died soon after he had finished the painting. It was a self-portrait. A gaunt, hollow face looks out at the world. But there is a glimmer in the big, staring eyes — and a moment of defiance, even triumph in the way he is brandishing in the air the first and second fingers of his right hand.

The translation of the inscription underneath says simply: 'For the friend I love'. (Dring 1986–87)

*   *   *

Principle 9: The child shall be protected against all forms of neglect, cruelty and exploitation. He shall not be the subject of traffic in any form.

The child shall not be admitted to employment before an appropriate minimum age; he shall in no case be caused or permitted to engage in any occupation or employment which would prejudice his health or education, or interfere with his physical, mental or moral development.

The only possible reaction to this principle is hollow laughter. In the First World the extent of child abuse and neglect in the midst of material plenty is only now being given the recognition it needs to be combated. To give just one example, in 1984 50,000 children were physically or mentally abused, neglected and emotionally starved in England and Wales. Of these, 600 had severe injuries such as broken bones and head injuries and 52 were battered to death. In the Third World an unknown number suffer these types of intrafamilial cruelty as well as the slow agonies of malnutrition and the preventable diseases that result from living conditions worse than those from which the RSPCA 'rescues' dogs in this country — conditions which are normal life for millions of slum and street dwellers. But the lives of slum dwellers require a different set of priorities — if Violeta's mother had been found shutting two toddlers in a windowless room in the United Kingdom, social workers would have removed them from her care and courts would have accused her of neglect and cruelty. In Lima, where few of the small numbers of social workers find the courage to descend to the area in which these people are forced to find some form of survival, she was actually protecting her daughters from worse dangers, while ensuring some kind of economic survival for them all.

Such families are citizens abandoned by their states, which determine priorities of warfare above those of welfare, nationalism above citizens' rights. In this they are aided implicitly by international attitudes and priorities. Such cruelty and neglect is the indirect outcome of the priorities of the First World, which place the acquisition of material goods and financial security above the needs of people who know nothing of either, for whom a gift of £5 to charity at Christmas is a large amount, while a gift of £150 for a computer toy for a nine-year-old child is cheap. From the unassailable moral position in which 'charity begins at home' is not infrequently believed to be a Biblical quotation, it is easy and comfortable to criticize those governments and groups that practise organized cruelty on small children. The inescapable knowledge that cruelty to children is an established feature of our own society, together with the abnegation of moral responsibility for the plight of children in other societies, must be borne in mind while we catalogue just some of the ways in which cruelty and exploitation are the lot of Third World children.

The facts of these cases alone speak for themselves:

> One night a young girl called Tahereh was brought straight from the courtroom to our cell. She had just been sentenced to death and was confused and agitated. She didn't seem to know why she was there. She settled down to sleep next to me but at intervals she woke up with a start terrified and grasped me, asking if it were true that she really would be executed. I put my arms around her and tried to comfort her, and reassure her that it wouldn't happen but at about 4 a.m. they came for her and she was taken away to be executed. She was sixteen years old. (Testimony of a female student imprisoned in Tehran between September 1981 and March 1982, from Amnesty 1987, *Iran: Violations of Human Rights*)

> It has been brought to our attention that on 11th October 1987 a 5-year-old boy, José Luis Perez Ochoa, died in the hospital of Torax de Tegucigalpa [Honduras] after 34 days in a coma as a consequence of serious wounds on his head and on other parts of his body.
>
> The boy's wounds were reportedly inflicted by the Police in an incident on 7th September 1987 in the 6th Avenue of Compayaguela opposite the market of San Isadora de Tegucigalpa. According to his parents, *Mateo Perez Garcia* and *Santos Isabel Ochoa*, stall marketeers, the child tried to stop members of the security forces from mistreating his parents and was consequently beaten himself. The Police say the child died of pneumonia. (Letter to the President of the Republic of Honduras, from a representative of an International Seminar on Children held by Amnesty International in London, 1 December 1987)

> Attorneys in the territories are reporting to us the continued use of violent interrogations to extract confessions, brutal beatings of children at the time of arrest by the IDF [Israeli Defence Force], and such violent treatment in prison that many are now in hospital. One such case is ----- ----- who received a written summons to appear for a Shin Bet [Israel's internal security service] interrogation. The boy was made to undress at the Gaza military

headquarters on 13 October and told that if he refused to confess to throwing a stone he would be raped by his Shin Bet interrogator . . . The boy is now in hospital suffering from what the prison medical person termed a 'nervous condition'. We have learned that his 'nervous condition' consists of serious injuries to his head, chest, liver and knee after a 12-hour marathon beating by four Israeli interrogators. He is still in hospital on the verge of a nervous breakdown. (Canon Riah Abu El-Assal 1987 *Children in Israeli Military Prisons*, Council for the Advancement of Arab–British Understanding)

A 16-month-old child, Natalia Garcia, . . . was imprisoned with her mother in a cell within close earshot of the one where her father was held. Both parents were tortured and could hear each other's cries. The child lacked proper food and care generally and the mother was unable to attend even to her most basic needs.

The mental traumas produced were of such severity that the child rejected the mother and suffered psychological disturbances so serious that her mental health was irredeemably impaired. A signed medical certificate states that 'the CNI returned a little girl, frightened, nervous, who can't sleep, with marks and blotches all over her body, and we still don't know whether they are caused by nervous reaction or infection. The nervous condition of the little girl is without doubt very serious and this is indicated by her insecurity and the fear of any person who approaches her; she becomes defensive and thinks she will be punished'. (Alan Grounds, 'Child's Own Story' in *Amnesty*, April/May 1987, p. 11)

State and para-state violence which is directed at individual families and their children will be relatively easy to target using the provisions of the Convention of the Rights of the Child. It is, however, much more difficult to target exploitation and cruelty which arise out of economic structures. A particular case in point is child work. We will be examining examples of this in detail in the case studies, especially those of India and Thailand, but the following examples from other Asian countries show how dangerous child work can be.

Jamilah was only eleven when she began work on a plantation. She did weeding, plucked and opened cocoa pods, sprayed pesticides and carried bunches of oil palm fruit to collecting points. Before she reached 18 Jamilah died of a form of respiratory cancer.

Raju, 13, helped his father who was an oil palm harvester to load the fruit bunches or collect loose fruit. One morning while his father was cutting a bunch, the sickle fell off the pole and fatally injured Raju.

Balu was a good student. He was ambitious and determined not to be an estate worker. But his dreams were short lived. At 11, Balu was asked to drop out of school to work in the estate. With ten mouths to feed and an elder brother in secondary school, the parents needed another wage earner for the family.

Shamsul Nizam was a bright and athletic 13 year old lower secondary school student in lower Perak, when he lost his right arm in March 1984 in an

ice-crushing machine in the fish factory where he worked.
    (All examples from *Child Workers in Asia*, 1986, Vol. 2, Nos. 2 and 3)

The International Labour Organization has guesstimated that there are 150 million child workers in the world, most of whom work alongside their families in agriculture. But gross figures of this kind do not help us to come to grips with the realities of individual cases like Jamilah. We need to know how these figures are related to other statistics about childhood and what effects other factors, like the economic system and welfare provision, have on their situation. But published figures do not often present this type of information and it is difficult to make comparisons between figures gathered for different purposes. Table 6 which combines UNICEF child health and demography figures with some estimates/guesstimates of numbers of child workers made by a Thai-based pressure group, should be taken only as a rough illustration of the situation for child labourers in some Asian countries. It does, however, enable us to look at some possible correlations.

Table 6
Child workers in Asia

	IMR	Population (millions)	Children under 4 (millions)	Child workers (millions)
Bangladesh	205	95.8	17.2	20.6
Bhutan	215	1.4	0.2	.30
Burma	95	37.6	6.0	6.57
China	55	1,039.0	95.0	84.9
Hong Kong	12	5.4	.5	.17
India	165	732.3	101.1	11.0
Indonesia	135	159.4	21.6	9.7
Japan	9	118.9	7.8	0.00
Korean Republic	39	39.8	4.0	.48
Malaysia	41	14.9	2.0	.22
Nepal	215	15.7	2.6	2.6
Pakistan	180	96.0	16.6	13.5
Philippines	85	52.1	7.6	4.6
Singapore	13	2.5	0.2	.06
Sri Lanka	50	15.7	2.0	.44
Thailand	60	49.6	6.5	8.5

Sources: UNICEF *State of the World's Children* 1983, and *Child Workers in Asia* Vol. 3 Nos. 2/3 1987.

What we can see is that there are no simple links between infant mortality rate and child work, even though a brief glance at the figures for Bangladesh, India and Japan, for instance, might indicate this. Hong Kong and Singapore still have high proportions of child workers, even though their infant mortality rates have fallen, from 80 and 55 respectively, in 1960. But this cannot simply be due to the influence of capitalist growth, because China's equally impressive reduction of IMR has not been accompanied by an eradication of child work, despite socialism. The incidence of child work is not determined only by poverty: cultural attitudes to childhood are also crucial. Organizations concerned about child work are only now beginning to recognize the difference between a child's right to do useful work under proper conditions and with fair pay, compared with the child's right to protection from exploitative labour practices which can mean lives and dreams lost for ever.

Policies about child employment which are now in use at various levels, both national and international, arose because of the way in which present ideas of childhood developed alongside those of work during the industrial revolution in Western societies. The ideas of work and childhood which we now use are recent developments. We are now accustomed to the idea that unemployment means lack of waged work and that this defines whole regions as poor. But unemployment does not mean idleness and would be an inconceivable notion in societies where people labour for subsistence rather than cash. These days 'work' in industrial and modern settings means employment, jobs and wage labour. It implies work outside the home, usually for a third party , normally taxed and controlled by the state.

In ancient cultures work is not separated from the individual and the household in the way that is common in modern societies. Nor is work separated from leisure or even, in some situations, from education. Child work is as inevitable as adult work, it is a natural part of the learning process and a necessary part of growing up. Child labour became a scandal when this learning ceased taking place within a household, when children were separated from adults and yet forced to do similar work alongside them. So the rhythms of household-based, apprenticeship learning were replaced by the harsher rhythms of the wage-earning workplace. At the same time, many of the teaching functions of the family were replaced by schooling which trains children in the skills needed by the industrial labour market; schooling simply intervened to prepare children for the adult world of work. Where it was not present, and the skills needed for factory production were low, then children, like adults, were free to seek a cash income in industrial production. In many cases they were preferred to adults because it would be argued that their smaller bodies required less food and they could be paid proportionately less. It could also be argued that they were less skilled, strong or useful than fully-grown people. Their lack of physical and political power made them a more amenable workforce and, for some tasks such as bobbin-filling in the spinning industry, their small size may have been advantageous for productivity.

But this 'Nimble Fingers' argument does not explain the whole of child labour. Economist Diane Elson argues that apparently economic phenomena, such as skill classification and wage levels, are not determined by purely economic factors, but by gender and seniority — social factors independent of industrial market economies. Even though jobs in industrial society are not gender-ascriptive they are nevertheless bearers of gender. Thus although a 'wage earner' is not necessarily male, in the sense that a husband or father must be so, it is usual practice to refer to employed males as 'workers' and employed women as 'women workers', which perpetuates sexual hierarchies. In the same way, economic categories are bearers of seniority. Even if children become skilled they cannot be regarded or paid as 'skilled workers' until they are adult males — in other words 'breadwinners' (Elson 1983). It is not difficult to see how this is related to the idea of the nuclear family as a man, a woman and one wage packet.

So the nuclear family is linked to the expressed need to protect women and children from the scandal of their exploitation in the workplace. There were three main influences on the development of child labour legislation in the West. First there was a body of philanthropic reformers who objected to menial work being performed in dangerous conditions by women and children. This point of view was reinforced by a new morality which separated men in the workplace from protected mother–child units in the home and was backed by both industrialists and trade unions. Industrialists aimed to eliminate labour as machinery became more capital intensive and especially to eliminate child work from (cheaper) labour-intensive competitors. It was also necessary for children to learn new skills, suitable for new production methods, in schools. From the point of view of trade unions, the existence of cheap, easily exploited child labour increased adult male unemployment and lowered adult male wages. When employment opportunities were scarce and adult wages did not support a family, unemployed or poorly paid adults were frequently obliged to rely upon supplements to the family income earned by their children. Few trade unions admitted young workers, even apprentices, to full membership. By supporting child and female labour prohibition in the nineteenth century, trade unions were promoting the interests of their adult male members. Meanwhile, women were instructed by doctors, psychologists, health visitors and popular literature in the health and morality of the family. Welfare legislation makes clear distinctions between male and female and entails that the family provides a suitable environment for the care of the future labour force.

Child labour legislation in the Third World has simply followed the lead of Europe and North America. The irony of legislation prohibiting child labour and providing compulsory education is that it does not prevent children working. If adults do not bring in enough money and family welfare payments are absent or inadequate, children may miss school to work at home or go out to work in conditions that are even more exploitative than the factories and mines from which they are excluded. Once minimum-age legislation is in force, unless it is backed up by adequate family allowances for unemployed parents, the result is a group of unprotected children. They are forced to go out to work in company with others who are excluded from protected legal employment: the old, the sick, women and illegal migrants.

*   *   *

Principle 10: The child shall be protected from practices which may foster racial, religious and any other form of discrimination. He shall be brought up in a spirit of understanding, tolerance, friendship among peoples, peace and universal brotherhood, and in full consciousness that his energy and talents should be devoted to the service of his fellow men.

Like Principle 9, this is mere rhetoric as far as most of the children in the world are concerned. Not only are children brought up in contexts in which all kinds of discriminatory practices exist, they are also among the first to suffer from them, either because they learn from them about other people or because they learn from them about themselves. The process by which a girl learns that she 'is' emotionally weak and illogical, or a black child learns that his skin is 'ugly' is long and slow. It takes years of implicit and explicit social instruction before a child learns to despise Jews or to consider blue eyes superior to brown, or to think of certain types of taste as inferior and lower-class. These types of difficult and utterly illogical lessons are learned by children throughout their childhoods in most parts of the world. Adults teach them these terrible untruths as part of the socialization process that prepares children to take their places in the real world, as citizens of hierarchical states.

One of the most insidious factors in this education is that such lessons are taught alongside others, which deal with important moral values. The things which might be considered worth dying or at least fighting for — truth and justice for instance — are all mixed up with ideas about the quality of one's fellow human beings. Thus the spirit of understanding, tolerance, friendship, peace and universal brotherhood is confused with other notions: patriotism, the motherland, fighting for one's own people, sacrificing one's life for one's country. The irony of a priest from a religion that preaches brotherly love and forgiveness blessing an aeroplane carrying enough bombs to kill and maim thousands of his brothers is not noticed amidst this nonsense. People who preach or practise pacifism are often silenced, imprisoned or killed.

It is, therefore, not surprising that children know about war and fighting rather than about peace and brotherhood. Nor is it surprising that, in most countries, the idea that it is noble to die fighting for one's cause or country is learned as early as and alongside the all-important lessons about the issues worth defending and the people worth attacking.

In October 1915, during the War to End All Wars, a Brooke Bond tea delivery boy left his job and enlisted in the British Royal Navy. His name was Jack Cornwell and he was a few weeks short of his 16th birthday. He was not a bright boy at school and had never distinguished himself in any activities during his short life, but he was ready to fight for King and country against the wicked forces of the Kaiser. Together with 600 other boys at Keyham Naval Barracks in Plymouth, he was hurried in six short months through a training programme which would have taken two years in peacetime. He was not very good at the gunnery course, which took up half of the time, but he did learn to obey orders without question and he passed out as Boy 1st Class, with pay of one shilling a week.

Less than a month later he saw action for the first time in the Battle of Jutland. In the early moments of the engagement he was mortally wounded, while all the adults around him fell dead or wounded. Communications were damaged and he received no orders, so he never even fired a shot at the enemies who killed him. Bemused and frightened, he remained standing upright by his disabled gun, not knowing what else to do, fully exposed to gunfire until the twenty-minute battle ended. He died of his wounds a day or so later.

Jack Cornwell became a hero and one of the youngest soldiers to be awarded the Victoria Cross. A painting of him standing gallantly by his gun soon occupied a prominent place in 12,000 schools all over the United Kingdom. He should have been a symbol of the wastefulness of warfare, an illustration of the inhumanity of employing children as killers, a reason for the adults on both sides to stop their foolish slaughter. Instead he became a means of enticing more young people to volunteer. Indeed he must have been a powerful symbol for adults too: the bravery of fragile children who fight must shame more than one 'real man' to take up arms.

The volunteer Iranian child soldiers who sought martyrdom in Khomeini's war with Iraq are only one example of present-day versions of Jack Cornwell. Estimates made by the International Red Cross, the International League for Human Rights and the Iraqi Red Crescent indicate that more than 50,000 children aged from 12 to 15 had died in the south-west of Iran before the end of 1983. In Kampuchea and Vietnam, children have been fighting since the early 1970s. In Nicaragua, members of the Alfonso Velásquez group of Sandinista fighters may be as young as seven, while the army takes recruits of both sexes from the age of 16. There have been reports of minors fighting in Ethiopia and Uganda, El Salvador, Colombia and Honduras. And boy soldiers are recruited not only by guerrilla forces or the governments of developing countries. In the technologically sophisticated Malvinas conflict, three British soldiers under 18 years of age died, while another 13 were wounded. None of these children could vote for the cause, or government, for which they risked death.

Children may be taught to kill and die not only from the inculcation of moral imperatives, but also from the experience of violence. In some cases, children may be witnesses to direct hostilities or gruesome atrocities; in others they are its victims. The psycho-social effects on both children and adults of living in an atmosphere of violence are little understood as yet. But it does seem clear that war has an overall impact on child development, attitudes, human relationships, moral norms and general outlook on life (see Freud and Burlingham, 1943; Horowitz and Solomon, 1975; Punamäki, 1982; and Fraser, 1974). Likewise the long-term violence of imprisonment in a refugee camp, as in the case of Palestinian refugees, leads to hostility and aggression.

If, like several of the children we have already mentioned, your parents had been killed or tortured in your presence, would you not have taken up arms in vengeance?

'I saw my mother being assassinated by Obote's people. I saw them come to my house and kill my father. I just ran away. Then I heard that Museveni's people were collecting boys and girls, so I joined them,' says 14-year old

George Kokosi, a corporal of the 11th Battalion, at present moving north towards Soroti and Gulu which are still under UNLA command.

Kabanda [aged 11] has strong feelings. 'The men who kill my mother, they make me angry. Me, I decided to go in the army. Me, I decide to beat them. If I find them, I kill.' But Kabanda is still a little boy. He is keen to show me how he opens up the heavy North Korean-made rifle that he carries, but the catch gets stuck and it's too stiff for him to budge. He looks up with a rueful smile; 'It is difficult, my friend.' I ask him how he cleans the gun. 'I have lost my cleaning rod', he confesses.

Corporal Kabanda already has an idea of what he would do, if given a chance. 'When the fighting finish, I stand back, I go for schooling. Soldier it is a bad thing. It is good if you are a child and they killed your mother and all your brothers and sisters, but when it is peaceful I would not go in for being a soldier. Me, I like to drive the motor car. I finish schooling, I go for work and earn money. Then I buy the motor car.' (L. Hilsum, UNICEF's Information officer for Eastern and Southern Africa, 'Not too small to Kill', *Children First!*, August 1986, pp. 17–18)

We are not suggesting that children cannot form political opinions, or have as much right to defend them as adults. Nicaragua has recognized this by giving them the vote at 16 if they are in the army. Moreover, children as young as ten are active in civil rights issues throughout the world. Often this means fighting, as in Northern Ireland, Lebanon and South Africa.

Such children have been born into situations of immediate and obvious violence. All members of the next generation, however, like all children born since Hiroshima, have been born into a situation of long-term fear of violence. We still remember our own post-war childhoods, how the siren wail was occasionally tested and how the fear this aroused in adults communicated itself to us, even though, unlike them, we had no memories of bombs dropping. But we also remember the fear of the unknown effects of nuclear warfare, how this seemed to strike us more than the adults around us. It was as if their experience of 'conventional' weapons could not (or would not) encompass this new and different threat. When we have been recently on local Civil Defence exercises, we have found that people of earlier generations still seem to think that the aftermath of a nuclear war will be rather like relieving what they persist in calling 'The War', despite the 120 fought since. There is talk of pulling together and digging latrines and the importance of hot water for shaving to keep up morale, which makes it rather scary to think that the people responsible for (not) starting a nuclear conflict at the moment are of that same earlier, naive generation.

Let us quote from a UNICEF document about children in armed conflict:

At present the world's nuclear arsenals contain over 40,000 nuclear warheads, which are roughly equivalent in destructive power to 1 million atomic bombs like the one dropped on Hiroshima. The nuclear explosive power is equivalent to 3 to 5 tons of TNT per capita. A massive attack using the present-day nuclear arsenal is likely to cause the death of hundreds of millions of persons and produce heat radiation, penetrating radiation, radioactive fall-out and a nuclear winter.

No health service in any area of the world would be capable of dealing adequately with the hundreds of thousands of persons seriously injured by blast, heat or radiation from even a single 1-megaton bomb. To the immediate catastrophe must be added the long-term effects on the environment. Famine and disease would be widespread, and social and economic systems around the world would be totally disrupted. (UNICEF 1986 (c), p. 34)

What is different about the next generation in the First World is that this is the third generation to be born into this nightmare. The first, which was our own generation, was still influenced by the relative innocence of past wars. The second, our own children, begotten in the era of peace and love of the 1960s, started life with our unrealistic optimism and is now rearing its own children in cynical pessimism and materialism. Research shows this third generation to be gravely concerned with the nuclear threat. It has been stated in both the United States and the Soviet Union that young people are forced to live with the sense that for them the future and adulthood do not exist. These findings have been replicated in Australia, Belgium, Canada, the Federal Republic of Germany, Finland, New Zealand, Sweden and the United Kingdom.

Meanwhile their brothers and sisters in the Third World also live with the very real fear that they will not live to be adults. Preventable disease, repression, 'conventional' warfare, the accidents inherent in poor housing, the infections that result from poor health care, sheer starvation: these are their immediate enemies. Yet these children too are affected by the two most terrible problems to have ever faced any generation: environmental destruction and nuclear war. No previous generation has been united by the same problems, yet, at the same time, no previous generation has been so divided by the inequality of the share-out of the products of the earth.

Part 2
Case Studies

Capital: Freetown
Area: 27,699 sq. miles
Population: 3,700,000
Urban population: 29% (1985)
Population annual growth rate:
  2.6% (1980–85)
GNP per capita US$: 350
  (1985)
Rate of inflation: 25% (1980–85)
Population below absolute
  poverty level { urban: n.a.
  (1977–85)   { rural: 65%
Population with access
  to drinking water: 22%
Life expectancy: 36

Sierra Leone
(U5MR = 297   IMR = 171)

Births: 174,000
Infants with low birthweight: 14% (1982–85)
Population 0–4: 600,000
Population 5–16: 1,000,000
Total population under 16: 1,600,000
Deaths 0–4: 52,000
Children 0–5 suffering from malnutrition:
  mid-moderate: 24% }
  severe: 3%   }   (1980–86)

One year olds { TB: 80%
fully immunised { DPT: 21%
              { polio: 21%   } (1984)
              { measles: 66% }

ORS per 100 episodes of diarrhoea: 57 (1985)
Primary school enrolment ratio male/female: 68/48
  (gross) (1982)
Grade One enrolment completing primary
  school: 48% (1976)
Secondary school enrolment ratio male/female:
  23/11 (1982)

(all figures 1986 unless otherwise stated

Sierra Leone

When a Koronko child is born the umbilical cord is taken and buried together with a kola nut seed, so that each individual has his or her own tree.

Sierra Leone was an English colony, but the population of around three million consists of no less than 18 distinct ethnic groups. Although 40 per cent are Muslim and about 8 per cent have been converted to Christianity, the remainder follow indigenous religious systems. English is the official language among this diversity, but the two main groups, the Mende and the Temne, make up 60 per cent of the total inhabitants. The Koronko live in the north-east and the Creole peoples, who play an important part in economic and political life, are concentrated around the capital, Freetown.

When Graham Greene arrived there on his way to Liberia in the 1930s, his initial impression was of the colonial influence:

> Freetown ... at first was just an impression of heat and damp; the mist streamed along the lower streets and lay over the roofs like smoke. Nature, conventionally grand, rising in tree-covered hills above the sea and the town, a dull uninteresting green, was powerless to carry off the shabby town. One could see the Anglican cathedral, laterite bricks and tin with a square tower, a Norman church built in the nineteenth century, sticking up out of the early morning fog. There was no doubt at all that one was back in home waters. (Greene 1936, p. 34)

Freetown has the third largest natural harbour in the world, but it is not used to capacity. The same can be said of the plains and plateaux of the hinterland, which has underused agricultural and mineral resources. Almost all the land is arable but most farmers are smallholders engaged in subsistence production, using slash and burn agricultural techniques to grow rice, which is the main crop and staple food.

Cash cropping and diamond mining have increased the standard of living for some, but intensified the imbalance between urban and rural areas in terms of service provision, especially in health and education. It is now regarded as prestigious to live in town, follow an urban way of life and buy imported foods and consumer goods. This does not mean that the indigenous political structure of chieftainships has broken down, for it has been incorporated into the national system of government and operates through a network of patronage that links rural and urban areas. The power of the modern sector to offer employment and, at the same time, to have the ability to expropriate land, leads rural people to seek links with patrons in urban areas. In this process, children are important agents of their parents' concerns, for it is through education that they can enter the modern sector (Bledsoe 1987 p. 2). In the autobiography of a Limba boy, written at the age of 19, we can see what this may entail.

> I was born out of a poor family whose main occupation was subsistence farming.
> At the age of 3 to 5, I was only permitted to scare birds. As I grew as a boy, my parents began to let me go on fishing trips where in seldomly, I was fortunate to catch fish [on a] large scale.
> My happy times arrived at the age of 7 years when all my brothers and sisters, both young and old, would gather together at night in the moonlight and start to narrate stories, and my most favourite story was: Prince Sarah, the cleverest of all kings.
> Early in the morning, we the children of the same age, will meet in a specific approved ground, where we have to perform a wrestling match, to know, what rank a person belong to.
> I fought with a boy from a village known as Kadanso; where we have the famous herbalists. He was a hero in their squad but I defeated him and got the name 'Yoboh' which means herb of the year. As I grew bold and troublesome, my father thought it wiser to send me to school.

At the age of 8 years . . . I was sent to school and to my amazement, I saw a white man, who was the first to see in my life. I ran back quickly home and told my Dad that I was not going to school again, but he encouraged me and I went back the next day. My close friend provoked me to anger, that I am a green because I feared a white man. With an immediate reaction I bounced on him without any complain, so the headmaster in revenge of the beaten child, gave me a thorough licking and told me to complain before reacting. So I adopted that manner, and the children ceased to provoke me.

Our headmaster passed a rule in school that every one go to church any Sunday, and I adopted that again since I feared him.

I was indeed fortunate to be made a class captain from class 1 to class 7 and even to reach the rank of a senior prefect of my school . . . From the origin, I have faith that, it was God who gave me intellect to defeat my comrades in both internal and external examination.

My elders and the big boys grew jealous of me and adopted the idea of beating me [on the way] home. So to prevent this I have to walk together with the teachers after school and when we arrive in town, I have to depart from them with a telivic [terrific] speed to my house.

I ceased going on fishing trips and attending wrestling matches. I preferred staying at home and go on reading my school notes and revising . . . selective entrance papers. I was victorious in the end for topping the squad that took the exams.

I departed from my mom and dad, but [they] were pleased because I never argued with them nor my mother's mates nor my elders. While I was in the elementary school, I often go to bush to fetch wood for my mother, or fetch water for her and also I did a lot . . . for my Dad and mother they felt it when I departed from them and often I go there [to] find blessings from them. My mother and Dad are always praying for me to have bright fortune in future. Thanks to the Jah [God], for out of the polygamous family that I originated from, I'm the only son to reach this level, as far as education or going to school is concern.

Thanks to God for making me to depart from my elders from the primary school whose aims were to keep on treating me as an enemy till I leave school. I am also glad that I have took to Christianity. I preferred staying in town rather than the village where the people take the law into their [own] hands.

Educational opportunity is limited because schools are not available, lack facilities and cost money. In 1970, adult male literacy was 18 per cent and female 8 per cent. Less than half the children who register actually complete primary school; nevertheless, literacy rose by 1985 to 38 per cent for men and 21 per cent for women. Literacy, however, is not a simple concept. Although it has the technical potential for changing the environment, it also adapts to the prevailing social and cultural environment. In other words, reading and writing are not inert skills; what is done with them depends upon how people perceive them. Literacy and education may be thought of in quite distinct ways by teacher and taught, particularly if they belong to different linguistic and cultural traditions. In a society like the Mende, which holds that certain kinds of knowledge are both secret and dangerous and must therefore be the preserve of secret societies open only to initiates, it is hardly surprising that literacy and educational knowledge should be regarded in the same light.

In Sierra Leone, literate knowledge is largely incorporated in written texts like the Bible, the Qur'an and government documents. People who can read and write thus have access to the means of personal advancement. In general, English is seen to hold the key to a more open type of knowledge in government and administration, and Arabic as the key to the secrets of healing and protective charms. Even though Western teachers think of schooling as the free spread of information, the Mende tend to manipulate it in the same way as they use their traditional, secret knowledge. Mende teachers have been known to exploit their position to obtain money and labour from pupils and their parents (Bledsoe and Robey 1986, pp. 217–20).

The idea of a national society is growing slowly; most Sierra Leoneans are rural and owe their primary loyalty to lineages and extended kinship groups, which define rights and duties according to ancient ideas of cohesion. What is the meaning of family to a child of the lineage? How meaningful would the rules of the Declaration about family life and biological parents be to these children? A Mende proverb, which states that 'a child is not for one person', contradicts in essence the principles by which nuclear families operate. Moreover, as the Limba boy made clear, polygamy is widespread in Sierra Leone.

Polygamy, which may be one man with more than one wife or (more rarely) a wife with more than one husband, is simply one of the many arrangements by which human societies ensure organized reproduction, care and socialization. Whereas nuclear families concentrate on the importance of paternity and the right of mothers and children to paternal support, lineage societies are more interested in the rights which adults have in children. Children are an important resource rather than a cost to parents. They are part of the unbroken chain of being linking all who have already lived and all who will be born. They are necessary as future lineage members, for their labour, and as part of the strength the group can use against other lineages in feud or warfare. Children provide welfare for old age and are needed to perform the rituals that incorporate their parents in the realm of the dead.

After the death of one of its members, the entire group gathers to reassert the continuing relevance of the dead to the living:

> This ceremony is for dead people. The people believe in the ceremony that whenever a person is dead they must have 40 days for him/her. As such they believe that after the death of somebody, that is from the first day up to the 39th day, the spirits of the person are in the house . . . after the ceremony . . . the spirits will leave the house and go finally to heaven. So that is why they always hold the 40 days ceremony after the death of a person.
>
> In this ceremony all of the family are bound to be present and they will invite friends from every part of the town and even outside of the town. Most of the people who are invited will come with some gift like rice, banana, palm oil, hen, sheep and goat etc., which have to be killed and cooked for the people. They also have to pound flour, which have to be eaten by the people.

They have to cook big rice of different type and a big pot of tea for the people to drink. And they will sing some songs for a long time. The ceremony will take place for about a day. (Secondary School essay on 'A Traditional Ceremony')

In the same way that chieftainship is incorporated into national structures it seems that polygamy is compatible with modernity. Polygamy can increase a family's chances of making better and wider patron–client relationships and become more politically powerful and economically secure. To have a large number of children is an advantage because it provides a larger workforce and also more chances of educational advancement. Another Mende proverb states that 'children are like a young bamboo tree: you don't know which of the shoots will be cut down and which will remain.'

Although there are internal household hierarchies between senior and junior wives, husbands are not supposed to show favouritism, and this means that, in practice, women are left to provide for their own children. The more wives a man has, the more male income is separate from female to avoid rivalry. Nevertheless, the status of a wife before marriage will be related to the links her husband has in the patron–client network through her natal family. This means that the children of more important wives will be favoured by their fathers, especially in providing educational opportunities, in order to forge closer links with the maternal kinship group.

Although, theoretically, all children have equal rights to inheritance, communal resources, like land, have to be managed by a family head and this can lead to sibling rivalry. But the most serious rivalries usually arise between co-wives, who co-operate to complete farming and domestic tasks but also compete with respect to their children. This is a result of the separation of male and female incomes and also of the common occurrence of divorce and widowhood. Mothers look to their children's advancement, especially through education, as an insurance against future impoverishment for themselves. It is common to hear this expressed among the Mende:

The father is so partial [to one wife's children] that he gets the uniforms, fees — everything for them fully . . . But for these other children, he doesn't do as much. This is a bad mistake. You cannot tell which of these children is going to be somebody tomorrow. And when that happens, then the child who becomes somebody will be ready to victimize these from another woman . . . (quoted in Bledsoe 1987, p. 11)

Fertility is thus crucial to personal survival and, in the past, if a woman failed to have children or her children failed to survive, highly fertile co-wives might be suspected of practising witchcraft. These days, examination failure is regarded as the possible result of witchcraft (Bledsoe 1987, p. 12). To guard against this possibility, children may be dressed in rags to show that they are not favoured, or be fostered out from quite an early age.

Fostering shows another aspect of the proverb that 'a child is not for one person'. It is an excellent mechanism for spreading the costs of feeding and clothing children and of spreading the benefits of their labour around the network of kin, friends and patrons. It is common throughout West Africa and has advantages for the children as well as for the sub-fertile, the elderly and the infirm, who may thus have access to social welfare. It is increasingly used to improve children's educational chances by sending them to live with an urban patron, as well as in the more traditional learning systems of apprenticeship and domestic work. Foster parents gain both present and future advantages, because foster children generally work harder than natal children and yet can often be relied on for the same economic help later in life (Bledsoe 1987, passim).

Underlying and cutting across the links of kin, friendship and patronage is the system of secret societies, which is crucial for children because it controls the passage from childhood to adulthood and structures the relationships between the sexes. Secret societies are only secret in that non-members cannot go to rituals and meetings and that the rites and knowledges of male societies are kept secret from female societies and vice versa. The main societies are Poro, for men, and Sande, for women. No adult status is possible without Poro and Sande which teach both ritual and practical skills in the initiation period which marks an individual's rebirth as an adult man or woman.

Secret societies maintain the social and natural order by being able to call upon the wisdom of the ancestors and the strength of the spirits, together with their ability to bring both blessing and punishment. They are responsible for the fertility of land and people alike and also for health. Without them there would be no social life at all and no continuity in the future. It is unwise to dismiss these activities as mere superstition, for they continue to adapt and have relevance to modern life for the majority of Sierra Leoneans. Poro, for instance, is overtly political and curbs the power of chiefs at the local level. Because of secret societies, women are quite powerful in some ethnic groups, sometimes as household or segment leaders and occasionally as paramount chiefs (MacCormack, 1979). The fact that most societies are limited to male or female membership does not indicate opposition or aggression between the sexes, but rather a complementarity in which men and women are separately responsible for particular realms of existence.

In the case of Sande, this responsibility is for all the aspects of biological womanhood, like fertility and birth, which are too important to be left to the whims of nature. These are matters of powerful social knowledge, which guide a woman throughout her adult life. Thus it is not surprising that one of the highest functionaries of any Sande chapter is a *sowo* or midwife. The age at which a child gains adult status is also not determined by the physical signs of puberty alone, but by initiation into Poro or Sande. Sande classes may range in size from three to more than 100 and ceremonies are held at variable time intervals, according to population density. Thus the girls who are initiated in a single class may be anything from 8 to 17 years old.

An important feature of rebirth as an adult is circumcision for a boy and clitoridectomy for a girl. 'As long as we are not circumcised, as long as we have not attained that second life that is our true existence, we are told nothing, and we can find out nothing' (Laye 1954, p. 106). The importance of the time when an initiate gives up childhood is described in the autobiography of a Malinké boy from neighbouring Liberia. Even though the operation was very quick it was still regarded as a dangerous business, but he states that he would not have dreamt of running away from the process:

> I knew perfectly well that I was going to be hurt, but I wanted to be a man and it seemed to me that nothing could be too painful if, by enduring it, I was to come to man's estate. My companions felt the same. Like me, they were prepared to pay for it with their blood. Our elders before us had paid for it thus, those who were born after us would pay for it in their turn. Why should we be spared? Life itself would spring from the shedding of our blood. (Laye 1954, p. 113)

A Sande initiate is sponsored by a mature Sande woman. She leaves the village or realm of normal social life and passes through palm fronds into the clearing or secluded place which is the Sande 'bush'. Initiation fees are paid, sometimes with recourse to a moneylender. The period of initiation now varies according to the girl's social and economic status, taking less time for girls who are at school and have to be initiated during the holidays. Through cleansing rites, they learn the cultural rules of cleanliness, such as the correct disposal of menstrual blood. Clitoridectomy, which is performed at the start of the initiation period, consists of the excision of the clitoris and part of the labia minora. It is also associated with cleanliness and brings respect for womanhood. Anthropologist Carol MacCormack claims that the pain of clitoridectomy is a metaphor for the pain of childbirth. In both cases the pain is shared with a Sande sister: the midwife performs and controls both processes. 'Womanhood is symbolically achieved in clitoridectomy and confirmed, under the midwife's hand, in childbirth' (MacCormack 1982, p. 121).

Fattening for fertility is an important part of the Sande ceremony. Extra food is sent to the 'bush' for the initiates. The ideal woman is plump enough to show creases at the neck, she 'is judged healthy, fertile and beautiful, in contrast to "dry" and barren girls' (MacCormack 1979, p. 33). The fattening process certainly helps the onset of ovulation and menstruation but Sande also emphasizes this in dance and ritual. A preference for having many children is widespread in Sierra Leone, which has one of the highest fertility rates in the world. Fertility rate measures the number of children a woman might expect to have during her reproductive life. In Sierra Leone women expect to have six to eight children and only 4 per cent of married women aged between 15 and 44 use contraception. The comparative figures in the United Kingdom are between one and two children and an 83 per cent take-up of contraception.

Three-quarters of births are not attended by any trained health personnel, and maternal mortality rates are high. Between 1980 and 1984, every 100,000 live births meant 450 women dying in the process. The equivalent figure in the United Kingdom is seven. The romantic image of women in Africa giving birth easily in the bush and carrying on with their work is a myth.

Throughout a normal childbirth the woman receives considerable social support from Sande women, just as she did during clitoridectomy. However, should a difficult birth continue until all hope is lost, social support is withdrawn from her. The fault must be the woman's. It cannot be Sande's. (MacCormack 1982, p. 129)

Sande's importance in matters of fertility is acknowledged by the health system. In the 1940s, on the suggestion of Dr Milton Margai, who was to be the first Prime Minister after independence, simple anatomy, physiology and modern methods of hygiene, first aid and sanitation became part of initiation skills. There are now some 12,000 trained traditional birth attendants. But the problem of their brief three-week training is that they tend to forget information. So umbilical cords may be cut in the modern way with scissors but, because the metal is not sterilized, the babies may still die from post-natal tetanus.

Illiterate women who attend ante-natal classes may find hospital-oriented language difficult to understand or remember. Persuading them to attend is not easy. Among the Koronko, for instance, it is not usual to make a pregnancy public until the sixth or seventh month. All reproductive matters are secret and the exclusive concern of the women's society, so they cannot be discussed with men, which means that male doctors are difficult to accept.

Breastfeeding on demand is the rule for up to 18 months. Mothers carry children on their backs during the day and sleep with them at night. But 14 per

Table 7
Improvements in infant mortality rate 1960–1986

	Under-5 infant mortality rate		Improvement (per cent)
	1960	1986	
Sierra Leone*	397	297	33.6
Somalia	294	255	13.2
All Very High IMR Countries**	308	211	31.5
India	282	154	45.3
Peru	233	128	45.1
South Africa	192	101	47.4
Nicaragua	210	100	52.4
Brazil*	160	89	44.4
Lebanon	92	53	42.4
China*	202	47	76.7
Cuba	87	19	78.2
United States*	30	13	56.7
United Kingdom*	27	11	59.2
Sweden*	20	7	65.0

Mozambique is not included because its IMR is so heavily affected by civil strife.
*   It is worth noting the differences between per capita incomes in 1985; Sierra Leone US$350; Brazil US$1,640; China US$310; USA US$16,690; UK US$8,460; Sweden US$11,890.
** UNICEF rating.
Source: UNICEF *State of the World's Children* 1988.

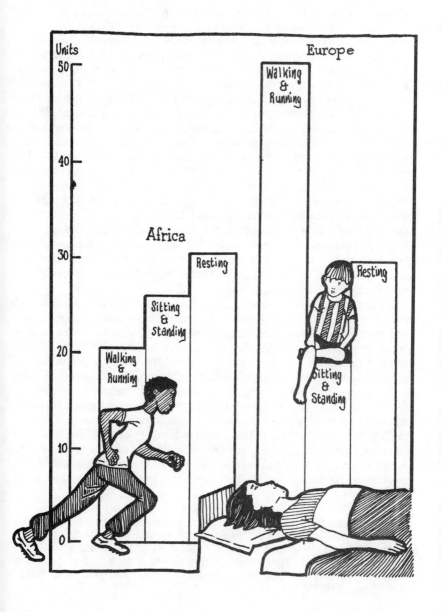

cent of infants are born with low birth weight of less than 2,500g (4½ lb). The latest figures available, which relate to the late 1970s, show that about a quarter of infants suffered from mild to moderate malnutrition (60–80 per cent of desirable weight for age) and 3 per cent from severe malnutrition (less than 60 per cent of desirable weight for age) with the net result that one third in the 1–2 year-old group show the wasting symptoms of acute malnutrition. One-third of children do not reach their fifth birthday. For the rest, energy and capacity to grow, learn and carry on their daily lives is to some extent impaired. African children, in general, are simply less active than their European contemporaries.

Malnutrition is the background against which children sicken and die from the diseases of childhood and from such tropical diseases as malaria, which was a major killer of children until the 1970s. In addition, morbidity rates increased; children easily fall ill with fevers and from infections caused by minor cuts and grazes which do not heal. The mortality rate for children under five is the third highest in the world, topped only by Mali and Afghanistan. The situation has improved slightly in the past two decades: in 1960 it was 397 per thousand, in 1986 it was 297 per thousand. Compared with other countries in our case studies over the same period, this is a significant achievement.

It is distribution of income, rather than national wealth, that determines infant mortality rates. Sierra Leone has a pretty creditable record, considering that 65 per cent of the population live below absolute poverty level and that only 6 per cent of rural people have access to clean water.

Western health services have an urban bias and suffer in Sierra Leone from shortages of human resource and equipment. Doctors are expensive to train and often become Westernized in the process. They are then reluctant to work in remote rural areas where equipment and facilities are rudimentary. Doctors and well equipped hospitals are not the answer to the most urgent health needs of Sierra Leone. The emphasis has to be on prevention and primary health care rather than cure: basic medicines, hygiene, nutrition and immunization. Because the 7.5 per cent of central government expenditure allocated to health amounts to only a few pence per head, it is official policy to seek development funding for health projects. This means a diversity of provision and poor administrative control with a concentration of services in and around the capital city. Child health can be improved if resources are made available and, more importantly, adapted to be relevant to local conceptual and social systems.

> Any truly appropriate primary health care system . . . cannot be narrowly based upon the Western 'engineering' approach to medicine where chemicals are prescribed as quickly and efficiently as possible for faulty organs. Rather, an appropriate system will have to recognise disease in whole persons embedded within social and moral contexts. (MacCormack 1982, pp. 118–19)

Somalia

There is no more powerful an image of Third World children in the 1980s than that of the dehydrated, starving baby we described in the Introduction: the tiny, unnamed child, taken from its mother's arms so that its pitiful, bare bottom could be exposed to the documentary film camera. The plight of Somali children is less well-known than that of their Ethiopian neighbours, whose desperate situation in 1985 shocked the First World into a more active public response to the problems of developing countries than had been the case with any previous disaster. Band Aid and Sport Aid achieved public mobilization of unprecedented proportions, and this was accompanied by further, less publicized, actions, such as the United Kingdom farmers' campaign to Send a Ton [of wheat] to Africa. Besides the relatively large sums raised by Band Aid, existing charities experienced a huge increase in public donations, and the Charities Commission was faced with processing applications for charitable status from a mass of new organizations, particularly those based on local initiatives.

In the long run, the amount of money raised was less important than was the increased interest in developing countries, particularly when this meant a demand for more information. It was as if people were asking each other, 'How could this happen?' and even 'Is this in some way my fault?' as well as the more usual response to previous disasters: 'What can I do to help?' School children of all ages worked on projects about Ethiopia. For the very first time the public conscience of the First World appeared to acknowledge that disasters of the scale of the Ethiopian famine have human as well as natural causes.

Three years later, however, much of the enthusiasm has waned. The First World is accustomed to rapid results and instant comfort. Consumer society is geared to the idea that all needs can be provided by money, that purchases solve problems. Women can have more time for careers if they buy washing machines. Illnesses can be cured by the purchase of drugs or machinery. Happiness is a cigar called Hamlet. Ugliness is eradicated by expensive surgery and friends will flock round if you use the right mouthwash. If there is a problem in an inner-city area, the government should spend more money, and it should also release more funds to find a cure for AIDS. Because the money collected for Ethiopia ran into far greater sums than most individuals will see in their lifetimes, it was expected that the famine would be bought out of

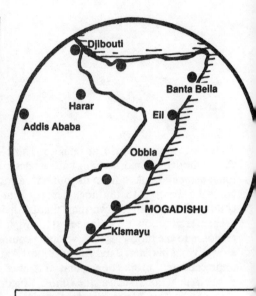

Capital: Mogadishu
Area: 246,200 sq. miles
Population: 4,800,000
Urban population: 35% (1985)
Population annual growth rate:
   2.9% (1980–85)
GNP per capita US$: 280
   (1985)
Rate of inflation: 45.4% (1980–85)
Population below absolute
   poverty level { urban: 40%
   (1977–85) { rural: 70%
Population with access
   to drinking water: 36%
Life expectancy: 42

Somalia
(U5MR = 255   IMR = 151)

Births: 226,000
Infants with low birthweight: n.a.
Population 0–4: 900,000
Population 5–16: 1,300,000
Total population under 16: 2,200,000
Deaths 0–4: 58,000
Children 0–6 suffering from malnutrition:
      mid-moderate: 16%
         severe: n.a.

One year olds { TB: 29%
fully immunised { DPT: 18%
{ polio: 18% } (1985–86)
{ measles: 26%

ORS per 100 episodes of diarrhoea: 27 (1985)
Primary school enrolment ratio male/female: 32/18
   (gross) (1983–86)
Grade One enrolment completing primary
   school: 33% (1980–86)
Secondary school enrolment ratio male/female:
   23/12 (1983–86)

(all figures 1986 unless otherwise stated

existence. Thus most people are puzzled that major relief agencies are calling for more funds because 1988 was expected to produce an even worse famine than 1985. Even though people are now better informed about the developing world, it is still a partial knowledge allowing much room for doubts and uneasy questions. Was all our money wasted? Did it get to the right people? How could this happen again?

One of the gaps that allows these questions to creep in is lack of knowledge about the structural causes of famines, and this is related to ignorance of the social situation in this part of Africa as a whole. One of our friends travelled to Addis Ababa, the Ethiopian capital, at the height of the famine. She is an archaeologist with much experience in that area of Africa and was astounded by the number of English people who expected her to be taking a month's supply of tinned food to sustain herself. The general view was that there was no food at all in Ethiopia and everyone was starving — this was the media picture presented. At that time we also asked a group of trainee teachers, in the course of a lecture on development education, to give one word to describe Ethiopia. The answers were 'wretched', 'starving', 'misery', 'hopelessness', all negative images. Even when pushed, not one student had any idea of the rich and ancient culture of Ethiopia, or of the history of the relationship between 'Abyssinia' and various European countries.

The fact that we started with a Somali baby and then wrote at length about First World ideas of Ethiopia is connected to this and also to Principle 3 of the Declaration of the Rights of the Child. This is the Principle which refers to identity and nationality. The reason it is important here has to do firstly with the ancient history of the Somali and Ethiopian peoples and secondly with the colonial period in this part of Africa.

Many people think about Africa as if it had had no history before the 'coming of the white man', as if the entire continent did not exist before it was 'discovered' by Europeans. This is not only wrong, but also muddled in the extreme, for Europe has been aware of Africa throughout all recorded history. The problem is that our historical thinking has lost geographical boundaries. There cannot be many people in England who did not learn at school about the wars between Rome and Carthage and about Hannibal taking elephants across the Alps. But most of us forget that both the famous Carthaginian general and the elephants came from Africa. We should be able to work out that the elephants were not natives of northern Africa, any more than were the lions that made a meal of Christian martyrs in Rome. Archaeologists tell us what our schoolteachers did not — that there were ancient and prosperous trade routes across the 'impenetrable' Sahara Desert, as well as sea routes around Arabia. Among the trade items from the region now known as the Horn of Africa, which Somalia shares with Ethiopia, were frankincense and myrrh. Thus two of the gifts which nursery school children mime the Three Kings from the Orient bringing to Jesus Christ at Christmas probably had their origin in Somalia, in what used to be called the Land of Punt, where these aromatic and medicinal resins are tapped from trees on the dry hills.

Although the Land of Punt is mentioned in documents relating to the coast of this part of Africa that date back to around AD 60, the origins of the Somali people and the date at which they settled the region are matters of debate among scholars. It is clear, however, that the Somalis were established here long before the first record of the use of their name in the early 1400s. We are not being simply academic in delving into this history, because it is important to understand the way in which Somalis think about themselves and the pride they take in their history. Somalis are almost all of the same Hamitic ethnic group, speaking or understanding the same language (Somali) and setting great store by their attachment to Islam and the connections which they traditionally trace from noble Arabian lineages and the family of the Prophet Mahomet himself. Somalia is, therefore, unusual in modern Africa in being a state in the process of transformation from a traditional African nation into a modern state. In this it contrasts with neighbouring Ethiopia, which, like nearly every other African state, is built on boundaries arising from European conquest from many different peoples, nations and tribes.

The relevance of this national pride to the present situation cannot be explained without also examining the colonial period and its aftermath. Somalia has retained its identity despite European attempts to dismantle it. The strength of its resistance is summed up by one researcher: 'economically their republic is one of the poorest in Africa. Yet they have baffled Western armies, resisted Western religion, made mockery of Western administration, and intrigued Western scholars' (Laitlin 1977, p. 20)

During the nineteenth century the Ethiopian Emperor Menelik helped Britain, France and Italy divide the Somali nation between five different colonial territories. European colonialism tended to favour fragmentation of this kind, or the formation of new territorial states from previously separate or conflicting groups. The policy of divide and rule has left the late twentieth century with a set of fragile and conflict-ridden independent states, desperately attached to the boundaries drawn by previous colonial rulers, which provide their only national identity, and trying to forge a national culture out of an enormous diversity of languages and societies. Somalia differs from this general picture to quite a large extent. The present state was formed from the previous sectors of the original nation known as the Italian and British territories. This means that the state itself enjoys cultural coherence, but also left three important Somali communities outside the boundaries of the state itself: the previously French territory of Jibuti (Djibouti), part of Ethiopia mostly situated in the Ogaden, and the northern province of Kenya. Thus when the Somali state was formed in 1960 it had a strong cultural imperative to expand to take in the whole Somali nation, which led to inevitable conflicts throughout the region. Thus the sins of the colonial fathers are visited on the present generation of Somali children.

Somalis form one of the largest single ethnic groups in the entire African continent. Because so many of them are nomadic, no exact census is possible, but in 1975 it was calculated that $3\frac{1}{4}$ million lived in Somalia itself, 200,000 lived in Jibuti, where they form half the population, 250,000 lived in Kenya and one million were in Ethiopia. Although Somalia is reported as having a population which had grown to 5.3 million in 1983, it is a thinly spread population by First World standards. During the worst periods of famine, relief agencies explained the difficulty they had getting food to starving people in terms of 'transport problems', but this was often difficult for the Western public to understand. The distances to be covered were seldom mentioned. Because Somalia has a small population and little political importance on the global stage, there is a tendency to think of it and even refer to it as a 'small' country. But in reality it is vast: from north to south it stretches over an area equal to the eastern seaboard of the United States. Imagine trying to drive a lorry filled with grain from New Orleans to New York without the benefit of petrol stations and highways!

One reason for the lack of highways is the lack of resources for colonial government to exploit. Somalia still exports frankincense and myrrh but has so far not revealed any of the natural resources that would attract funds from public or private development agencies. There is no gold or any other valuable mineral, no oil or other energy resource worth exploiting at this stage, and the land is too poor to attract agricultural development schemes of any size.

The dry savannah of Somalia is mostly home to nomadic pastoralists herding sheep, goats, camels and cattle. Some of the country is so arid that it can support only small numbers of both people and beasts. In the south, which is watered by two permanent rivers, there is also an arable area growing sorghum, maize, sesame, beans, squashes and manioc, with some sugar and fruit plantations. Given the poor environmental situation, the prospects for economic growth are slim and people are accustomed to being at the mercy of a relatively unreliable climate. For the nomads, when and how much rain falls each year is crucial for the survival of their livestock and themselves. It seems that the climate has worsened during this century and also that the human and animal populations have increased, making further demands on both water and grazing. The sparse mountain forests have been plundered for fuel and this has led to almost instant desertification in the harsh climate. With such a marginal ecological situation the nomadic herders were forced traditionally to make decisions as harsh as the climate itself. William Travis, who was in Somalia during the 1960s, recreates what had sometimes to be done to ensure community survival when the seven-year cyclic drought struck:

> A fertile woman was of more value than her baby and their beliefs could not countenance the blood guilt of child murder. But for all to live the extra load must be shed, and so when the 'seventh' made its terrible demand the two-and-unders were discarded and left behind, whilst the others struggled on . . . (Quoted in Laitlin 1977, p. 22)

The adjectives used by trainee teachers in England with respect to Ethiopia spring readily to the First World mind at this point: 'wretched', 'starving', 'misery'. Perhaps a child who may be deserted to such a fate doesn't have an identity in the way we understand it and a documentary film maker is justified in taking it with little ceremony from its mother's arms. Perhaps, in the face of such a history of deprivation, the people are not endowed with the same kind of humanity. But this is not the case. Our problem is that we are such strangers to deprivation and so accustomed to associating comfort with purchasing power that we have a low opinion of humanity. We can only imagine how badly we would behave in the face of loss of all that we count as civilization. In 1985, a television drama which tried to show what would happen in the wake of a nuclear conflict involving the USA showed only the inhumanity that would supposedly result from the loss of all the props which make modern cultures possible. It was a terrifying picture of selfishness, individualism and greed.

Our imaginations are so limited by our comfortable existence that we cannot even learn from the examples of devastation at our disposal. Although Somali culture has little in the way of material wealth it has one uniquely human achievement — its language. The nineteenth-century European explorer, Richard Burton, said that 'the country teems with poets'. This has increased with modern means of communication.

> Poetry . . . today as much as in the past, plays a vital part in Somali culture, and the extensive use of radio broadcasting has enhanced rather than diminished its significance. Often a poem is not merely the private voice of the author, but frequently the collective tongue of a pressure group, and propaganda either for peace or for war is more effectively spread through poetry than by any other means. (Lewis 1980, p. 5)

This is surely why the Somali language has been adopted as the official language of the state, superceding either Italian or English, which might have been regarded as more internationally useful. The script for the Somali language has been a sensitive political issue from the date of independence in 1960, and Somali script was established in 1972. Its use in government abolished the previous language barrier between those educated in foreign colonial scripts and their illiterate countrymen. The Supreme Revolutionary Council, which came to power in 1969, established the Somali language as the single official language of the country. As the Somali poet, Maxamad Ismaaciil, wrote:

> Protesting children are compelled to learn foreign tongues.
> And make a universal cry for that sweet flower: their own native speech.
> (Quoted in Laitlin 1977 p. 133)

Somali democracy weakened at the end of the first decade after independence, ending with the assassination of the president and the start of military rule. When it assumed power through a *coup d'etat*, the military junta announced the end of corruption and tribal nepotism and, on the first anniversary of the coup, proclaimed a doctrine of scientific socialism. Nevertheless, President Barre, who has ruled for 17 years, has many relatives in high positions and the country continues to be governed by clan allegiances. President Barre has brought the country a kind of stability with social and economic progress but his administration also shows the authoritarianism one expects from military regimes. The problems are compounded by the country's strategic position on the Red Sea and the United States' base at the port of Berbera. This means that any changes within the fragile power structures are important way beyond its borders. In 1978 Somalia broke off diplomatic relations with the Soviet Union and expelled Soviet personnel from the capital, Mogadishu, because of Russian and Cuban support for Ethiopia in the Ogaden War. In recent years there has been some thawing of relationships with both the Soviet Union and Ethiopia, but economic problems brought on by bad management, drought and the large numbers of refugees crossing into Somali have made the country dependent on financial aid from Western and Arab nations.

Scientific socialism retains the Somali interest in language and also encourages literacy, but in 1983 only 11 per cent of adult men and 3 per cent of adult women were literate. This is not a substantial improvement on the figures of a decade before, which were 5 per cent and 1 per cent respectively.

Gender differences are also reflected in primary school enrolment ratios, with just over half the children registered being girls in both primary and secondary education. Somalis see some point in providing an elementary education for girls, but they see no reason why this should continue beyond the age of first menstruation and, if girls do not start school until they are 8 or 9 years old, they may not complete many years of education. For both sexes, school enrolment figures remain low. Only one-third of boys are enrolled at primary level and less than one-fifth attend secondary schools, while fewer than one girl in ten manages to enrol in secondary education. The government has tried to combat this with a philosophy of trying to accommodate the largest possible number of students, putting special emphasis on female education and gearing both content and methods to Somali culture. All schools are under government control and Islamic teaching is integral.

Nomadism is a major problem for education planning, particularly given the sparse grazing in Somalia, which means not only that herds have to move frequently in search of food but also that they have to be grazed over a wider area, using child workers to guard small groups of animals. One answer to this is to send teachers to travel with the groups rather than expect children to attend schools; but this is a poor use of scarce teaching resources. At the turn of the 1980s, a three-year educational programme for nomadic children took advantage of seasonal herding patterns. When conditions permitted, children attended school for half the year and then followed the herds with their families for the remaining six months. It is possible for families to board a child in a permanent settlement, but this entails considerable cost.

The resources for this are well beyond the means of most Somali families, particularly in rural ares where 70 per cent live below the poverty line. Government expenditure is unable to meet the costs of either education or health care: not only are the resources slim, they are also subject to an unsustainable loading resulting from the influx of refugees from other parts of the war-torn Horn of Africa, most of whom are ethnic, but not national, Somalis who, in a sense, are returning to where they belong.

In 1979, the Somali government appealed for help to the United Nations

High Commission for Refugees, but no request for international aid was made by the Secretary-General for six months. There are no exact figures available for the number of refugees. The Somalis themselves estimated 310,000 when they first requested help but this had risen to 750,000 by the time action had been taken and it seems that by early 1981 there were 1.3 million living in camps and a further 700,000–800,000 trying to adjust their nomadic life style to urban living. The effects of this enormous influx of refugees over a period of about 18 months on a desperately poor population, which itself numbered only three million, can scarcely be imagined. Proportionately, the United Kingdom would have to assimilate 14 million people. A paper submitted in Geneva to the International Conference of Assistance to Refugees in Africa by the Somali government sums up the impossibility of the situation:

> the citizens of our country have in effect waived their whole development budget and have now most seriously deflected their natural resources and food reserves . . . the truth is that we have only marginal resources with which to be generous . . . (Quoted in Fitzgibbon 1982, p. 70)

The significance of this new Somali nation which does not have the benefit of nationality is that it does not seem to have the same age and sex structure as it would have had in its places of origin. Some reports suggest that 90 per cent of the refugees are women and children. In April 1981 the Somali government estimated that 60 per cent of the people in camps were under 15, about a quarter more were women and the remainder mostly elderly men. In the mid-1980s a team of epidemiologists from the Center for Disease Control of the United States Public Health Service sought to determine the demographic characteristics of a sample of refugee camps and found the under-fives made up 15–18 per cent of the camp population; those from five to fifteen, 45–47 per cent; the 15–44-year-olds, 29–33 per cent, and the over 45s, 6–8 per cent. It should be remembered that the life expectancy at birth in Somalia is 43, so these figures mean that a disproportionate number of people in refugee camps are in fact children.

Children in the camps are particularly badly malnourished. Like the baby in the BBC documentary, they are weak, wizened and tiny. A survey of refugees in the Gedo region showed that 17 per cent of all children were below the critical 80 per cent height-for-weight standard and they were very susceptible to death either from severe malnutrition soon after arrival, or from the epidemics of measles and diarrhoea which sweep through the camps. In a sense, reaching the camp is only the start of a new set of problems. Food and shelter are in short supply even there. Refugees live in huts which are rapidly made from wattle and branches, for which the surrounding area is denuded, leaving no vegetation and little in the way of fuel for cooking or warmth at night. In any case, the ad hoc nature of much of the response to the refugee influx means that many camps are badly situated for either the use of local resources or the transport of aid.

For Somali children in general, the presence of these other Somalis means that progress in health, education or welfare resources will be slowed or will even stop. The situation in rural areas was not good before the refugees arrived and many rural Somalis have migrated into urban areas where they are joined by some of the refugees, who do not stay in the camps but make straight for the apparent opportunities in towns like Mogadishu. More than 90 per cent of poor households in the capital have a rural migrant as household head.

It might be tempting for Westerners to imagine that the capital of a largely nomadic nation like Somalia would be like a desert town in a Hollywood film. This is not the case. Despite the Islamic qualities of its architecture and the fact that 40 per cent of the urban population live below poverty level with no access even to clean drinking water, Mogadishu has its modern commercial centre as well as middle-class districts and tourist and leisure areas. There is little industry, of course, and employment tends to be in small craft workshops and the service sector, especially informal work that lies outside state control. Childhood is thought to end at 15; few children attend school and so it is not surprising to find that many of those whom we would think of as children are in full-time work. The most visible child workers are found around the commercial area of Xamar Weyne and the area of bars and restaurants, known as the Lido, situated near the beach. Rooba, who was 13 years old when interviewed by development workers in 1986, worked selling plastic bags in the street in the Xamar Weyne area.

> Except when sick, Rooba works every day, for eight hours a day. She earns about 200/- a day, depending on sales. All her money is given to her mother, although sometimes when she is late for work she gets money for her bus fare.
>
> Rooba copes with the risks of street life by imposing strict rules upon herself. She knows most of the working children there but does not involve herself with any of the children engaged in jobs other than plastic-bag selling. Normally she sells only from one place to avoid interference by other children. Rooba is part of a group of four girls who sell bags and who all look out for one another. Near where Rooba sells bags there is a woman selling eggs who is a neighbour of Rooba's family. She looks out for Rooba.
>
> Rooba does not mind working but she would rather stay at home, and sometimes her mother has to push her to get up and go. Rooba hates this, which is not surprising because she is always tired. (CIIR, 1987)

Although she attended school as far as Grade 3, her parents feel that schooling is not as important as learning a trade and they have sent her twin brother to train as a mechanic. They would like Rooba to be trained in sewing and tailoring, but do not yet have the resources to do this.

Living in a family which is well integrated with the surrounding community, Rooba is in no danger of being a street child, even though casual observation of her at work in her apparently precarious employment might lead people to think that she is one. Catholic Institute of International Relations researchers estimated that at least 190 Mogadishu children did indeed live in the streets, sleeping out at night in the main market areas and other public places. They were aged from 6 to 14 years old and grouped partly by territory and partly by age. This description of them would fit street children in almost any part of the world:

[They] were exposed to more risks than other children, but also to more excitement. Constantly using their wits to survive, but poorly nourished, the children appear quick thinking, but seem to concentrate less easily than other children might, and are as quickly taken with the mood of the moment. Loyalty and friendship are as frequent as fighting and argument; street life is physically and emotionally exacting, but most children do not want to return to their former lives. Street children are partly, but by no means entirely, victims of circumstance. There is an element of choice in living in the streets, and although determining factors, such as family breakdown, appear to be a recurrent feature in child backgrounds, street life is not without fun: one child . . . was seriously ill, but after 2 days away from the street he ran back again, still sick. His reason was 'Xaraarad ayaa i qabatey' ('I was craving for the street'). (CIIR 1987, p. 255)

If we were romanticizing at this point we might suggest that this child's craving for the freedom of the street shows a preference for a nomadic life style. But not one of the children in this research had a rural background. There are, in fact, no comfortable stereotypes to draw upon. Not all the children were driven out of home by poverty; one came from a relatively wealthy background. The freedom of the streets is combined in most cases with an addiction to sniffing glue. One older, ex-street child was even found to have settled down into more or less respectable family life. But the real point is that these children, together with working children like Rooba, are far from being the stereotypical starving babies of the documentary. Even though they have little education in our sense, they are heirs to a great poetic tradition which they share with the nomads of rural areas. Moreover, the poverty that reduces their chances of improving their situation is not the result of being left behind by history, but rather the result of colonialism and its aftermath. Even the Somali baby in the documentary probably did not have Somali nationality.

Mozambique

Boy with bare feet
boy of my country

The world is green and bitter
and despite capulanas
and the black man humbled in the sand

a black boy
like you

died murdered
broken up in the puddle your flesh ripped apart
by racist hatred

From green eyes
of the rising sun
and the violet hiss
like birds of the dawn

A black boy
who was running on bare feet
like you

Opening his unknowing arms
in the sonorous bow of the morning

We begin with a poem of the Mozambican revolution by Kalungo, translated by an English schoolteacher, Chris Searle, who, in the early, optimistic days of the FRELIMO government, went to share in the revolutionary process by working as a *cooperante* teacher in an elementary school (Searle 1982, p. 52). Schools are a major component of Mozambican reform, and education takes up about a quarter of public spending. In the 13 years since independence, adults and children have been able to take up educational opportunities which had been denied to black Mozambicans by the Portuguese colonists. As a result, the adult literacy rate has increased from 7 per cent to 28 per cent, and many children now complete primary education. Despite scarce resources, teachers who are barely trained themselves, and a curriculum and school system still based largely on the Portuguese model, there have been innovations in both content and method. Materials and textbooks suited to Mozambique and Africa are now being produced. Schools in rural areas, like the one in

Capital: Maputo
Area: 302,227 sq. miles
Population: 14,300,000
Urban population: 20% (1985)
Population annual growth rate:
  2.6% (1980–85)
GNP per capita US$: 160
  (1985)
Rate of inflation: 25.8%
  (1980–85)
Population below absolute
  poverty level { urban: n.a.
                  rural: n.a.
Population with access
  to drinking water: 13% (1980)
Life expectancy: 47

Pemba
Zumba   Bomba
Lusaka
Quelimane
Harare
Belra
Chicualacuala
MAPUTO

Births: 651,000
Infants with low birthweight: 15% (1982–85)
Population 0–4: 2,500,000
Population 5–16: 4,000,000
Total population under 16: 6,500,000
Deaths 0–4: 161,000
Children suffering from malnutrition:
          mid-moderate: n.a.
          severe: n.a.

One year olds   { TB: 45%
  fully immunised   DPT: 32%   } (1985–86)
                     polio: 32%
                     measles: 39%

ORS per 100 episodes of diarrhoea: 10 (1985)

Primary school enrolment ratio male/female: 94/74
  (gross), 53/45 (net) (1983–86)

Grade One enrolment completing primary
  school: 26% (1980–86)

Secondary school enrolment ratio male/female:
  9/4 (1983–86)

Mozambique
(U5MR=n.a.*   IMR=n.a.*)
*Figures are available for 1960,
U5MR = 302   IMR = 174

(all figures 1986 unless otherwise stated)

which Chris Searle worked, have been built by village communities. Pupils often grow their own food-supplies (Searle 1982, p. 52 and Quan 1987, p. 22).

Portuguese colonial history is a sorry tale of slavery, racism, outright exploitation and sheer neglect. Mozambique, like Angola, gained independence late — in 1975. Few nations have had such an inauspicious beginning as Mozambique. The Portuguese simply left; only 15,000 of the 250,000 expatriates remained. All but 7 per cent of the population of Mozambique were illiterate, and 70 per cent lived out of reach of any health care. Even though the land is generally fertile, especially in the north, the agricultural potential had not been developed. Most families lived by subsistence farming and a large part of the country's labour force depended on wages earned as migrants in South Africa, where they were forced to seek cash incomes because of harsh taxes and a forced labour system. This meant that children and women had to do the bulk of the work on family farms, which were under-productive as a result. Migrant workers' earnings, as often as not, were spent on acquiring animal stock, which led to overgrazing.

Despite this, the Marxist-inspired FRELIMO government, led by Samora Machel, began with high hopes and high ideals. Behind it was a history of 11 years of armed struggle. Undeterred by the hasty flight of the Portuguese, which left almost no one in the skilled labour force, the government acted swiftly to nationalize health and education. The spread of literacy and schooling also made known the ideas behind the government's central planning, based on co-operation, self-help and democracy founded on local-level popular assemblies.

Since independence, Mozambique has continued to be involved in warfare, but the government has managed to approach its problems with a pragmatic realism that does not lose sight of its ideals. In some cases these ideals have cost the country dear. By joining in the international sanctions against Rhodesia in 1976, for instance, it lost foreign exchange earnings from transport routes to Rhodesia, which were the only major source of such income apart from remittances from workers in South Africa. Moreover, by allowing the Zimbabwean liberation movement to operate within its borders, Mozambique attracted retaliatory action from Rhodesia, allowed a focus for anti-FRELIMO dissidence and put its foreign earnings from South Africa at risk. South Africa's recent decision to use the port of Maputo less and to reduce its employment of Mozambican mineworkers has dealt a crippling blow to the economy.

From the very beginning, therefore, a fragile economy was laid open to further threat. Moreover, attempts to strengthen the agricultural base were not always wisely conceived. Initially the stress was put upon expanding the modern agricultural sector, using state farms and large-scale machinery, especially in the fertile north. But results did not come up to expectations. One factor in this is the paradox that Mozambique simply cannot afford to increase food production because prices cannot compete with subsidized produce from Europe and North America.

In addition to the political need to subsidize their own farmers, the developed countries have a vested interest in keeping food prices low. It allows them to encourage developing countries to produce export crops and import food. (Hanlon 1984, p. 267)

Meanwhile, subsistence family farming failed to receive the support it needed. Another plan, reminiscent of the Ujamaa villages of Tanzania which sought to make use of traditional African cohesive mechanisms, tried to organize the previously scattered family farms into communal villages. There have been conflicting reports of the success of this programme. Some communal endeavours, such as schools and health posts, succeeded, but the collective organization of agriculture suffered, as it did in Tanzania, from over-bureaucratic central planning. Peasant farmers are not easily persuaded to change, particularly if they have not been involved in the planning, and particularly if the promised support for change is not forthcoming. In addition, the loss of remittances from migrant workers leaves marginalized farm families utterly dependent on under-productive subsistence activities.

As if this were not enough, the climate takes a hand. The west of Mozambique has always been subject to flooding and the south to drought. At the end of the 1970s, the Limpopo and Incomati rivers flooded and yet, early in the 1980s, drought became widespread in several provinces. There were major cyclones in 1979 and 1984; in 1984, 1985 and 1986 there was further flooding. There is a National Disasters Office, and Mozambicans have organized an impressive response to all emergencies. But enough is enough. The government appealed to the international community for help in 1983 and has continued to require foreign aid, which is often given in ways that conflict with the government's basic ideals. Furthermore, aid cannot be truly effective because of continued civil strife. The MNR (Mozambique National Resistance), backed by South Africa, attacks transport routes and devastates villages, adding more internal refugees to those already on the move because of the drought. In 1986, after leading the struggle for 11 years, Samora Machel died on his way back from a summit meeting in Zambia, when his plane crashed into a hillside just inside the South African border.

The present task for Mozambique seems to be like that facing Sisyphus in Greek mythology:

> The gods had condemned Sisyphus to ceaselessly rolling a rock to the top of the mountain, whence the stone would fall back of its own weight. They had thought with some reason that there is no more dreadful punishment than futile and hopeless labour ... Sisyphus, proletarian of the gods, powerless and rebellious, knows the whole extent of his wretched condition ... (Camus 1955, pp. 96–7) ... the fundamental subject of the myth is this: it is legitimate and necessary to wonder whether life has a meaning; [but] although the myth of Sisyphus poses mortal problems, it sums itself up ... as a lucid invitation to live and create, in the very midst of the desert (p. 7).

Samora Machel's phrase for the children of Mozambique was 'the flowers that never wither'. The next generation continues to be the focus of optimism and the target of policy, despite adverse conditions that might also cause it to be termed the children of Sisyphus. Because of the very high infant mortality rate at independence in the mid-1970s, the new government gave priority to Maternal and Child Health. The centrally planned primary health care programme was allotted 11 per cent of the national budget, which may not seem much, but in international terms is unusually high — compared, for example, to the 5.9 per cent of the United Kingdom budget set aside for health. As a result, over 6,000 paramedical health workers were trained and more than 1,300 health posts were built. The Third Congress of FRELIMO stated that it aimed to make 'each citizen a sanitary agent and to arm and organise the people to defend themselves and their health' (in Cliff et al 1986, p. 7). The Mozambican equivalent of barefoot doctors are called *Agentes Polivalentes Elementares*. They are not employed directly by the government but by their local communities, more than 400 of which were communal villages. With the escalation of warfare, however, it is now difficult for APEs to be supervised or supplied. Nearly half the health posts have been damaged and no one now knows how many paramedics are still working in the disrupted countryside.

There were other initial success stories which improved the conditions for child health. Sanitation has been improved by a National Latrine Campaign, with 600,000 simple latrines constructed in urban houses. Mozambique's sanitation record is now very good in African terms. There are 17 per cent more latrines in cities and 25 per cent more in rural areas than the African average (Cliff et al 1986, p. 14).

Preventive health measures for children also increased. By 1979, 95 per cent of urban and 44 per cent of rural children were fully immunized, an impressive achievement in the time and under the circumstances. UNICEF reports that, in areas most disrupted by war, a 'silent' communications strategy has been adopted by health workers. The workers themselves call on all the relevant families in the area shortly before vaccination takes place, rather than make a public announcement, which could alert MNR forces to the opportunity to strike at a public gathering (UNICEF 1987).

One of the most impressive successes of the early years of independence was the basic drugs policy, which is a part of primary health care programmes that often remains underdeveloped. It is designed to combat the power of major international drug companies to market expensive, brand-named drugs aggressively and to offload unsuitable or dangerous drugs on developing countries. The World Health Organization has produced a list of basic medicines but it is difficult to combat the sales power of transnational companies, especially if they are manufacturing in a satellite factory in the developing country concerned. Mozambique took a tough stand on this. It produced a National Drug List of 343 essential medicines and banned the import of others, creating a state company, MEDIMOC, to import and distribute all drugs. By this means it kept the national medicine bill to only 20 per cent of the health budget, which is far lower than the Third World average of 30–40 per cent. But, by 1984, the government found itself close to bankruptcy through loss of foreign earnings and spending on defence. Although US$10 million had been budgeted for that year, only US$6 million was actually available, and this was released only in early 1985. During 1985 it was not possible to raise more than 5 per cent of the planned budget. Chronic shortages meant that external aid became a vital necessity (Cliff et al, 1986).

What this history means for children is that the figure given for infant mortality at the beginning of this section is as much a myth as the story of Sisyphus. Given the progress made in the early years of the FRELIMO government, the under-five infant mortality rate should now be around 185 per 1,000, but UNICEF estimates it now to be the highest in Africa, and perhaps the world, at 325. Should this figure be confusing after reading the demography at the beginning of this study, where we do not show a 1986 figure, it is because UNICEF itself has left that detail blank in the 1988 *State of the World's Children*. Neither it nor any other body can be sure. In 1986 Afghanistan was the highest at the same figure, 325, but after showing an improvement over two decades; Mozambique, on the other hand, appears to be deteriorating. Rather than creating a contradiction, we hope that this illustrates the contradictions that arise when one attempts to collect data, and the difficulties in reaching any kind of accurate figure in the first place.

The difference is due to the war alone. To put these figures into human terms, 602,000 babies were born in 1985. If we work out how many would have died if infant mortality had been decreasing, as one would have expected with the health services provided, and subtract this from the number who actually did die, we are left with something like 80,000 'excess' deaths. As if this were not obscene enough, it seems that the MNR targets health workers, health posts, teachers and foreign aid workers, as part of its policy of inciting disaffection with the government. It might as well target children directly, for the net result is that all the services that might serve children are being destroyed.

All wars are waged against children, but few have had such explicit effects:

- health workers are killed, wounded or captured, so preventable diseases continue to kill children;
- health posts are destroyed, so antenatal care, growth monitoring and immunization are virtually impossible, with the result that preventable diseases continue to kill children;
- dislocation of rural life and food production means children do not have enough to eat;
- dislocation of rural life means that cash crops cannot be exported and the government has insufficient foreign exchange to provide education, health and other essential services to children;
- disruption of transport means that food aid cannot reach famine areas, so people die of starvation, and the first to die are usually children;
- disruption of transport means that medicines do not reach those who need it, many of whom are children;

- 42 per cent of the national budget is now allocated to defence; less funds are available for other sectors of public spending, which means decreased services for children;

- MNR attacks on rural communities disrupt families and leave people homeless refugees, unable to contact other family members. Most displaced persons are women and children. Many unaccompanied young children cannot remember their family names or where they came from;

- many of the dead civilians in terrorist attacks are children;

- many MNR soldiers are children, reportedly kidnapped and pressed into service as fighters for a cause they do not understand.

Perhaps the most distressing stories to come out of Mozambique recently have concerned the apparent brutalization of both sides in the unrest.

One of the deadliest weapons of the war is mass terrorism carried out by forces which have burned crops and farmhouses, pillaged and destroyed schools, clinics, churches, mosques, stores and villages, poisoned wells by throwing bodies down them . . . The carnage has been indiscriminate, with infants and children not exempted. The results are clear and tragic: death for many, and for the survivors fear and flight, destruction and displacement. (UNICEF 1987, p. 18)

Displaced refugees told Oxfam worker Julian Quan: 'We have come to the conclusion that the bandits [MNR] don't have human hearts' (Quan 1987, p. 3). Stories of atrocities, of disembowelling, executions, children being burned and hacked to death, or kidnapped and forced to fight for the MNR are now too common to be mere media scandal-mongering. They appear regularly in the reports of reputable relief agencies. It is not surprising that people retaliate.

The Bandits are the enemy of the State and of the people. They only want to kill people. When they catch children they kill them. How could they govern if ever they get power? What will they be like if they kill children? . . . If a Bandit is caught they should do to him what the Bandits have done to the people. (Senhöra Paulina Chauque, midwife, quoted in Bray 1987, p. 37)

The destabilization policy of South Africa aims to create dependence in what are now called the Front Line States. It operates at economic, political and terrorist levels. It was inevitable as soon as such countries as Mozambique, Angola and Zimbabwe became independent and broke the protective cordon of white governments by which South Africa maintained its local economic and political dominance. There is no target more vulnerable or more important than the next generation of the Front Line States.

During the late 1980s, aid agencies have paid increasing attention to Mozambique. In March 1988, 100 agencies, including many from the United Nations, met in Maputo to plan a programme of emergency aid with a total budget of £155 million. The statements made were unusually forthright. An Oxfam official was reported as saying that 'This is not a famine, this is a war situation', while a Save the Children Fund representative said that the 'most significant' cause of the emergency is 'the war being waged by terrorists trained, armed, or otherwise assisted by Pretoria' (Brittain, 1988). An emergency recovery programme, launched after negotiations with the International Monetary Fund and the World Bank in 1987, has improved the economic situation despite the MNR's persistent undermining of constructive efforts. Nevertheless, the country continues to depend on foreign aid. In UNICEF's words, 'They cannot protect and preserve the lives of their children without international assistance and solidarity' (UNICEF 1987, p. 22).

Such solidarity has not always been so forthcoming. International aid was restricted in the early days by Western governments' reluctance to support an explicitly Marxist regime. Moreover, Mozambique was making a positive effort to avoid the trap of dependence, and discovered many of the problems of accepting aid when it was necessary to ask for help with the health budget. Foreign consultants arrive with little prior notice and no consent from the Mozambique government. They usually have no relevant language skills or regional experience and present formulae already worked out to 'solve' problems, ignoring local expertise and government policies. Their very presence puts a strain on local resources, drawing Health Ministry staff away from dealing with everyday management tasks. The idea of simply providing funds with which indigenous policies can be implemented is alien to foreign aid, which assumes that the need is due to incapacity, and usually ends by creating dependence. Aid is not always as useful as it may appear, or even as much as it is trumped up to be. When external finance accounted for half the health supplies in 1984, only one-third of the US$2 million-worth of medicines that arrived were on the National Formulary of 343 essential drugs; many were dangerous drugs banned by the World Health Organization, packaged using languages unknown in Mozambique, and had already expired or were close to their expiry date. The WHO actually encouraged dependence, and implicitly denigrated local policies, by recommending that Mozambique should not buy its drugs on the open market according to decisions made at Ministry of Health level, but should be supplied with goods exclusively from UNIPAC. Moreover, promises of help are often misleading. One agency which announced that it would be sending US$500,000 of supplies eventually sent goods worth only US$11,000, while costing health officials much extra time and work (Cliff et al 1986, pp. 11–12).

The modern Sisyphus not only has to toil uphill with his boulder, he also has to contend with continual danger from the war raging around him and the negative effects of the help he receives. What is remarkable is that so much of the positive optimism of the early days of independence in Mozambique survives. Some economic improvement has occurred recently. Many children are immunized, receive health checks and go to school even in the present state of emergency. Paramedics and schoolteachers in rural areas are reported to be staying at their posts, despite danger and failures of communication and supplies. The government did not collapse into factional fighting after the death of President Machel, but has continued to pursue an overall consistent ideological approach. Despite the rhetoric of aid, and the need of millions of displaced and destitute children for immediate help, it is not simply financial help that is required to allow the next generation in Mozambique to benefit from the gains of independence. One pressing requirement is international solidarity with the Front Line States to stop the imperialist wars being waged by South Africa in this region. But this generation also has much to give the world, through the lessons of solidarity that seem to have been learned by many through the spread of ideas in the early FRELIMO education programmes. It would be easy to derive a negative, needy image of Third World children from the plight of Mozambique's children of Sisyphus, as it appears in the advertisements of international charities. Their situation is desperate but the sentiments expressed in a school song of the 1970s show that, if the future is to be better, it will not be charity alone that has brought it about:

> If all the world's children
> wanted to play holding hands
> they could happily make
> a wheel around the sea
>
> If all the world's children
> wanted to play holding hands
> they could be sailors
> and build a bridge across the seas
>
> What a chorus we would make
> singing around the earth
> if all the humans in the world
> wanted to dance holding hands.
>
> (In Searle, 1983)

Capital: Delhi
Area: 1,229,215 sq. miles
Population: 772,700,000
Urban population: 26% (1985)
Population annual growth rate:
2.2% (1980–85)
GNP per capita US$: 270
(1985)
Rate of inflation: 7.8% (1980–85)
Population below absolute
poverty level { urban: 40%
(1977–85) { rural: 51%
Population with access
to drinking water: 54%
Life expectancy: 57

India
(U5MR = 154   IMR = 101)

Births: 22,477,000
Infants with low birthweight: 30% (1982–85)
Population 0–4: 99,000,000
Population: 5–16: 198,400,000
Total population under 16: 297,400,000
Deaths 0–4: 3,455,000
Children 0–5 suffering from malnutrition:
        mid-moderate: 33% }
        severe: 5% }   (1980–86)
One year olds { TB: 29%
fully immunised { DPT: 53%
{ polio: 45% }   (1985–86)
{ measles: 1% }
ORS per 100 episodes of diarrhoea: 5 (1985)
Primary school enrolment ratio male/female: 107/76
(gross) (1983–86)
Grade One enrolment completing primary
school: 38% (1978)
Secondary school enrolment ratio male/female:
45/24 (1983–86)

(all figures 1986 unless otherwise stated)

India

> To my mind, the defining image of India is the crowd, and a crowd is by its very nature superabundant, heterogeneous, many things at once (Salman Rushdie, *Guardian*, 25 March 1988).

These are the words of Salman Rushdie, who coined the phrase 'Midnight's Children' to describe a generation born at the same time as the independent state of India over 40 years ago. One thousand and one children are believed to have been born at the midnight hour of freedom, 1 August 1947. The present Prime Minister, Rajiv Gandhi, was only three years old at the time. For him and his contemporaries, Rushdie's phrase is a familiar slogan that identifies a generation too young to remember the struggle for independence. The next generation might well be described as Midnight's Grandchildren. What they inherit is an independent but not united India, although its disunity is less severe than that which split Pakistan and Bangladesh apart. India has 800 million people, 15 major languages, many minor tongues, and no united race, religion or culture.

To people born in the United Kingdom, India may seem more familiar than any of the other case studies in this book: after all it was part of the British Empire. Most of us have an image of what India is like, full of heat and dust, vibrant colours, exotic smells. We know about the British Raj, and we may know a bit about the mystical, mysterious, and exotic aspects of Indian culture, all of which have been reinforced in our minds by such films as *A Passage to India* and *Heat and Dust*. We have some idea that it is a nation made up of many diverse cultures, languages, religions, localities, peoples; we are forever being given the impression that it is paradoxical, impossible to understand, ineffable. We are partially aware that India has been through many transitions, from ancient culture, through imperial British rule to being the largest democratic nation in the world. It is one of the few foreign countries to whose traditional customs we xenophobic islanders give any status. Despite racism within the United Kingdom against Asian immigrants, we still probably have more jokes about French culture than about Indian. It is so recently that we were there and appropriated for our own use such words (and styles) as jodhpurs and such ideas as 'sacred cow'. There are certainly more Indian than French restaurants in England.

Lavishly illustrated Indian cookery books give us the impression that everyone in India eats like a king or queen: 'From childhood onwards, an Indian is exposed to more combinations of flavours and seasonings than perhaps anyone else in the world' (Jaffrey 1985 p. 10). Yet we also read newspaper reports about children dying of hunger in remote villages as India's worst drought in 100 years begins to take its toll, illustrated as usual with pictures of anonymous starving children. Poverty mixed with mysticism probably sums up the British view of the sub-continent and yet this is a nation which is, on paper, self-sufficient in foodstuffs and among the top industrial countries of the world, with a high technology production sector and its own space programme, even while most of its agriculture is of a technology low in the extreme.

Tourists arrive in search of a mystical India, but cannot avoid coming face to face with relentless poverty. Some take the first plane home, others turn a blind eye, still others try to come to terms with it, using explanations along the lines of 'well, their religion makes them accept their lot in life, there's nothing we can do about it'. To the Western tourist, Indian children are too often little nuisances who incessantly call out 'What-is-your-name?', 'One pen', 'Which country?'. Few travellers stop to think about the lives these children lead.

Children who know a few words of English may at least go to school, although some may have learned from tourists in the harsh education of the street. The less vociferous beggar children on the railway stations almost certainly have never gone to school. Tourists may encounter the odd working child, an under-age rickshaw driver, or a couple of little boys ferrying people around in *shikaras* on Dal Lake in Srinagar; or perhaps they may notice children working in the fields as the train passes through the great plains. They may notice Rajasthani village women breaking stones on building sites in the centre of New Delhi, their children crawling around in the dust, or small cigarette sellers and *paan* stall-holders in the streets of big cities, boys pumping up bicycle tyres in cycle repair shops along the sides of the road, or selling food on railway platforms. Above all they will notice children begging. But what the tourist does not see are the thousands of children who work in factories and sweatshops all over India.

Child workers are a common feature of the Indian labour market and children work in industries ranging from lock-making to agriculture. The International Labour Organization has estimated that there are more than 16.5 million child labourers in India, over 90 per cent in agriculture and associated rural occupations, less than 10 per cent in urban areas. According to an Indian Planning Commission estimate, made in 1985, there are more than this (*India Express*, 12 August 1987). If one takes into account children who work as part of a family group there may be as many as 44 million child workers.

One of the first images that springs to mind when child labour is mentioned is the carpet industry, the products of which are luxury items hung up for sale in ethnic shops and department stores throughout Europe, where the image of the small fingers which may have made them is banished. Currently the major weaving centres in India are the Mirzapur–Bhadohi area, Agra, Jaipur,

Srinagar and Amritsar. The Mirzapur–Bhadohi area accounts for almost 90 per cent of India's total production, with some 40,000 people working in the carpet-weaving sector. Most of the work takes place in villages. Men and boys weave, while girls and women spin the wool. Weavers often own one or two looms, which are set up in their homes rather than being located in and owned by a factory. This means that production is a family or group activity which needs different levels and types of skills. Merchant middlemen often suggest to families that they employ children under 12 years of age, in order to keep production costs low (Morrow 1987 pp. 2–4).

Outside the more benign cottage industry, there are regular stories in the Indian press about the wrongful confinement and physical abuse of child weavers. In 1979, a report that a small boy was branded with a red-hot poker by a supervisor for not obeying instructions provoked an official enquiry into the conditions of children in the carpet-weaving industry in Kashmir. It was established that 150,000 children aged 8–10 were earning a daily wage of 2 rupees. The children were found to be working in poorly ventilated, badly lit rooms, laden with dust and fluff from the wool or cotton, squatting on the floor hunched in front of the looms, staring at their work for very long periods. For growing children, the consequences of working in these conditions are far more serious than they would be for adults. According to one medical report, carpet-weaving children are significantly under weight and malnourished, they suffer from headaches, blurring of vision, backaches, abdominal pains, limb pains and respiratory tract infections (*British Journal of Industrial Medicine* cited in Juyal 1987). There are also frequent reports of forced labour that amounts to little more than slavery. For example, in 1987 the journal *Child Workers in Asia* published allegations that 30 children aged between five and twelve had been kidnapped in Bihar. They were taken to the Mirzapur district of Uttar Pradesh and obliged to weave carpets for as long as 22 hours a day. According to the report, they were tortured, scarred, beaten and paid nothing.

Traders make profits of up to 300 per cent on Indian carpets. Both the traditional Indian craft 'beloved of Western trendies' and the 'pale and fashionable imitation' . . . 'designer durries' (*Observer Colour Supplement*, 3 February 1985 pp. 35–9) are part of an international trade in luxury goods stretching from remote villages to Western high street stores, by which we in the West decide who in the East gets fed. The industry has a history stretching back to the seventeenth century, when a company was founded in Lahore by English merchants. After a relative slump in the eighteenth century, interest was rekindled by displays at the Great Exhibition of 1851, and foreign firms returned to India to establish factories. After independence the Indian government took an active interest and now gives encouragement in the form of export incentives to producers in this and other handicraft industries.

The handicraft industry gives employment to children throughout the small-scale sector, which survives by sub-contracting work to ensure lower production costs and higher profit margins. If it is more profitable, large factories and mills are closed and the work transferred to small units, which employ women and children. Child labour cannot be justified purely on the grounds of poverty when adult unemployment and underemployment is high throughout India. It is commonplace to suggest that children are forced to work because of family poverty but this is ironic if the poverty is caused by parental unemployment. Neera Burra, who has researched many industries in which children are employed, makes this very clear. Although it is true that child labour is associated with poverty, she says, 'this argument is frequently overextended to justify its continuance as a necessary evil' (Burra 1986 p. 241).

In reality, employers have a vested interest in expounding this argument: children work because their labour is cheap and because their collective bargaining power is minimal. Another myth is that children are employed because their small fingers are more nimble at certain tasks (like knotting carpets) than adult fingers would be. But just try to imagine children as watchmakers in Switzerland! Even the skills these small workers acquire are of little use to them in the labour market. As they get older they are replaced by yet another set of young, cheap, manipulable children. It gives a new meaning to such terms as 'redundancy' or 'early retirement'.

The Child Labour Bill of 1985 (Child Labour (Prohibition and Regulation) Act, 23 December 1986) was intended to prohibit employment of children below 14 years in *bidi* [cigarette] making, carpet-weaving, cement manufacture, cloth printing, dyeing and weaving, manufacture of matches, and a number of other specific industries. But the Act is inadequate. By specifying some forbidden industries, it ignores others, which are equally hazardous, such as the glass industry (Burra in *The Times of India* 7 November 1986). Neera Burra found that some 50,000 children below the age of 14 work in the glass industry at Firozabad, forming about a quarter of the total workforce. Children carry out a wide range of tasks, but most carry molten glass on iron rods 'from the furnace to the adult glass worker and back to the furnace again'. They

> sit in front of the furnaces where the temperature is said to be about 700°C. In many of the factories where the children were drawing molten glass from tank furnaces in which the temperature was between 1500° and 1800°C, the face of the child was within 6–8 inches from the opening of the furnace. Since he was small in size, he had to put his arm right inside in order to draw adequate quantities of molten glass. As a result, his body was almost touching the furnace. (Burra, in *Economic & Political Weekly*, Vol XXI, No. 47, 22 November 1986)

The Act also fails to take account of children's work that is subsumed under the labour of the family as a whole. It is practically unenforceable and yet there are constant calls in Indian national newspapers for the Child Labour Act to be 'strictly' enforced. The Indian government finds itself in a double bind. It wants to encourage the export of luxury goods to bring in foreign currency, but the most profitable way for such luxury goods to be made is on a small-scale, labour-intensive basis.

India has a rapidly growing population and people flock to towns in search of work. The urban population of India as a whole has risen from 25 per cent of the total in 1971 to nearly 50 per cent in the 1980s. Informal small-scale industries and the service sector of the street, albeit unstable and liable to crisis, provide an unsatisfactory solution (but a solution none the less) to what seems an intractable problem. Yet poverty in the city is harsher in many ways than it is in the countryside, and the pavement-dwelling families of major Indian cities, unable to enjoy any of the benefits of city life, exist in some of the worst conditions found anywhere in the world. As Indian development worker Adarsh Sharma points out, 'The brunt of this is borne by the child' (Sharma 1987 p. 5). She quotes a report from welfare workers:

> On the floor in a dark *Jhuggi* [living quarter of mud hut with thatched roof] an infant lies quiet, not even whimpering. He has just been given the daily dose of opium and his mother has left for the day's work . . . sewage pipe being replaced on the edge of the road, men and women sweating and dragging, the toddler from the pavement runs on the road, the screech of brakes of a passing scooter rickshaw and wails of the mother rend the air . . . Two children six and seven salvaging bits of paper from a trash heap off the road, their two year old sister in the middle of it all, flies buzzing around. These are . . . images that fall upon our retina every day in this city. (Sharma 1987 p. 5)

Ironically, it is rag-picking, scavenging the streets for any resaleable item, that has become one of the most lucrative and least dangerous forms of child labour in India today. On a good day a child can earn up to 12 rupees (about 75p or US$1) without being immediately exposed 'to any danger or health hazard' (*Child Workers in Asia*, Oct–Dec 1985). In Asian terms, compared to the glass industry workers of Firozabad for instance, this may be true but, as the ILO points out, the dangers may simply be less obvious.

> The most unhygienic working conditions are those endured by the children who collect rags and other waste materials. Even a casual look at their physique and clothing reveals the extent of their poverty and deprivation; even in the most severe winter, they can be seen working in the open without a single sweater or other protective clothing. (In Mendelievich 1979 p. 84)

It is, after all, a matter of perception. While development plans stress the need for population control and campaign posters state 'SMALL FAMILY, HAPPY FAMILY', a more pragmatic voice can say, 'What the devil that means to an agricultural labourer who knows that a 5-year-old child is a breadwinner is anyone's guess' (Brown, *Guardian*, 14 August 1987). For most Indians a new child is less an extra mouth to feed and more an extra source of income. The reasons why parents send their children to work are complex and cannot simply be understood either as cruelty or as the result of sheer necessity. In the course of her research into the gem-polishing industry of Jaipur, Neera Burra interviewed the father of an adolescent boy who, like his brother and three sisters, had first started working at the age of six. The father said:

> I am a *khula mazdoor* [casual labourer], working in shops loading and unloading goods. I sent this boy to school for a year or two but then decided that it was better to get the boys to learn a decent craft. So I brought them to

the *ustad* [master craftsman]. Even if they don't earn anything in the initial years, they will earn enough later on to make a decent living after five or six years. My son has been spared the indignity of manual labour. (Burra 1987 p. 40)

Mohammad Ali, who belonged to the roof-thatching caste, confided to Burra that he worried about his eight-year-old son working in gem-polishing: 'such a small child away from home can easily get into bad company'. But he had withdrawn the boy from school after only a couple of years of education.

My wife was keen that the child learn to work rather than study. She would point to all the other families where children were working and not going to school. So I agreed to send him to work. After all, Bablu is never going to become an officer. If he can be spared taking up our traditional occupation, that's good enough (Burra 1987 p. 40).

Caste, which divides the Indian population according to occupation, is one of the most difficult aspects of the culture for a Westerner to comprehend. It can determine an individual's status in life from birth to grave and should never be ignored as a factor in individual choices and decisions. Gender is another profound aspect, which affects the treatment children receive from early infancy. Sons are favoured by child-rearing customs, often receiving better nutrition than their sisters. In a reverse of Western patterns of thought, boys are regarded as flowers to be nurtured with care, while girls are like stones that can get along with any kind of treatment.

A further crucial factor in the life of the poor is debt, which may arise from loans to pay for festivals and family occasions such as weddings, or from financial crises caused by illness or the need for small farmers to pay for seed or even food to see them through shortages. Moneylenders and exploitative landowners still practise the now illegal system of bonded labour, by which adults and children pledge their labour to repay debts and loans.

In really desperate situations families pledge their children to contractors, sub-contractors or landowners to tide them over a financial crisis. Children are sometimes used to replace a parent who was bonded many years earlier, because manipulation of interest rates or the need to extend credit have made the original bond into a form of perpetual slavery. Such parents are not heartless, for they have little choice but to survive in this way. Hilary Coulby spent two years living and researching in a small village in Orissa. This is one of the poorest parts of India, where land for smallholdings is scarce and landlords are economically and politically dominant in ways now unknown in the West. Despite the grinding poverty of daily life, young children are given a great deal of freedom to play and enjoy themselves. Hilary Coulby comments that this seems to be a way for their parents to give them at least a short experience of freedom, because they become economically viable workers around the age of eight and are pledged to work for a landlord to pay off their families' endless debts. Before sunrise they leave home and walk many miles to work a full day in the fields, returning after dark for their one meal of the day (Coulby, personal communication).

It is ironic to think of mothers borrowing small amounts to pay medical expenses and pledging their children in return to work in *bidi* manufacture, where they contract respiratory infections and tuberculosis, thus incurring further medical expenses and greater loans. Fathers tend to run up much bigger loans and, when the debt is a matter of thousands of rupees, the *bidi* workers admit that their children may be bonded for the rest of their lives (*The Hindu*, 12 July 1987). Although parents are not deliberately cruel in treating their children in this way, even the least powerful has enough power to dispose of their children without reference to them, and landlords are able to exploit children because of the power relationships within families.

It would be wrong to imply that every Indian child is a child labourer. Even the 44 million who are believed to be so are only 13 per cent of the nation's 336 million children under the age of 15 (Paul 1987). Nevertheless, the quality of life of most of them is below the standards desired by national policy makers. There are high rates of infant mortality, malnutrition and nutrition-related diseases, leading to temporary or permanent disabilities. It is estimated that 40 million children under the age of six do not have access to the basic minimum needs of health and nutrition (Sharma 1987 p. 4). Literacy remains low and, for the reasons we have already seen, there are high rates of school dropout. In all these situations there are wide variations across regions, economic class, caste, cultural group and gender, which reflect the superabundant heterogeneity of Indian life (ICDS 1986). Socio-religious factors, traditional values, differential sex upbringing and the health and nutritional status of mothers make the problems relating to child care and development extremely complex.

This does not mean that nothing can be done or that nothing is being attempted. The Integrated Child Development Service (ICDS) was introduced by the Indian government in 1975 to try to improve the situation: 'to increase child survival rates among the poorest and enhance the health, nutrition and learning opportunities of pre-school children and their mothers' (ICDS 1986 p. 00). The scheme not only tries to draw together the forces of a multitude of different child-related services, but it is also pledged to reach out beyond existing health and education systems to children and their mothers in villages and slums, and to deliver them an integrated package of services.

At the heart of the ICDS strategy is the provision of *anganwadi* centres, in both villages and urban slums. Each *anganwadi* is in the charge of a specially trained woman who is familiar with the area and its people. She receives a small monthly payment and spends most of her time teaching families better hygiene and nutrition, organizing supplementary feeding for children seriously at risk, providing non-formal pre-school education for children, and conducting functional literacy classes for women. She is the focal point for integrating all other child services to that community. Immunization teams work through the *anganwadi* centre, where common local illnesses are also treated. It is a focal point for the community, where families can bring their children in the knowledge that either the *anganwadi* worker herself will be able to help, or she will call in whatever help might be necessary (UNICEF 1984).

A UNICEF assessment of an *anganwadi* centre in 1984 found that, in the three years after it had been established, the proportion of children immunized against diphtheria, whooping cough and tetanus had risen from 5 per cent to 35 per cent. Protection against tuberculosis doubled to 44 per cent. Sixty-one per cent of children received health checks, which was a massive improvement on the 18 per cent before the centre was opened. Nutrition also improved: over half the children were receiving Vitamin A supplements, as opposed to only one-tenth before; the proportion of children receiving supplementary food had doubled to 55 per cent; and the proportion of children found to be severely malnourished was down from 19 per cent to 11 per cent (UNICEF 1984).

Other practical solutions have been attempted, such as providing health care and some education where children are to be found, rather than building schools and health centres and expecting children to find and use them. An example of this is the Mobile Creches organization of Delhi and Bombay, which organizes day-care centres for children of migrant workers on construction sites, providing integrated services of health, education and nutrition. Construction workers are themselves mobile, usually staying on a site less than three months at a time and living with their families in makeshift labour camps: 'the child on the construction site is linked only to his family, a nuclear situation made more severe by constant changing of the camping site' (in Naidu & Kapadia 1985 p. 98). The only way to try to prevent these children from lifelong illiteracy, poor health and a future of casual labour has to be from services provided on site and according to need.

One of the most heartening aspects of the situation of children in India is the quality of work and workers who are committed to tackling the seemingly overwhelming task of helping children to survive the worst consequences of India's vast social transition.

> For most Indians this transition is an extremely painful struggle because they are deprived of the basic necessities of life which are taken for granted in developed societies. Moreover, while a tiny minority among us have already arrived, an overwhelming majority of us are still groping for a better today and tomorrow. (Naidu & Kapadia 1985 p. v)

The generation of Midnight's Children and its children's children has emerged with a greater awareness of social inequality than had previously been possible (Ali Baig 1987 p. 145). Besides the often creative approaches to pressing problems, it is clear that these workers are not content merely to ape the models of social and economic development that have been appropriate in the 'modern' West. The wish to lay the groundwork for the next generation on the firmer basis of their own cultural environment: complex, difficult, heterogeneous superabundant as this may be.

> Many such groups today are increasingly prepared to make considerable sacrifices to change the realities of daily life in the forgotten areas of our country. Unaffected by the money values of the city, they realize that there will be no India unless hard work is done to activate and preserve the work and lifestyle of the common people. Children would then grow up with the

justice conferred by natural rights, without this becoming simply a legal word meaningless in the context of this very ancient civilization. (Naidu & Kapadia 1985 pp. 145–6)

Capital: Lima
Area: 496,222 sq. miles
Population: 20,200,000
Urban population: 68% (1985)
Population annual growth rate:
  2.3% (1980–85)
GNP per capita US$: 1010
  (1985)
Rate of inflation: 98.6% (1980–85)
Population below absolute
  poverty level { urban: 49%
  (1977–85) { rural: n.a.
Population with access
  to drinking water: 55%
Life expectancy: 61

Peru
(U5MR = 128   IMR = 91)

Births: 708,000
Infants with low birthweight: 9% (1982–85)
Population 0–4: 3,000,000
Population 5–16: 5,600,000
Total population under 16: 8,600,000
Deaths 0–4: 91,000
Children 0–5 suffering from malnutrition:

  mid-moderate: 38% }
          severe: n.a. }   (1980–86)

One year olds { TB: 53%
fully immunised { DPT: 50%
  { polio: 50% }   (1985–86)
  { measles: 41% }

ORS per 100 episodes of diarrhoea: 15 (1985)

Primary school enrolment ratio male/female: 125/
  120 (gross) (1983–86)
Grade One enrolment completing primary
  school: 51% (1980–86)
Secondary school enrolment ratio male/female:
  68/61 (1983–86)

(all figures 1986 unless otherwise stated)

Peru

'Peru is Lima, and Lima is the *Jiron de la Union*' states a well-known dictum, quoted in Salazar Bondy's book, *Lima, La Horrible* (Bondy 1974 p. 28). This slim volume of ironic essays sums up many of the geographical, architectural, racial and economic divisions that characterize Peru. On the Jiron de la Union these are all displayed for public view. This street, which is now a pedestrian precinct, links the two main squares of central Lima: Plaza San Martín, flanked mainly by smart hotels, airline offices and restaurants, and the Plaza de Armas, which is dominated by the Presidential Palace and a baroque cathedral. Running parallel to this, the Jirones Carabaya and Camana contain offices of most of the banks and businesses of Peru, forming the main arteries of a grid of intersecting streets full of hotels, offices, shops and restaurants.

Jiron de la Union has the superficial air of a Mediterranean holiday resort. In the daytime, it is nearly always thronged with middle-class businessmen and secretaries, taking the air away from the office; or young people strolling along wearing fashionable, imported clothes, among tourists easily recognizable by their height, blonde features, backpacks and assortment of recently-purchased 'ethnic' clothing. Skirting these are poorer Peruvians, usually alone, or in groups no larger than three, many of them youths or children in dull grey uniforms. Most are bent on commerce: selling handfuls of cigarettes or biscuits, demonstrating clockwork toys or, especially at the San Martín end, dollar touts with pocket calculators ready to rush any tourist.

Lining the precinct at regular intervals, seated in front of shops that display assurances that the proprietor speaks English and takes credit cards, are the practised Jiron beggars, almost all of whom display some infirmity. In the Jiron de la Union one rarely sees the absolute poverty of a mendicant peasant woman with her begging bowl and dirty infants. That form of begging is more successful around the pavement cafés of the seaside area. In the business-like atmosphere of the Jiron de la Union, beggars have to show good reason, such as infirmity, why they should be asking for alms.

The Jiron de la Union links the power of state and Catholic church to the economic power of foreign exchange in banks and hotels. But Lima is more subtle and more complex than this. While the centre for the Western-oriented city is the Jiron de la Union, the centre for Indian Lima, and for the provincial hinterland, is just five minutes' walk away in La Parada. This is the wholesale and retail market area which serves thousands of smaller markets throughout the vast urban sprawl of shanty towns, with market sellers arriving to purchase goods before dawn, carrying their wares back in huge bags on their local bus or *micro* (minibus), or on their own *tricycle* (bicycle with a cart in front). A great many *micros* terminate here, as do the long-distance lorries and buses that bring people and goods from the countryside. It is also in La Parada that the best-known street children in Lima are found: the *pajaros fruteros* (fruit birds), so called because of their habit of stealing fruit from the wholesalers, either to eat or to sell. Here they have found a variety of income opportunities, from unloading trucks to prostitution and stealing, often organized in gangs by older youths or adults.

We think of these two hearts of the capital city as representing the two faces of Peru. The *criollo* heart is in the Jiron de la Union, dominated by Western races, languages and economics and tracing its origins to the Spanish conquest, and its traditions to the mixed inheritance of coastal Indians and the rule of Spanish Viceroys. This is now formal-sector Lima, engaged in economic activity in the corporate sphere, often with foreign finance, for which reason the unit of accounting is the dollar and the language of commerce often North American English. The map of this Peru starts with the Jiron de la Union and the broad avenue leading to attractive coastal residential areas, together with the two other arteries that lead through the main industrial area, where many of the signs indicate European and North American factories, to the airport, or the Pan American and Central Highways which lead out of Lima to the major cities of the hinterland as well as to beach and mountain resorts. The major forms of transport here are private cars, taxis and aeroplanes.

The heart that beats in La Parada also knows two languages, but they are Spanish and the different dialects of Quechua or other indigenous languages. This is informal-sector and provincial Peru, where commerce is reckoned in *Intis*, although payment in kind is not unknown. The people are as diverse as the languages and activities: migrant *cholos* who are assimilating the superficial aspects of *criollo* culture; *serranos* from the Andes; a few *nativos* from the Amazon basin; *zambos* (negroes) and *chinos* (orientals).

The attitude of the minority *criollo* population to the *cholo* and Indian inhabitants of Peru is characterized by fear and by romanticism, both of which are fed by ignorance of the way in which they live. In Lima, the poor and migrants live in slums and shanty towns which they alone enter, served by the *micros*, which the middle classes seldom use. The poor are feared as a potentially criminal or revolutionary mob and treated with a mixture of disdain and paternalism. Peruvian society is deeply racist, and this fundamentally affects the world in which its children grow up. Indian features are not favoured for children and *cholo* is a term used alternately as an insult, meaning ignorant and uncultured, or as an endearment which also implies denigration. Indians from the Andes or Amazon are also assumed to be uneducated, dull and stupid, particularly about the ways of the modern world. In everyday life as servants, in legal and commercial transactions, in education and in administration, their indigenous ways of thought and culture are discounted and despised. In recent years they have also been the target of suspicion, because many of the guerrilla forces, which have disrupted the country during the 1980s, have their bases in the countryside.

At another level, the middle classes romanticize an idealized indigenous, Incaic culture, on which their own identity and the tourism industry are founded. Although the tourist image of Peru is of a country of colourful peasants and jungle Indians, more than two-thirds of the total population now live in towns and nearly two-fifths of these are in Lima. Peruvian children are now largely urban, growing up in a concrete or shanty-town environment.

Thus it matters very much to a Peruvian child not only what colour you are born but also where you are born. The story of Manuel, which we told in the foreword, would have been very different if he had been light-skinned and well dressed and perhaps also if it had not later become apparent that he was accompanied by *gringos* (white foreigners) like ourselves. The differential figures for infant mortality rates in Peru, which we discussed under Principle 4, bear this out.

The legal provisions for children in Peru bear no relationship to this reality. Peruvian children are protected by the Codigo de Menores of 1962, which is based on the protective principles of the Declaration of the Rights of the Child. This began an era of changes in the relationship between the child and the state, by establishing the child's right to protection and guardianship if parental protection is absent or defective. One of the doctrines of the new attitude led to ideas about the child's right to a family and a home, the use of foster homes and the easing of restrictions on adoption. The 1979 Constitution also contains certain articles regarding the status of children and their need for protection and education. In addition, the Labour Law refers to certain aspects of the conditions of working children, and the 1984 Civil Code made some innovations in family law, particularly concerning parental rights and obligations. The 1979 Constitution makes it clear that the family is thought of as nuclear and that it is the basic unit of society, with some distinctions made between rights and duties of fathers and mothers. The age of majority in Peru is 18. Young people under this age may not marry without parental permission, girls at 14 and boys at 16, although consensual unions are not unusual for girls as young as 12 and boys from 15 onwards, particularly in rural areas. According to the 1981 census, 7 per cent of 15–19-year-old women were already mothers. This is the lowest figure in Peru. In the jungle province of Madre de Dios, a quarter of girls that age have children.

The paradox of protective legislation in Peru is that, while the nuclear family is the model unit of society, the mechanism by which it operates entails the domination of women and children by adult males. This is because the prevailing ideology of gender and age structure in urban and Hispanicized Peru is based on *machismo*. The logic of this is that men have the right to control, castigate and beat their womenfolk and their children. The exercise of male violence within the family, sanctified by ideals of family life, serves to emphasize male identity. Violence to children is related to an authoritarian ethos in social life generally. Physical punishment is the norm in homes and schools. Domination is the social, political and family symbol in Peruvian society (Barrig 1982; Ennew 1987). Thus, parental authority is manifested in the exercise of the capacity to use force. Protective legislation is contradicted by the actual conditions of childhood within urban families of all classes. The result is that, '. . . it is possible to state unequivocally that the incidence of failure to thrive, accidents and violent injury is generally extremely high as reported by hospital authorities in Lima' (Boyden 1986, p. 70).

Rural areas have different rules of social life, which retain ideas of family cohesion based on mutual responsibilities, including children's duties to other family members. Children there are subjected to another violence, caused by lack of health and welfare provision, for all such services are heavily concentrated in the capital. Inequality of access to health services is accentuated by lack of water, sewerage and good housing. Many Peruvians never see a doctor, but the use of herbs and other traditional medical techniques is very common, even among the urban elites. There are insufficient resources, both human and economic, for the public health agencies to provide free or controlled-price services. Peru is a huge country, encompassing enormous geographical differences, from coastal desert plains to high mountains and deep jungle. Administration is costly and transport difficult. At least a quarter of the population is prevented from using health services by geographical remoteness, which is a major cause of rural/urban migration.

But there are further inequalities in provision that directly affect children. The number of hospital beds for children in the whole of Peru is only 3,500. Eighty per cent of both private and public health services are for adults, which leaves precious little for children and pregnant women. Half the annual deaths in Peru are individuals under five years of age and 81 per cent die from preventable diseases. Many families are well below the daily calorie intake for malnutrition and it is men who tend to benefit from state nutrition programmes; only 10–12 per cent of state expenditure on this is for school-age children and only 5 per cent for pregnant and lactating mothers and school-age children.

Malnutrition is widespread. Violeta, who we described in our discussion of Principle 5, had other checks on the development of her natural abilities besides being shut in the house all day. Several children in her class always covered the paper they were drawing on with large circles, which they would describe as 'bread' or 'potatoes', 'their only dream', commented their teacher.

> These children take no breakfast at home except tea [without sugar or milk]. They have a meal of soup, Quaker [oats] without milk or sugar and perhaps a bread roll all day . . . They have little milk. These children have no defences, they are always ill. When they are taken to the doctor they can't buy the prescriptions. Because they are always undernourished they have difficulties of coordination, they are always tired.
>
> [They] live without gardens and without stimulation; for example they don't know how to use scissors, they don't know colours or shapes. They lack fine movements. They are very torpid. If they cannot come to a nursery school, they will repeat the first grade of primary school and, because of the

cost, their parents will take them out of school altogether (Johan Flores, quoted in Ennew 1985 pp. 77–8).

Until very recently, illiteracy was widespread in rural areas and it is still higher among women than men. In 1940, around three-quarters of rural adults were illiterate. During the 1948–56 presidency of General Odria, there was a concerted national effort to expand primary education, and enrolment doubled in the 1960s. Between 1950 and 1970, secondary school enrolment increased tenfold. But there are still many more who benefit only from primary education, because secondary schools are heavily concentrated in provincial towns and in Lima. In urban areas the school enrolment and attendance figures show lower numbers for slum areas and shanty towns, where parents also show a higher degree of illiteracy and incomplete education. The search for education is a major reason for rural–urban migration and also motivates poor urban families to send their children to private academies or to schools in better areas. The search for education also causes children to migrate.

In 1982 we recorded the life histories of boys and men who were attending a night shift at a central Lima school, most of them after a full day's work. The overwhelming majority had been born in the provinces and their life histories often described their early environment with pleasure and nostalgia, despite references to poverty. In contrast, many stated that Lima is hard and unwelcoming. They had all come to Lima for work and education, sometimes with a group of siblings or cousins and some to stay with members of their kin group who were already established in the capital. But some were entirely alone. Illness, poverty and the need to work to support themselves meant that many in their late teens and even twenties were still slogging their way through primary school grades. Many had been independent of parents from the age of 12 or under, one from the age of seven.

> I started the first grade of Primary at five years old [in Punol]. I studied in the daytime living with my parents. At the age of 11 I finished the fifth year of Primary and then at 12 years old I separated from my parents and came to Lima with the aim of continuing my studies. But I wasn't with my parents then, I was alone. I started to work in a *bodega* to cover the necessities I was faced with and I still didn't have time to study in the daytime. So I entered a school night shift, but I failed the first year. I didn't finish and I abandoned it for one year. Then I registered again in [this college] but I'm actually working in a mechanics workshop . . . (18 years old, Final year of Secondary).

Legal provision regarding the employment of children is made in the *Ley de Trabajo de Menores y Mujeres*, which also deals with women and has been modified by subsequent Acts. The basic principles regarding child work are that the minimum age for admission to employment is in general 14, except in exceptional poverty when children aged 12–14 are permitted to work at simple tasks only. For minors to be able to work, the general legal requirements are an authorization from the Ministry of Labour, issued on presentation of a birth certificate and permission from parents and a magistrate. This does not apply to work done under the authority and supervision of parents, nor to domestic service or non-mechanized agricultural labour. Higher minimum ages apply in the case of industrial work (15), commercial fishery (16) and nightwork or certain dangerous categories of employment. There are certain specific rules laid down for the employment of girls and young women, the most important of which is that they cannot work as licensed prostitutes under the age of 21.

Despite legislative prohibitions, the economic and social realities of Peru ensure that many children work illegally, work under age, or work without being registered as employed because they work independently of either parents or employers. Many of those who do work in a family context labour in conditions, or for hours, that endanger their physical or intellectual development. Many lack the requisite documents, such as birth certificates, that would enable them to register as working.

In view of the lack of welfare resources, adult unemployment, and the fact that the social security payments are tied to adult formal sector employment, there is a large active informal-sector child workforce. It is so obvious that in 1982 one could see children in school uniform selling copies of the Education Act outside the Ministry of Education.

A further factor influencing the employment of children is that many people earn less than the minimum wage, which is in any case too low to provide for the needs of a family. Thus many families have to use the labour of all available family members to survive. Even in the formally registered labour force many workers are minors. Over 7,000 10–14-year-olds formed 1.5 per cent of Lima's economically active workforce in July 1982, while 15–19-year-olds accounted for 8.2 per cent. They are paid significantly less than adult workers, generally about half the adult wage.

In the mountains, children begin to take on family responsibilities very early. Their work varies according to age, sex, family size and family land holding. A typical pattern in the Andes would be:

- from four years old: caring for guinea pigs, which are an important source of animal protein;
- from 6 or 7 years old: discouraged from playing, may have sheep to look after and their own fields to cultivate;
- from 10 years old: given donkeys and cows to care for;
- by puberty: have full adult responsibility. (Bolton and Bolton 1982)

The 1981 Census records that 78,387 children in the 12–14 age group were registered as working, mostly in agriculture and services, but later surveys have shown that up to 25 per cent of children have some kind of employment in urban areas and some are forced to do as many as three types of work in order to survive (Ennew 1985).

The influence of family or domestic group seems to be a key factor in the process of becoming a worker. The family of one 11-year-old shoeshine boy we interviewed in Lima seemed to maintain this trade for all its young sons between the ages of 10 and 13. At the age at which they started secondary school, the box of dusters and polishes was simply handed on to the next boy in the family. Even though many child street vendors work independently, their choice of wares tends to fall within those sold by their parents, who have contacts with wholesalers. An eight-year-old who cleaned cars started work when his sister became ill and needed medicine. The only equipment he needed was a bucket and a cloth, which he was able to borrow from home. He set out for the nearest commercial centre, where he paid the equivalent of 50p a day to the caretaker of the building fronting the 'patch' of road on which he worked. This was partly rent but also enabled him to have access to water. It represented half his daily income. He was lucky to find a space, because all the profitable car-washing areas, which are outside major office blocks, hotels and supermarkets, are closely guarded by gangs of older boys and adults, renowned for their fighting and pickpocketing.

It is clear that many Peruvian children work despite, or perhaps because of, prohibitive legislation. Although many are subjected to conditions and hours of work that may be detrimental to their development, it seems that there are many cases where the money they earn is crucial for any development at all to take place. It can also be beneficial for children to shoulder some responsibility and take pride in their contribution to family survival. But the inequalities of Peruvian society, which mean that it is predominantly Indian, rural or slum-born children who are forced to work to survive, while their white contemporaries enjoy a standard of living higher than most Europeans and North Americans, is iniquitous. We have one abiding image of Peruvian children and it is not of Manuel, Violeta, Fidel or Oscar. We see a pavement café in the seaside suburb of Miraflores. A family is sitting at a table under the awning. The parents are sleek and their two attractive, well dressed but fractious children are tucking into huge ice-cream sundaes. A little boy in laceless plimsolls and torn, dusty shirt and shorts approaches the table and wordlessly holds out his hand for alms. The parents brush him away with threats and terms of abuse, while his two compatriots of the next generation, their lips smeared with chocolate, gaze at him in disdain.

Capital: Pretoria
Area: 471,818 sq. miles
Population: 33,200,000
Urban population: 56% (1985)
Population annual growth rate:
  2.5% (1980-85)
GNP per capita US$: 2010
  (1985)
Rate of inflation: 13% (1980-85)
Population below absolute
  poverty level { urban: n.a.
                  rural: n.a.
Population with access
  to drinking water: n.a.
Life expectancy: 55

Births: 1,272,000
Infants with low birthweight: 12% (1982-85)
Population 0-4: 5,400,000
Population 5-16: 9,000,000
Total population under 16: 14,400,000
Deaths 0-4: 128,000
Children suffering from malnutrition:
       mid-moderate: n.a.
             severe: n.a.

One year olds   { TB: n.a.
fully immunised { DPT: n.a.
                 { polio: n.a.
                 { measles: n.a.

ORS per 100 episodes of diarrhoea: n.a.

Primary school enrolment ratio male/female: n.a.

Grade One enrolment completing primary
  school: n.a.

Secondary school enrolment ratio male/female:
  n.a.

South Africa
(including the 'Homelands')
(U5MR = 101   IMR = 75)

(all figures 1986 unless otherwise stated)

South Africa

> The child is not dead
> the child lifts his fists against his mother
> who shouts Africa! shouts the breath
> of freedom and the veld
> in the locations of the cordoned heart.

With these words of Ingrid Jonker, the Afrikaner poet whose despair led her to suicide in 1965, Oliver Tambo, President of the African National Congress, began his speech to an international conference on Children in South Africa held in Harare in 1987 (Tambo 1987 p. 1). Apartheid probably attracts more attention than any other human rights issue in the world. It has its apologists and opponents throughout the ideological spectrum from right to left and is often wholly condemned by governments of nations whose practices are, in reality, little better. It is the keyword for all discussions on South Africa. Because of this it is common knowledge that this is a society racially divided into whites, blacks, 'coloureds' and Asians. The reality is more complex, for South Africa is also a multicultural and multilingual nation, divided by class, gender and age.

The Afrikaans word 'apartheid' simply means 'separateness'. The closest word in the English language is 'separation'. The separation is of people into racially segregated groups, which definition has more basis in ideology than in biology. When combined with other 'natural' distinctions such as gender and age and the economic divisions of class it means that rich, white, adult males have the greatest power in society while poor, black, female children are the most powerless group of all.

This hierarchy serves its purpose in maintaining the structure of apartheid. As Oliver Tambo says, it 'persists because without the death of innocents, it cannot be' (Tambo 1987 p. 2). Apartheid is known for its overt brutality, but the deaths it causes from disease and starvation are even greater than those from beatings and torture, which are better known. The effects of racially biased health care allocation are clear, even in official South African infant mortality rates. In 1982, in South Africa but not including the homelands, 80 black children out of every 1,000 born alive did not reach their fifth birthday, compared to 59 'coloured', 21 Indian and 13 white children (Race Relations Survey, 1984). One source cites 68–107 for urban Africans and 240–378 in rural areas in 1980 (Jewkes 1984 p. 6). The same report states that in May 1983 the *Cape Times* had told of a 55 per cent IMR in Worcester in the Cape. Suspicions about this differential should arise from the observation that the UNICEF estimate, which takes into account the 'independent' homelands, was 101 in 1986, which compares most unfavourably with many countries with the same per capita income: Mexico for instance is 71 and Malaysia 37 (Jupp 1987 pp. 21–2).

The situation in the homelands themselves is far worse. It has been reported that the Transkei IMR is 190 and some commentators claim that the overall IMR in the homelands is 14 times that for whites (Jupp 1987 pp. 1–2). The irony is first that the homelands would not be economically viable at all without the remittances sent home to their families by male migrant workers in South Africa. In the second place, the homelands also serve the purpose of producing and nurturing the next generation of such workers, and they do this outside the South African system proper, at minimal cost to that system. The wastage of human life is immaterial to South African capitalism, as long as enough future workers are produced.

These figures reflect the racially biased allocation of health care. The new South African Constitution divides health and welfare into three 'own affairs' organizations: for whites, for 'coloureds' and for Asians. Blacks in white-designated areas come under the administrative division of 'general' affairs. Each of the ten self-governing homelands has a health minister; but resources are not evenly distributed. In South Africa, whites have 330 patients per doctor but blacks have one doctor for 12,000 patients. Looked at in the context of rural and urban settings there are 750 patients per doctor in cities and 25,000 patients per doctor in the countryside. The situation is far worse in the homelands: in the Odi 1 area of Bophuthatswana there is only one doctor for every 365,000 people (Jupp 1987 p. 22). The consequences for child mortality and morbidity are obvious. One survey of primary school children in the Eastern Transvaal found that 46 per cent of the children had active tuberculosis and 16 per cent were debilitated by bilharzia, but local doctors could treat only 15 per cent of those in need because of limited resources (Jupp 1987 p. 22). Another study shows that in an area of Natal where domestic water was drawn from an unsafe supply, 50 per cent of children probably suffered from bilharzia (Jupp 1987 p. 23).

It is always the white advantage over the black that stands out. The two minority non-white groups are so safely contained between them that we see and hear little about them. Occasionally Asians are turned on by blacks and respond as aggressively as their white counterparts; 'coloureds' have less public profile. That 'coloured' and Asian populations are generally overlooked in discussions is extremely important. Although proportionately few, their numbers are not insignificant. A large part of their population is also children, who are as relevant to the issues as is the highly oppressed black child. No less important are white children, who are victims of their socialization and may be drawn into the front line after the inevitable change from white to black domination in their country. Simply because they live in an apartheid state, all

South African children are vulnerable: 'Those who are white, face a legacy of donning the SADF uniform, whether they like it or not, to defend a system they may or may not want to uphold' (Langa 1987 p. 9).

Apartheid has been systematically applied in all aspects of life to perpetuate strength and weakness. In the face of the law, the uneducated black is always disadvantaged in comparison with the Asian or the 'coloured' and has no equal footing with whites worth considering. Even the liberal white opponent of apartheid still has far more chance of fair treatment in law than a black. It is not only the division of society into these groups but also the degree of privilege enjoyed by each group that prepares them for unequal treatment. Education is one of apartheid's more loyal servants.

The infamous Bantu Education Act of 1953 was summed up in one of Hendrik Verwoerd's speeches. Verwoerd was an ardent believer in the inferiority of the black (Bantu was the commonly used term in his day) and influential in creating the rigid framework of apartheid. He said, 'There is no place for [the Bantu] in the European community above the level of certain forms of labour . . . For this reason it is of no avail for him to receive a training which has as its aim absorption in the European community' (as quoted in Jupp 1987 p. 34).

Thus the pattern was set. The Minister of Education in 1984, Barend du Plessis, argued in parliamentary debates on education that more than five million black children were then at school, compared with about 800,000 in the 1950s. Laying the blame for the inferiority of education at the feet of the blacks themselves, he claimed that the 'drastic increase' in numbers of black people was 'hampering the quality and provision of African education' (in Jupp 1987 p. 35). He claimed that this took up an ever-increasing slice of the budget and that, unless the blacks embarked upon sensible family planning schemes, the government would eventually no longer have the resources to provide education.

The information we have tells a different story. Whilst there is free and compulsory education for whites, it was not until 1980 that it was introduced for 'coloureds'. They should attend school between the ages of 7 and 14 in Cape Province and 7 and 16 in Natal. It is nowhere near as universal as the white education from 7 to 16 years of age and it has been reported that compulsory education for 'coloureds' is still not being enforced (Jupp 1987 p. 35). Asians have had compulsory education where possible. This naturally means that where it is difficult or impractical to provide education, there is none.

Since 1976, education for black children aged 7 to 11 years has been compulsory. On the other hand, education is still not free for all black children: although registered schools receive subsidies from the government, pupils may still need to pay fees, and less than 12 per cent of black schoolchildren actually attend school. There are only about 7,000 black public schools outside the homelands under direct government administration (Jupp 1987 p. 36). Many black children — estimates point to about 20 per cent — live on white-owned farms. It is up to the farmer to build a school, decide that one cannot be built, or close an existing school. If a farmer allows a school to be run, then the state subsidizes construction and pays the teachers' salaries. Ultimately access to rural education depends on private landowners, who control wage opportunities for black parents. If black workers object because their children are not obtaining an education, it may be at the expense of their jobs.

There are ten grades in the school system. It has been estimated that, overall, white children spend an average of 13 'man-years' in school to obtain their Standard Ten Certificate against 225 'man-years' for blacks. This correlates with drop-out rates, rather than with specific educational failure. The pass rates for 1983 show that 50 per cent of blacks who sat the final grades passed, as compared with 80 per cent for whites, 72.5 for 'coloureds' and 86 per cent for Asians (Reynolds 1987). School success can be similarly viewed by looking at the numbers of children from whole school enrolments who are in the Standard Ten grade. The figures for 1982 show that of 3,603,039 black children, 41,127 were Standard Ten, whereas, of 975,414 whites, 55,216 were at that grade. Nor are 'coloured' or Asian children as successful at reaching the final grade as they are at passing the Certificate: of 767,340 coloureds, 10,844 were in the tenth grade and of 224,322 Asians, only 8,576.

> The 579 black squatters' children who attend the Thembilihle or 'Good Hope' school of Inanda Township, 14 miles north of Durban, barely have a roof over their heads. The school is ineligible for government subsidy and subsists on fees paid by the impoverished parents. There are only eight teachers and only one book for every twelve pupils. Deprived of chairs, desks, and pens, the children do not know that education is their right. They assume that the systemic inequality that they struggle against is normal (Reynolds 1987 p. 41).

It is this inequality in education that has drawn black South African children into the forefront of the violent struggle against apartheid. In 1976, the first violent protest by schoolchildren against the state took place. Since then schoolchildren and students have clashed continually with the state, thousands of them have been injured or killed in ferocious street battles and during police raids on demonstrations in schools. A series of school boycotts reached its peak in 1985–86 when an estimated 220,000 primary and secondary school children were reported to have stayed away from their schools. In contrast to Western child liberation lobbies, this is not a cause taken up on their behalf by adult champions. Children themselves are demanding rights. They want scientific subjects to be taught in English rather than Afrikaans. They want student representative councils. They demand an end to excessive corporal punishment and to the sexual harassment of schoolgirls. They call for the age limit to be scrapped, for qualified teachers and for supplies of books and materials to be provided free. These are not, or should not be seen as, revolutionary demands. These are the demands of young people who want to learn. But the government regards their actions as revolutionary and represses them violently. The result is that, 'Black South African children now have to make decisions usually made by adults, face choices they should not have to face as children and face battles they should not be fighting' (Chikane 1987 p. 3).

As the Secretary-General of the South African Council of Churches notes, much repression is specifically addressed to people under 25 and the main target of terror is children. This is not surprising because, since 16 June 1976, 'the most militant, energetic and courageous fighters against apartheid have been the youth and children' (Chikane 1987 p. 7). The South African government has decided that, in order to break the spirit of protest, you have to break the spirit of youth, which means a repression felt by young people who may not even be activists. For example, one 15-year-old boy, who had never taken part in protests, was walking home from school with a friend. They saw a transporter full of policemen approaching, and the friend ran away. This is what the boy says happened next:

> Six police, two white and four blacks, got out of the Combi. The white policemen knocked me down with his gun and then three of them took me to the street corner . . . [they] assaulted me with rubber truncheons. They threatened me with a knife. One of the policemen told me to run so that they could shoot me . . . They drove me to the schoolyard where they assaulted me again. They hit me with rubber truncheons and sjamboks. Then they blindfolded me with a greasy cloth and tied my hands behind my back with my belt. (Quoted in Chikane 1987 p. 7)

He was detained for three days for suspected car theft, then released without a reason.

In a small Orange Free State community called Petrus Steyn, on 2 September 1987, secondary school children called a boycott of classes to protest at the detention of two activists and against corporal punishment by the principal. Children from primary school were sent home as a precaution. But as the children went home, police arrived and attacked them with sjamboks from which some children received serious injuries.

Almost every day, press reports tell us of the latest dispute or unrest in South Africa. Frequently these accounts are supplemented by case histories of men, women and children who have been subjected to injustice and physical abuse. Some die in horrifying public circumstances, others in the hands of the police or other official bodies, who never reveal the truth. Conflicting figures of detainees reach newspapers equally frequently, often telling us about large numbers of minors. Due to the different sources of reports, and to censorship, it is difficult to know exactly how many children are in detention.

South African law makes the following provision for the detention of juveniles:

> In terms of the common law, a child younger than seven years old cannot be held responsible for his or her criminal conduct. Children between the ages of seven and fourteen are presumed not to be criminally responsible and this must be rebutted by the state in order to convict the child accused. It is therefore theoretically possible for a child above the age of seven years old to be imprisoned. In addition, the Children's Act, No. 33 of 1960, includes a police cell in the definition of 'a place of safety', so that a child may be placed in a police cell without having committed any alleged criminal offence at all (Section 1).

The new Child Care Act, No. 74 of 1983, which has been enacted but is not yet in force, does not specifically include a police cell in the definition of a 'place of safety'. This Act instead provides that a 'place of safety' includes any place suitable for the reception of a child, into which the owner, occupier, or person in charge thereof is willing to receive a child (Section 1 (xxviii). Once this legislation is in force, the use of police cells as 'places of safety' suitable for the reception of children should be challenged in the courts. (McLachlan 1986 p. 347)

It is clear that the power to detain children in prisons has, thus far, not been illegal. But the new Child Care Act, although not including police cells, does not specifically legislate against their use and, until that has been challenged successfully, children will continue to be detained in them. If it was simply that children were detained for short periods until handed over to their parents or guardians the issue would never have attracted much attention. The reality is that detention is frequently long. Fiona McLachlan cites instances of 13 months on a criminal charge, of rape by other inmates and of the disorientation of a 15-year-old who had been detained for 14 days. In a 'Preliminary Report on South Africa', Geoffrey Bindman, who was one of the four lawyers on a mission for the International Commission of Jurists, states that the Detainees' Parents Support Committee (DPSC) informed the Commission of several children aged 10, 11 and 12 who had been in detention from the beginning of emergency regulations (12 June 1986) until their visit in early February 1987 (Bindman 1987).

Although detention can be rationalized in terms of a 'place of safety', which keeps minors out of harm's way, children who are detained have consistently complained of assaults and abuse. A sample of 40 statements by detainees under 18 contained 24 allegations of torture, which included:

- kicking, sjambokking, caning, slapping and beating
- forced exercise for extended periods . . .
- electric shock treatment
- hanging by the neck
- drowning
- being made to hold a hand grenade
- being forced to lick a soldier's blood
- being suspended and then dropped to the floor
- having water thrown over them and being made to sleep on it
  (Jupp 1987 p. 57)

A quarter of these statements included the complaint that intimidation had been used in an attempt to make them become informers which, if true, would put the children at risk of reprisals when they return to their own neighbourhoods. Intimidation included threats that they would:

- be killed
- have their homes petrol bombed
- be detained for . . . up to 15 years

- be locked in a cell for 5 years
- have a tyre placed round their necks and set alight
- have petrol poured on their heads and hands and then set on fire
- be hanged
  (Jupp 1987 p. 58)

Medical examinations have verified many such allegations. Children have also died in detention (DPSC Press Statement, Harare 1987). A 13-year-old boy died on 5 July 1985, after being taken into police custody and held 'in connection with public violence'. His parents were told that during a routine cell visit he had been found dead. A post mortem was carried out five days later and it was reported that the pathologist attributed the cause of death to brain damage and a fractured skull. These injuries were sustained during detention by the police.

Quite apart from the infringement of international agreements, the use of torture and the conditions of imprisonment are contrary to South African law. The Prisons Act states that unconvicted prisoners under the age of 18 should not be held in prison or police cells unless it is necessary and no suitable place of detention is available. They are not to be confined with anyone older than 21, unless such a person is a co-accused or the association would not be detrimental to the child. There are also provisions about access to food, clothing and reasonable conditions in detention (McLachlan 1986 p. 355). In reality parents and children are often totally ignorant of the rights and privileges of unconvicted persons, especially juveniles. What white South Africa has created is a legal system with so many loopholes that it is impossible to contain the most simple principle, such as 'place of safety', within reasonable parameters. Not only is Justice blind, but in South Africa there is great caution taken to see that she does not recover her sight.

The under-educated oppressed majority of black children cannot even be properly counted. The United States Census Bureau of Statistics estimated in 1981 that 42 per cent of the population of South Africa was under the age of 14. In August 1986, the Deputy Consul-General for South Africa stated in New York that more than half of the black population of 23 million is under 15 years old. It has also been guesstimated that there are about 12 million blacks under 18 years old. This number is somewhat larger than the combined populations of white, coloured and Asian South Africans of all ages. 'I have heard a new slogan among the children,' said Pius Langa at the Harare conference. 'It is symbolic of the resistance pervading the country, it is a chilling reminder to us all of our responsibilities: "Freedom or death!"' (Langa 1987 p. 9).

Capital: Managua
Area: 57,143 sq. miles
Population: 3,400,000
Urban population: 57% (1985)
Population annual growth rate:
   3.4% (1980–85)
GNP per capita US$: 770
   (1985)
Rate of inflation: 33.8% (1980–85)
Population below absolute
   poverty level ⎰ urban: 21%
   (1977–85)   ⎱ rural: 19%
Population with access
   to drinking water: 56%
Life expectancy: 63

Births: 145,000
Infants with low birthweight: 15% (1982–85)
Population 0–4: 600,000
Population 5–16: 1,100,000
Total population under 16: 1,700,000
Deaths 0–4: 14,000
Children suffering from malnutrition:
   mid-moderate: n.a.
   severe: n.a.

One year olds   ⎰ TB: 95%   ⎱
fully immunised   ⎰ DPT: 45%   ⎱ (1985–86)
                   ⎰ polio: 80%   ⎱
                   ⎰ measles: 51% ⎱

ORS per 100 episodes of diarrhoea: 92 (1985)

Primary school enrolment ratio male/female: n.a.
Grade One enrolment completing primary
   school: 27% (1980–86)
Secondary school enrolment ratio male/female:
   n.a.

Nicaragua
(U5MR = 100   IMR = 64)

(all figures 1986 unless otherwise stated)

Nicaragua

Nicaragua is 'somewhere' in Central America. That is all most people can tell you, if they realize at all that there are countries between Mexico and South America. The map of the world tells us that between Mexico and Colombia there are seven small countries; Nicaragua is nearly in the middle. These are not facetious comments. It seems to us that Nicaragua exists in the international consciousness more as a T-shirt and poster slogan than as a country. It is a place to show solidarity with, rather than to have information about. Similarly, all most people know about Nicaraguan children is that many of them are active soldiers.

We can illustrate this lack of knowledge with an anecdote. In 1986 we were at an undergraduate seminar about Nicaragua. One West African student had read of 'problems on America's back door'. He assumed that, since the 'front' of the United States was across the Atlantic, Nicaragua must be on the Pacific coast, near California. A vehemently anti-American Iranian told the African he was stupid and ought to know that Nicaragua was part of his own continent. Out of a group of about 16 or 17 students, only four could place Nicaragua approximately. Even a woman from Guyana refused to accept the possibility of there being only four countries and about 1,500 miles between the border of her birthplace and Nicaragua. All of them were pro-Sandinista, supported revolutionary Nicaragua and considered the United States-financed 'contras' to be a threat to liberty and democracy.

Such debates take place all too often. Details of the political and social history of Nicaragua or of the physical conditions appear to be irrelevant. Without wishing to divert from the subject of children in Nicaragua now, it is worth presenting a short history of the nation they have inherited. It is a story of chronic instability and imperialist intervention. Ironically, part of Nicaragua is the 'Mosquito Coast', known by aficionados of tales of high-seas piracy as a haven for their heroes. If we may draw on that and suggest a comparison between fact and fiction, and then compress the history down to a three-hour Hollywood epic, we could be sure that much of it would require Errol Flynn, Douglas Fairbanks, Stewart Grainger and other great swashbucklers to play the leading roles. Only in the later scenes would a less famous actor enter the scenario, one Ronald Reagan.

Nicaragua stretches from a chain of volcanoes on the Pacific coast, over a range of high, damp, cold mountains which slope down to the Atlantic. Like most of Latin America it was conquered by Spain in about 1523 and remained a colony until 1821, originally as a province of Guatemala. Britain occupied part of the Atlantic coast, giving political and military support to the Indian population, as part of the rivalry with Spain and France for control over the Caribbean region. Moskitia, which we know as the Mosquito Coast, became a *de facto* protectorate in the eighteenth century, leaving a mark on cultural traits, and 'coastal English' in Nicaragua. It was not until the dictatorship of General Zelaya, at the turn of the century, that the region was really integrated into the nation.

The history throughout most of the nineteenth century was one of war and dissent. A liberal constitution, inspired by that of the United States, was written in 1826 and replaced by a conservative one in 1858. Both constitutions freed peasants from the obligatory labour that had been the rule under Spanish domination, and slavery had already been abolished in 1824, although it took most of the century actually to disappear. Throughout the nineteenth and well into the twentieth century there was endemic warfare between the León 'liberals' and Granada 'conservatives', who were, respectively, supporters of the ideas of the American and French Revolutions, and traditionalists who were attached to Hispanic aristocratic values. The reality of government by either side made very little difference to the common people.

When, in the early 1850s, the 'liberal' Castellán lost against the 'conservative' troops of Chamorro, he looked for outside support. William Walker, a journalist from the southern states of the USA, was recruited. The Accessory Transit Company was eager to secure a hold over the inter-ocean routes in the area and provided financial backing. Walker, an ardent supporter of slavery, turned against his liberal friends and seized power. He hoped to unite the five isthmus states into a single white republic with a model slave society. In 1858 he had himself 'elected' president of Nicaragua. Slavery was reintroduced. English was declared the official language and property seized from the 'enemies' of the Republic and given over to naturalized Nicaraguans. The President of the United States, Franklin Pierce, instantly recognized Walker's government. Nevertheless, Walker was overthrown by Central American troops, backed by the British government and the Accessory Transit Company which had earlier financed his rise to power.

Thereafter there was an uncertain peace during about 30 years of conservative rule. During that period, however, the aristocracy tried to create a basis for expropriation and forced labour, and a reactionary law in 1877 brought about an Indian uprising that lead to massive bloodshed in 1881.

In 1893 the nationalist head of the Liberal Party, General Zelaya, became president. His 16-year dictatorship attempted to modernize the country, thereby creating the basis for modern capitalist production through stark authoritarian rule. This was cut short by an invasion of US Marines. Zelaya had defied the USA by negotiating a loan from a London syndicate and beginning to negotiate with Japan over an Atlantic–Pacific canal through his country.

It was essential for the United States to have control over such a canal. Although it was eventually built in Panama, the US Marines occupied Nicaragua in 1912 and the country was to remain under the control of its northern neighbour until 1925. After withdrawal, the Marines returned to Nicaragua in 1926 because a civil war had broken out, provoked by the results of an election initiated and supervised by the United States. Augusto César Sandino refused to accept the US-imposed solution to Nicaraguan problems and resisted with guerrilla warfare. By 1931, the United States had begun a gradual withdrawal after creating a local military force, the National Guard, leaving its commander, Anastasio Somoza, in control of the country. Subsequently, Somoza became President, his two sons following him as hereditary dictators of Nicaragua in a dynasty that ruled for 43 years.

Nicaragua is a country that has seldom known stability and has been governed by external forces in part or in whole for hundreds of years. Whenever post-colonial Nicaragua attempted to assert itself as a nation, the USA was instrumental in bringing it 'back in line'. Thus recent history is nothing unusual.

Before the successful 1979 revolution there were no infant development services in rural areas; by 1983 there were 24 services, for just over 2,000 children. Prior to 1979 there were no communal kitchens in rural areas; by 1983 there were 32, for well over 5,000 children. It was for reasons such as these that Sandinista forces overthrew the Somoza regime. To take another example affecting children, under the dictatorship military spending was 50 per cent higher than spending on education. The build-up to the overthrow followed the massive earthquake, which left 15,000 dead and devastated the capital, Managua, in 1972. Large parts of the international aid for victims and reconstruction went to line the pockets of the Somoza clan; very little of the money was ever used to reconstruct medical or educational services. Instead, Somoza introduced an Immediate Action Plan for Education in 1973 to reduce the school week from 30 to 20 hours, and reorganized the school calendar to fit in with coffee, sugar and cotton harvests, which provided the main exports. Much of the profit found its way into Somoza or *somocista* bank accounts. What this legislation amounted to was legal exploitation of child labour in order to help generate a false economic boom.

There were no educational incentives. Not only was education scarce but attendance reflected feelings about its value. In 1976, only 6.7 per cent of young children had access to pre-school education. Eighty per cent of those places were in the private sector and were, therefore, well out of the economic reach of most families. Primary education, for 7–12-year-olds was the only education universally available. In 1976, only about 70 per cent of more than 400,000 children had school places, and about half dropped out within a year. Ninety per cent of rural schools had only one teacher for all six grades. As a result, children commonly took eight or nine years to complete six grades, and most failed to complete at all. Many pupils were required to look after younger siblings whilst parents worked, and so rarely, if ever, attended. It was an education system divorced from the realities of Nicaraguan life, with books that taught on United States models, while the rich elite had their own private schools and often sent their children abroad for education. After 1973, schools were forced to reduce their teaching capacity radically. As a result, only slightly over one-third of all schools offered more than the first three grades. Secondary education for 13–16-year-olds was available only for children who had achieved all ten primary grades, therefore very few peasant children ever got that far; this was a privilege reserved for a few urban children. Even fewer reached the pre-university grades; there were fewer than 35,000 children at that level in 1972. According to 1976 figures about 0.3 per cent reached higher education.

Since the successful overthrow of the Somoza regime, Nicaragua has faced a period of transition which is fraught with problems caused largely by external pressures, in which 'aggression by the US-backed "contras" is a backcloth to everything else that goes on' (Massey 1987 p. 11). According to newspaper reports, President Daniel Ortega goes jogging daily with a Kalashnikov rifle in his hand, to show his constant preparedness for an invasion. It is a situation he has shared with his contemporaries since childhood:

> From an early age he was politicised. At 14 he was throwing stones at Somoza's hated National Guard. In 1960, at the age of 15, he participated in attacks on the two National Guard barracks and was arrested and tortured for the first time (Jenkins 1985).

He was to experience arrest and torture four more times before he was 19 years old.

But his was not an isolated case. Children were in the front line of Somoza's aggression and it seems as if he tried to wipe out an entire generation of males in what some have called a 'Herod Policy', after the Biblical tale of the king who ordered that all male children in Bethlehem should be slaughtered when he heard that a king who would be greater than him had been born there. In the case of Nicaragua, the order went out in May 1979 that the National Guard should enter slum areas of major cities to seek and kill all male children over 12 years of age, although some slum dwellers state that the policy actually started with eight-year-olds. In any case, the Guard were unlikely to be asking for, or to find, birth certificates. As a result, thousands of young boys were faced with a decision. They could stay and die in their own homes, they could flee to the countryside, or they could join the undifferentiated mass of the people ranged against Somoza and fight. Many chose the last course and helped on the Sandinista barricades.

> Those who chose to stay and fight were called heroes and those who died martyrs. The aggression and violence exhibited by many of these youngsters armed with anything from automatic weapons to Molotov cocktails were praised and given real prominence by the Sandinista Liberation Front for its final victory on 19th July 1979 as 'skillful, intelligent, resourceful, mature and loyal'. (Taçon 1981 p. 24)

The Nicaraguan Revolution is better known for its fighting women than for its fighting children. The active role of both social groups in the armed struggles is strikingly different from the expected roles of women and children in male-dominated Latin American societies. Yet it is by no means unusual to see photographs of tough women and battleworn children carrying heavy weapons and wearing combat gear. The caption of one newspaper image in 1987 reads, 'Carol Pineda, a Sandinista soldier, demonstrates a Russian-made SAM-7 rocket launcher during a visit to a Managua school' (*Independent*, 12 November 1987).

Carol's confident posture, balancing the heavy weapon, with one elbow on her out-thrust hip and clad in serviceable battle fatigues, is a long way from the ideal woman of *machista* society who emphasizes girlish helplessness rather than competence and, swinging her hips for a different purpose, teeters on high-heeled shoes as obvious prey for males. The children in the picture take her confidence for granted; all their curiosity is reserved for the SAM-7.

The situation of women in Nicaragua has been described more fully, and is better understood, than that of children. Women have been given a prominent part in Western literature of the Sandinista story. It is clear that, by joining the overall battle to overthrow Somoza alongside men, by sacrificing separatist feminist goals and fighting only for short-term strategic gains for women, the Nicaraguan sisterhood has placed itself in a position in which its strength is politically acknowledged and a return to the oppression of *machismo* has been avoided (see, for example, Molyneux 1985). Such advances for women inevitably have consequences for children, by altering the conditions of dominance within the family and in society itself. Advances in female literacy also have beneficial effects for children, for maternal education has been found everywhere to correlate to child health status.

Roughly half the 3,400,000 Nicaraguans are now under 16 years of age and about one-third of those are five years old or less. Parenthood begins young, so the number of children is growing fast, at an estimated rate of about 3.4 per cent per annum at present. On their behalf, it appears that the Sandinista government has begun to fight problems inherited from the Somoza dynasty. The mortality rate for infants under 12 months has been halved from 120 per thousand in 1978 to just over 60 in 1984. Similar success has been achieved in helping children to reach their fifth birthday. The rate is now less than half that of 1960, but 100 per thousand in 1986 keeps Nicaragua in the High Infant Mortality Rate category of countries, according to UNICEF's ranking system. On the other hand, this record should not be underestimated. It has been achieved with a per capita income of US$770, when South Africa, which stands just above Nicaragua on the ranking, has a per capita income of US$2,010.

In 1978, the principal causes of death in children were measles, diphtheria, malaria and polio. In 1983, there were only 102 recorded cases of measles, three of diphtheria, 407 of malaria and one of polio, and children did not necessarily die from any of these illnesses. Immunization programmes have been successful in so far as they have been extended to larger numbers of children. United Nations figures for 1985–86 show 51 per cent of children immunized against measles, 45 per cent against diphtheria, 80 per cent against polio and 95 per cent against tuberculosis. Moreover, the primary health care message is clearly reaching mothers and children throughout the country, because 92 per cent of children suffering from diarrhoea are reported to have benefited from oral rehydration therapy. On the medical front at least, the fight to save lives is gaining momentum. The problem, as we stated in our discussion of Principle 4 of the Declaration of the Rights of the Child, is that lives rescued from early childhood diseases are often lost in the wastage of warfare. Between 1982 and 1986, 9,638 civilians were wounded, kidnapped or killed. About half of these casualties are likely to have been children and these figures do not include the children of 12 and over who are wounded and die in the army or with 'contra' groups. The war has lasted 13 years. The Red Cross estimates that 40,000 to 50,000 Nicaraguans died prior to 1979. Children who had survived this slaughter, who celebrated reaching their fifth birthday at the same time as the success of the revolution, are now 14 years old and being drafted into the army.

Besides being healthier soldiers, young Nicaraguans are also better educated. Standards of schooling have improved dramatically. Up to 1978, half the population was illiterate; since the Somoza regime was overthrown this has been reduced to about one in ten. In 1978, there were only 24,000 high school students; now there are over 35,000. The number of just over half a million middle school pupils has grown to $1\frac{1}{4}$ million, and the less than 400,000 places in pre-revolutionary primary schools has grown to well over 600,000. Pre-school facilities formerly provided for only about 9,000 children; now nearly 70,000 have access. Where there were few community schools there are now several hundred. The budget has increased from 341 milion córdobas in 1978 to well over 2,000 million in 1983. Nevertheless there is still a long way to go: recent United Nations statistics show that only 27 per cent of children enrolled in grade one ever finish primary school.

Immediately after the revolution, the National Association of Nicaraguan Teachers (ANDEN) was formed to oppose and replace the unions that supported the Somoza regime. Within a very short time it had about 10,000 members including the reinstatement of 450 who had been sacked by the Somoza regime. One thousand two hundred Cuban teachers went to Nicaragua in 1979 to help reconstruct the system. Child Development Centres (CDIs) were set up by the Ministry of Social Welfare to organize small-scale development centres at local level.

None of the measures taken to improve child health or education can be expected to succeed fully in the present economic situation. Nicaragua has a negative growth rate, and in the early 1980s inflation was nearly 34 per cent. The peasant economy has been disrupted by warfare continually during the past two decades; trade embargoes imposed by the United States have dealt heavy blows to an already stricken economy and the country is dependent on outside aid, which is not always forthcoming. As in Mozambique, civil warfare has disturbed whole sectors of the population, displacing them from their homes and livelihood. There are an estimated 250,000 displaced persons within Nicaragua, a further 220,000 in the United States, and 102,000 in other parts of Central America (including 20,000 Miskito refugees in Honduras). Altogether about 16 per cent of the Nicaraguan population has been forced from hearth and home (*Central América*, 1987–88 No. 36 p. 5). The effects on the next generation, which is, as always, disproportionately represented among wanderers, is incalculable.

José Polanco moved with his family close to the border with Honduras in 1980, seeking a quiet life and the possibility of continuing subsistence farming without violent interruption. In 1985 he said, 'At first the revolution was good. They built a school nearby; they came every year to vaccinate the children; . . . Now the school is closed, no one comes by. They are frightened by the fighting' (Quoted in Jenkins 1985).

Another typical report of 1987 shows that Daniel Ortega is not the only Nicaraguan who is alert for invasion,

> Every night the children go to bed in El Cedro cooperative in the knowledge that before dawn they may be running over the hill to flee another attack by the . . . Contra guerillas. They have done it more than once before and most of their lives are now spent just waiting for it to happen again. (*Guardian*, 2 July 1987)

The war between the supporters of the Somoza dynasty and the Sandinista revolutionaries continues as the United States-backed 'contras' fight relentlessly against the new regime. The cost for children in front-line areas is high. They have been killed, kidnapped and allegedly pressed into serving in 'contra' guerrilla forces.

Because children are not organized as a group, in the way that women are, their post-revolutionary gains are not so marked politically. Children are oppressed within patriarchal families not only by men but by all adults who, in *machista* society, use authoritarian methods and corporal punishment to control children's behaviour. It is hard for a war veteran, who has been praised for the use of lethal weapons, to return to the submission of childhood. In the early days of the revolution, the rehabilitation of heroes of the revolution was not always smooth and was related to a continued street children problem in urban Nicaragua. As Peter Taçon, the Director of Childhope, asked:

> Why should we expect Juan Carlos at age twelve, having put his life in the balance and having taken the lives of others as an instant adult and freedom fighter, to return to grade four in short pants with a suddenly reconstituted childhood? (Taçon 1981 p. 25)

As things have turned out, 'Juan Carlos' was not able to return to childhood because his services, and those of his sisters, continued to be required by the revolution. It is an irony that the only real advance in children's rights in Nicaragua is the lowering of the age of majority for soldiers to 16, in acknowledgement of the importance of children in warfare and in direct contradiction to more than one of the Principles of the Declaration. Even if a secure and lasting peace is reached very soon and United States threats of intervention are forgotten, few children will have been free of the threat of war. Their elders will have known very little but armed struggle and will never fully readjust to peacetime conditions. Like those who lived through both World Wars, they will almost certainly remember days of hardship and of comradeship. Children born without the war experience will inherit the history and perhaps guard against foreign dominance and national tyranny. The next generation is the important fresh start. If they are heirs to a nation in peace then they might just make it. If so, they will be the first generation for 400 years to do so. The lessons of history are unfortunately against them.

Brazil

What do most people know about Brazil? That it is the name of a nut, has the Amazon River and jungle, Rio de Janeiro, Carmen Miranda headwear during carnival, Ipanema Beach, maracas and music and . . . 'They've got an awful lotta coffee' . . . Some people will know about Brasília, the capital built in the wilderness. Followers of economic affairs will know that the state has the fastest rate of growth and biggest foreign debt in the world, some will have noted that it is among the top five or so armaments exporters at present. But not one of these scrapbook facts is about children.

One highly successful film, called *Pixote*, brought Brazilian street children to international cinemas in the early 1980s. We ourselves first saw it in Lima, with a largely English group of aid workers who, like us, were spending much of their time trying to do something (anything) about street children there. It was a surrealistic experience, sitting in a comfortable row of seats, looking up at the huge images of children like those who normally appeared to us as tiny figures tapping our arms for attention, trying to slip watches off our wrists or huddled in small bundles in shop doorways at night. The depiction of an ugly, violent reformatory, of drugs, sex, death and danger, the speed of street life and its fleeting relationships was accurate beyond belief and we were glad it would reach a wider audience. The child actors were real street children, but the real *Pixote* did not find fame and fortune; he returned to the street after his brief acting career and died in 1987, while still in his teens. Meanwhile, the streets of Brazil's cities continue to be home to many thousands of Pixotes, the marginalized scapegoats of the country's economic miracle.

Probably you have read newspaper stories or seen television documentaries on the 'sale' of children for international adoption or about street children in one of the principal Brazilian cities. The international image of Brazilian children tends to be dominated by exposés. Poverty is so widespread in the Third World that it is not interesting to newspapers unless it can be incorporated into the pornography of misery, accompanied by a massive famine, flood, earthslide or other natural disaster, or by the picture of a grinning urchin.

Brazil has a paradoxical public image, which combines the gloss of success and the patina of wretched, sordid disaster. It is the fifth largest country in the world. Although it is still counted as a Third World nation, its immense wealth

Capital: Brasilia
Area: 3,286,488 sq. miles
Population: 138,500,000
Urban population: 74% (1985)
Population annual growth rate: 2.3% (1980–85)
GNP per capita US$: 1640 (1985)
Rate of inflation: 147.7% (1980–85)
Population below absolute poverty level { urban: n.a.
{ rural: n.a.
Population with access to drinking water: 76%
Life expectancy: 65

Brazil
(U5MR = 89   IMR = 65)

Births: 4,039,000
Infants with low birthweight: 8% (1982–85)
Population 0–4: 18,200,000
Population 5–16: 32,800,000
Total population under 16: 53,000,000
Deaths 0–4: 359,000
Children 0–17 suffering from malnutrition:
      mid-moderate: 55% }
         severe: n.a. } (1980–86)

One year olds fully immunised { TB: 58%
DPT: 62%
polio: 86%
measles: 63% } (1985–86)

ORS per 100 episodes of diarrhoea: 28 (1985)
Primary school enrolment ratio male/female: 108/99 (gross) (1983–86)
Grade One enrolment completing primary school: 20% (1980–86)
Secondary school enrolment ratio male/female: n.a.

(all figures 1986 unless otherwise stated)

and level of capitalist development make it a very rich state indeed. It has enormous geographic and climatic variation, and a range of resources that beggars description. Brazil's population is about the seventh highest in the world: over 138.5 million people live in some 3,286,488 square miles, giving a population density of about 42 persons per sq m, compared to over 580 in the United Kingdom. About 74 per cent of the population, or close to 102.5 million persons, live in large urban areas. Between 1970 and 1980, the rural population grew by less than 10 per cent, the urban by about 50 per cent.

Unlike other Latin American nations, white colonial domination did not lay the groundwork for a specifically racist social inequality. Outside the Amazonian regions, well over half the population is white, which means that, although the ruling elite is almost exclusively European, so too is the bulk of the impoverished population. Mestizos, blacks and Asians are equally likely to be part of the lower range of the middle classes. The most powerful people in Brazil are still the old landowning elites, who have retained rural power bases whilst involving themselves in the booming manufacturing sector. Less than 0.1 per cent of the big landowners own more than 15 per cent of the land, while over 50 per cent of smallholders own under less than 3 per cent of the total between them.

One Portuguese word has become familiar through exhaustive media exposure: *favela*, the word meaning shanty-town, squatter settlement or slum. It is an urban phenomenon, which is not to say that similar settlements do not occur in rural areas. New *favelas* grow up wherever migration brings people. *Favelas* are haphazard collections of dwellings built of mud, wood, cardboard, palmstraw matting, or whatever material happens to be most easily available. There is no water supply in the houses, no sewage outlet, no waste and garbage collection. Electricity supplies, where they exist, are fragile and extremely dangerous, invariably tapped from an illegal connection.

The dwellings average two rooms, used as bedrooms, kitchen and dining room as occasion demands. Often there is only one bed, sometimes none. Children and adults sleep together without the separation and individual living space so often recommended by child psychologists. Infant mortality rates have been closely related to levels of development in specific areas. Low incomes and cramped, unhygienic conditions with too little money for food have meant that the *favelas* of this wealthy country have some of the highest infant mortality figures in the world.

Yet people still flock to the cities because rural poverty is often far worse. In the most depressed areas of the north-east, droughts, famines and gross mismanagement of the economy have driven to the cities those who could afford to leave. Those left behind scratch a meagre living from the exhausted soil. Children as young as three years old accompany parents to the fields; by five they are cutting sugar cane. Education makes brave attempts to get children to attend school, but all members of families need to work in order to ensure that at least some survive. Those who do not are, as always, infants and children whose short lives literally wither away. In the Amazonian jungle regions, disease and what can only be described as persecution drive infant mortality rates even higher.

Brazil is thus a wealthy but grossly unequal state. The children of the urban *favelas*, of poor agricultural workers, of the jungle and of the streets live in dire poverty and suffer the double disadvantage of being children: powerless, vulnerable and unable to gain access to health care or 'free' education. According to the World Health Organization, the health-care system is substandard, and about 40 per cent of Brazilians lack adequate medical coverage (Nyrop 1983). An extensive programme of immunization of children has reduced the incidence of diphtheria, tetanus and whooping cough and virtually eliminated polio. But high death rates continue to be caused by parasitic and infectious diseases. Poor sanitation, lack of clean water supplies and nutritional deficiencies have stood in the way of long-term improvements in health conditions and prevention of disease. Parasitic diseases account for more than 15 per cent of deaths in Brazil, with rates about twice as high in the poorest areas of the north-east and north. It is not disease alone that kills, because the principal factor in mortality for infants and small children is malnutrition, which weakens resistance to illness and hinders recovery (Nyrop 1983).

Despite national wealth, which gives a nominally high income for each citizen, the Brazilian figure for medical practitioners is well below the Latin American average in terms of population served. In the late 1970s there were about 80,000 doctors — one for every 1,500 persons. Half of all doctors were practising in São Paulo and Rio de Janeiro, and overall the largest cities and state capitals have four times as many doctors as other parts of Brazil. In rural areas, paramedics often carry out the little work that is done. Medical services such as hospitals and clinics also tend to have paramedical staff; physicians are mostly private practitioners and inaccessible to the poor.

Welfare programmes merely scratch the surface of poverty. Federal food programmes offer supplements to the most vulnerable: pregnant and lactating women and small children in low-income groups. They attempt to promote better distribution of foodstuffs and lower costs in depressed areas. But all programmes of social welfare are urban-based and rely on people being in regular waged employment. Unemployment insurance, for instance, works as follows: employers are required to deposit a portion of each employee's earnings in controlled accounts. These can be withdrawn on retirement, drawn on for the purchase of a house or as benefit if the employee loses his or her job. Thus most people in urban areas, who work in casual labour, and most of the peasants in the countryside, are unprotected. There are maternity benefits supervised by the National Social Security Institute, but the problem, again, is that only formally employed women benefit. Payments rarely extend to cover all the requirements of large families.

Elementary education is free and compulsory between the ages of 7 and 14, but it is estimated that only 75 per cent of children between those ages were attending free schools in 1978. Free secondary education for four years was attended by about 13 per cent of 15–17-year-olds the same year. There are large numbers of private institutions at all levels of education. UNESCO records

208,663 schools, staffed by 934,282 teachers and attended by 24,304,875 pupils, in 1983. Yet, at about the same time as UNESCO gathered those figures, there were over 30 million children under nine, and nearly 27 million aged between 10 and 19. If we guesstimate half of the lower group, about 13 million, and just over half of the older ones, about 14 million, we come up with 27 million children of primary school age. Those aged between 14 and 17 who could go to schools are obviously not going. Balancing the guesstimates, we must assume that many children of all ages simply do not go to school.

These back-of-an-envelope statistics are proved correct by research which shows that 70.2 per cent of household heads started their first jobs when aged 14 or less, in other words before they would be expected to have completed their education (Pastore 1982 p. 71). A further 17.7 per cent of 15–17-year-olds, who could have been at secondary school, also started work. This means that 87.9 per cent of heads of family enter the labour force before the age at which they would have completed secondary school. These figures relate to urban areas and, in most cases, to men; the situation for girls and for anyone living in rural areas is probably much worse.

Full-time employment is illegal for anyone below the age of 14, although licences can be obtained for restricted work for children aged between 10 and 14. Little attention is paid to this detail. It is especially difficult for children whose parents were too poor to register their births: no birth certificate, no licence. A work licence signed by the employer provides some guarantees in the working relationship, but no guarantee against work in unhealthy and dangerous conditions, against being required to work more than the eight-hour limit daily, or against night work. Moreover, licences mean nothing to the vast majority of children who work informally.

Children see getting a job as part of their obligation to their families and their parents. It is expected that boys in working-class areas will start to earn around their thirteenth birthday, while girls of this age are usually occupied looking after younger children or in other domestic tasks. This is because adult women will be able to earn higher wages than the girls. One researcher in São Paulo found this reflected in internal household budgets: 'Three girls who defined themselves as workers and were thus included in the sample were paid by working mothers to take care of younger siblings and do housework on weekdays' (Gouveia 1983 p. 10). It has been reported that children feel that the status they acquire by working gives them a greater sense of freedom from family supervision, and entitled to adult privileges. They feel that they can answer back to their parents and need not submit to harsh discipline. Work has a positive advantage for parents too, quite apart from the extra income:

> It is generally believed that to be busy working is safer than to wander the streets. Most families have access to TV which publicizes the street violence and dangers. According to some youngsters, their parents' encouragement to start work was justified in terms of their concern about moral integrity. Drug addiction and gang delinquency are frequently mentioned problems (Gouveia 1983 p. 10).

This concern with morality shows again the lesson learned from Klong Toey slum in Bangkok: not all poor children are either potential criminals or street children. Nevertheless, the persistent image of the Brazilian child is that of Pixote.

Grubby-faced little urchins pose grinning for cameramen from the world's glossy magazines; children are shown sleeping in rows on the streets of São Paulo or Recife; children who, we are told, are thieves and murderers. Nevertheless, even this is a false image. The majority of street children are boys and girls aged 17 or less who spend a lot of their time on the streets working. Their work is any one of an enormous range of informal economic activities. They are on the streets either to maintain themselves or help maintain their families. They work long hours at their chosen occupation and then the majority of them go home. Home and the family still provide the basic framework of their lives. Some, however, do not go home at night because they have lost contact with their families, or are not welcome, or are orphaned. These are the true street children.

Marginalization has made street children into 'criminals'. Some of them do steal but many more are beggars. Beggars are seen as vagrants unless some kind of disability presents an obvious reason for unemployment. Children accompanying parents are party to the act, therefore they are as vulnerable as those begging alone. Frequent 'visits' to police stations, homes, detention centres and prisons certainly induce some children to be criminals. Gangs operate in a highly professional manner, ruling territories and preparing members for a life of crime. It is an alternative that suits the need to survive. Glue-sniffing is especially common as a way of escape and it also provides a profitable trading opportunity for older street children. It is not crime that has created the environment, but the environment that has created criminality. The *trombadinha*, the small boy who bumps into people to distract them whilst he picks their pockets, is simply surviving as best he can. In a gang, chances are better. It is a hard, lonely life in a big world when you are eight and on your own.

Juvenile delinquency is often rationalized by sociologists in terms of the poor quality of life and living conditions of lower-class children and youths. The reality is that a much larger number of children from the same conditions are not delinquents. Most of them are trying to have a childhood, many of them are struggling to survive a mockery of childhood, usually in ways less drastic than resorting to prostitution or crime. But political propaganda and the media try to convince the public that up to 80 per cent of all offences in Brazil are committed by juveniles. It is a scapegoating of the next generation which results in public demands for closed institutions for punishing child offenders. Children are criminalized by reputation, imprisoned as if they were criminals and, like adult prisoners everywhere, robbed of their human rights. Thus the full force of mainstream society is ranged against a group of children who are particularly powerless.

The champions of street urchins are few. Dr Walter E. Garcia of the Catholic University of São Paulo uses harsh words to criticize the closed institutions proposed for children who, in the usual euphemism of Latin America, are 'in irregular situations'.

> These institutions practise a repressive pedagogy, by means of isolating children from their environment, not taking into account the social context that produces their marginality, educating them with conservative principles and giving a kind of professional training that is not desired by the children themselves (quoted in Taçon 1981 p. 136)

The government agency *Fundação Nacional do Benestar do Menor* (the National Foundation for Child Welfare or FUNABEM) has a different remit. According to Law No. 4.513/64, Article 7–VI, FUNABEM '. . . shall mobilise . . . the indispensable participation of the entire community in seeking a solution to the problems of children'. Unfortunately, the reality described by Dr Garcia shows that, if they receive any treatment at all, children are shut away from the community. It is a situation underlined by Peter Taçon when he was UNICEF's Special Adviser on Street Children in Latin America: 'Such problems could not exist in a country which really took its collective parenthood seriously' (Taçon 1981 p. 89). Taçon himself believes that street children could disappear by the year 2000, but only with community co-operation so that society works alongside rather than against street children. This is not just the dreaming of a Canadian outsider. In 1981, the State Secretary of Labour of Rio Grande do Sul

> was emphatic in saying that the problems of child abandonment and family deprivation and disintegration could be resolved at the community level — but only with the community's full participation and with the proper delivery of services such as water, sewage, electricity, land entitlement, health, education, nutrition and employment (Taçon 1981 p. 116).

Just as we felt that we knew the reformatory shown in *Pixote*, Peter Taçon having described a closed government re-education centre he visited in 1981, he wrote, 'I knew that I had seen this place too many times before in Latin America'.

> They will stay until they are 18 in this dark and dreadful shell, living their daily lives in crowded dormitories, mass bathrooms, and ill-equipped dilapidated craft-shops, eating the bland common fare dipped out of the one common dinner cauldron brought in from outside. Their only sense of anything even remotely resembling freedom will be the bare half-acre central courtyard (Taçon 1981 pp. 59–60).

Of course, preventing children coming on to the streets in the first place would be the best answer. But, for those already there, the solution probably lies in projects like *Republica del Pequeno Vendedor* (The Little Street Vendors' Republic), set up by Padre Bruno Sechi in Belém. This is a small city in Brazilian terms, with a population of about 1,000,000. The Republic launches an attack on the problem on two fronts: on the one hand it tries to improve the lives of Belém's street children, on the other it is trying to change the community's view of these children and to improve their chances of reintegration in a highly competitive world.

The Republic's practical work provides six months' intensive training for youths in mechanical workshops. Once this is finished, they are given assistance to set up their own co-operatives. An annual display of the young people's capacities is used as a one-day campaign of collecting used furniture, household goods, clothes, bicycles or whatever happens to be available. This is seen as the best way of getting the general public to participate and aid the children's work. The children repair the goods in the project's workshops and then sell them at markets or in the project's second-hand shop. The scale of the one-day drive is immense; in 1987, over 80 trucks were commandeered for the campaign. The children chose their own slogan: '*Queremos a forca da comunidade*' — 'We want the strength of the community'.

Such projects are few, but they contribute to the possible emergence of a broader awareness of the problems of childhood in Brazil. In May 1986, the first ever National Meeting of Street Children was held in the capital, Brasília. Four hundred and fifty children from throughout the country assembled there to tell the National Congress about their problems. They told senators about their health, education and work problems, adding dimensions in a range of areas as diverse as family relationships and police violence. Suggestions were made about measures to restrain violence against them — for example, that police should talk to children before beating them! Their demands were not entirely selfish, as the suggestion for changes in education show: they asked for higher salaries for teachers and a maximum of 25 pupils per class. They also wanted the government to support the alternative schools being developed in poor areas. Work was handled with an equally mature approach, they suggested that their work should become legally recognized and that it be protected by labour laws guaranteed by the federal Constitution. The Meeting received much publicity, and both national and international support. It showed how reasonable these criminals of the street really are. But it brought no change in their situation. The sad fact is that the rhetoric of pity for street children is no more help to them than the forces of repression which criminalize them and blame them for all manner of social ills. Only a major redistribution of wealth in Brazil will help children already on the street and stop thousands more from joining them. But that would be a miracle in human terms not just confined to economics.

Lebanon

It was a bright spring day outside, but, in the meeting of non-governmental organizations which met before the UNICEF Executive Board annual meeting in 1985, the only light was artificial. We were in a plush suite, equipped with all the technology of simultaneous translation, somewhere in the heart of EUR, the massive suburb of Rome that is almost the sole reminder of Mussolini's imperial ambitions. The topic was Children and War and the speaker was from Rädda Barnen, the Swedish Save the Children Fund. He had recently returned from Beirut and, of all the stories he told, none struck home like the words of a Lebanese child who had asked her mother: 'What is The War, mummy?'.

To a child who has never known a reality without fighting and bombs, without fear and days when it is impossible to go to school or accompany her mother shopping, who has heard adults speak of 'The War' as a threatening, but undefined, entity, this is a logical question. Adults and teenagers in Lebanon can remember a time without The War, and therefore imagine a future without bloodshed and danger. But the children of Beirut have known no other environment but this, they cannot understand the reasons for The War and have no way of thinking about Peace. No child alive in Lebanon has ever experienced peace. Since the Arab–Israeli War in 1967, the whole area has been volatile and, during the past 13 years, Lebanon has been a patchwork of varied and often overlapping violence.

Of all the case studies in this book, Lebanon is the most difficult to comprehend. We share that child's puzzlement. It is a country created by foreign powers, with no natural boundaries, no single ethnic identity and no easiiy definable geographical reason for existence. It is basically a twin mountain range, stretching from Homs in the north to Mount Hermon in the south, which was formerly a part of Syria. The first steps towards its independent existence occurred when the district of Lebanon was separated from the Turkish *pashalik* of Syria in 1861 and put under a Christian governor soon after major bloodshed had taken place between Maronites and Druzes. The modern state was established after the First World War, when five Turkish districts or *sanjaks* were detached from the defeated Ottoman Empire in 1920 and, along with Syria, awarded to France under a League of Nations mandate. At that time the Maronite Christians outnumbered the Muslims, but today the balance has changed, laying part of the basis of the present conflict.

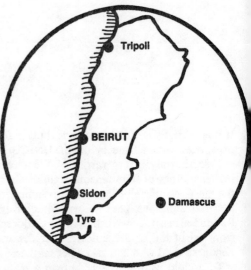

Capital: Beirut
Area: 4,000 sq. miles
Population: 2,700,000
Urban population: 81% (1985)
Population annual growth rate:
  1.6% (1980–85)
GNP per capita US$: n.a.
Rate of inflation: n.a.
Population below absolute
  poverty level { urban: n.a.
                { rural: n.a.
Population with access
  to drinking water: 92%
  (1980)
Life expectancy: 67

Lebanon
(U5MR = 53   IMR = 41)

Births: 80,000
Infants with low birthweight: 10% (1982–85)
Population 0–4: 400,000
Population 5–16: 700,000
Total population under 16: 1,100,000
Deaths 0–4: 4,000
Children 0–5 suffering from malnutrition:
  mid-moderate: n.a.
  severe: n.a.

**One year olds
fully immunised** { TB: 4%
                  { DPT: 30%   } (1985–86)
                  { polio: 30%
                  { measles: 30%

ORS per 100 episodes of diarrhoea: 2 (1985)
Primary school enrolment ratio male/female: 105/95
  (gross) (1983–86)
**Grade One enrolment completing primary
  school:** 66% (1980–86)
Secondary school enrolment ratio male/female:
  57/56 (1983–86)

(all figures 1986 unless otherwise stated)

Under French rule, a Constitution was drawn up by a joint commission of Lebanese and French 'authorities, although this has been subject to many alterations. Because of the long history of division among the population, the electoral system has been structured to provide proportional representation by religion as well as by region. The President is traditionally a Maronite Christian, the Prime Minister a Sunni Muslim and the President of the Chamber of Deputies a Shi'a Muslim. But the population is made up of a myriad of religious communities. Christians include Maronites, Roman Catholics, Greek Catholics, Syrian Catholics, Armenian Catholics, Chaldeans, Greek Orthodox, Armenian Orthodox, Nestorians, Syrian Jacobites and various denominations of the Protestant churches. Followers of Islam include the 'heretic' Druze as well as the Sunnis and Shi'as, and there are also a small number of indigenous Jews. Within and between these communities there are bitter conflicts and fierce loyalties. Lebanon is characterized by an overall primacy given to the family by all religious groups and by unbreakable ties between families forged through patronage and godparenthood.

It is difficult to remember Lebanon before the present conflict, now that we are accustomed to images of concrete ruins and tanks and gunfire, the appalling devastation modern weapons cause in a built environment. Yet Lebanon is a breathtakingly beautiful country and Beirut used to be a city of luxury and both ancient and modern architectural splendour. The rich are still able to enjoy some of their former lifestyle and to take pleasure in the Mediterranean beaches, despite the frequent bloodshed and the destruction of familiar landmarks and former meeting places.

The War, which the little girl asked her mother about, became inevitable because of major changes in the Near Eastern region following the Second World War. Lebanon was completely separated from Syria and given full independence and sovereignty in 1946. At about the same time, Jordan and Syria gained sovereignty, the state of Israel was created and the Palestinians left stateless. From that time, Palestinian children have always been denied the benefits of Principle 3 of the Declaration of the Rights of the Child; they have no nationality in any meaningful modern sense of the term. Many live in exile; there are an estimated 400,000 of them living as refugees in Lebanon. 'I was about eight years old when I realised that I had no country. I became aware of being a Palestinian when I was six. I began to wonder why I didn't have a home, other people had their own country and we didn't', says Leila Ahmed, a Lebanese-born Palestinian Sunni Muslim woman, in a Thames Television documentary film, *Barricades*, made in 1985. Then aged 31, her education cut short, a widow 'perhaps' because of The War, one child severely disabled because of The War, she lives in a single room with her small daughter and is somehow able to say 'despite all that has happened, I still have hopes'.

The present, seemingly insoluble, war began to all intents and purposes in 1975 and has been further aggravated by conflicts between various Lebanese Islamic groups, between Palestinians and Lebanese, Syrians and Israelis and also by invasions and occupations of Lebanon by Israel and Syria. Although women like Leila may still have hopes, it is in the face of a perpetual struggle to achieve some kind of childhood for their children, to find security, shelter, food, health care and education. Nothing abuses children more than War. It is not just that conflicts fought out between adults with lethal weapons injure and kill children. These are the external, physical abuses. Underneath, wars inflict serious psychological, social and moral damage which is likely to be incurable.

In terms of direct physical injuries alone, the conflict in the Lebanon has had effects equal to any epidemic or famine. It has been estimated that there were over 120,000 deaths due to civil strife between 1975 and 1985. This conflict is particularly modern, which means that an unusually high number of casualties, about 90 per cent, are civilian victims of war, rather than the 'tame' homicidal maniacs whom we dignify by the term 'soldier' — or in Lebanon, 'militia'. The number of child victims in that period is difficult to calculate, but it is likely that, in any one incident, the proportion of child deaths will range from 15 to 35 per cent. This means that, from 1975 to 1985, between 18,000 and 42,000 childhoods were cut short as a direct result of The War (Shamma' 1987 p. 86). Alongside these direct victims are those who died as a result of diseases that could have been prevented by immunization or by access to clean water and adequate food: gastro-enteritis, measles, diphtheria, diseases related to malnutrition, and respiratory diseases. The irony is that these figures are counted and classified in public health statistics, and not related to The War. War is not recognized by either national or international classifications as a public health problem (Shamma' 1987). Child war casualty figures are thus impossible either to collect or to compute, while information about the deaths and deeds of brave soldiers is usually easy to come by. In *Barricades*, Leila describes how, pregnant with her third child, she ran desperately from clinic to clinic under shell- and gunfire, carrying her son who had a high fever caused by drinking contaminated water, which could not be boiled because gas and electricity to the camp had been cut off. There was no medicine available, not even aspirin. Her son was left severely paralysed, her baby was born dead. But her bravery under gunfire and the wounds to her and her family are part of the hidden story and hidden statistics of The War.

The physical wounds that modern weaponry inflicts on children in Beirut are horrific, as Pauline Cutting's description of Bilal shows. Limbs are blasted off by mines and car bombs; hideous damage is caused by high velocity bullets hitting tiny, vulnerable bodies; small individuals are crushed and suffocated by falling masonry. And children are heroic too. Not just in the way they bear the pain and fear of their suffering, but also in the deeds they perform.

Cutting describes many such incidents, such as the time four girls, aged between 7 and 13, who volunteered to brave the bullets of Amal gunmen to cross the open ground around the besieged Bourj al Barajneh camp to fetch medicines; on their second trip,

> as they crossed the distant sand-hills . . . they were seen and a fusillade of bullets raised puffs of sand around them. They dived to the ground, then pelted down into the cemetery, into the arms of the waiting men. They were frightened but miraculously unharmed (Cutting 1988 p. 193).

This particular incident was also recorded by the camera of television journalist Brent Sadler, whose visit to Bourj al Barajneh was later followed by that of two *Sunday Times* journalists. It is an irony of enormous consequence that, while these little girls had to risk their lives for 'four carrier bags full of medicines, bandages and gauze' (Cutting 1988 p. 193), large sums of money could guarantee the relatively safe entry of the media into besieged camps. As Cutting states, 'It seemed that if one had the resources it was becoming quite easy to bribe one's way into the camp' (p. 195). This makes nonsense of the UNICEF idea that children should be a 'Zone of Peace' in war-torn regions. Although days of tranquillity and cease-fires can be negotiated so that children can receive immunization, and even though journalists do put themselves at some risk, it seems that hard cash and the Western public's voracious desire for spectacular news can create peace zones all their own.

Amidst the urgency of dealing with physically injured children, there is little time and few resources with which to tackle the psychological damage they suffer. The reported effects seem similar to those shown by many abused and unhappy children in our own environment: disturbed sleep, nightmares, regressive behaviour and increased fearfulness. Such children find it difficult to form relationships. They are insecure, have poor self-images, are depressive, have feelings of guilt. Some are highly dependent while others are isolated, and still others have developed rigid super-egos (Yacoub 1978; Nassar 1985). Many are fascinated, even obsessed, by violence and killing (Abu Nasr et al 1978). Amal Shamma', who is a paediatrician in Beirut's Barbir Hospital, reports that 82 per cent of children injured as a result of the war suffer moderate to severe injuries, with major handicaps occurring in 13.5 per cent of cases. Nevertheless:

> A common scene on a paediatric ward where casualties are treated is to see the injured play with their favourite toys: toy machine guns and toy soldiers. These same children may fantasize that their injuries were inflicted as they 'butchered their enemies'. Children wander in to hospital grounds and help pick up pieces of bodies and carry the dead to the morgue. In their homes, children talk of gory scenes, massive injury, and death of neighbours, with remarkable detachment. The streets are usually the arena for the war-games of children emulating their heroes, the militia-men of the neighbourhood (Shamma' 1987 p. 88).

Detachment from the effects of violence is matched by distancing from moral judgements about killing. If The War is all their reality, how can it be wrong? Thus games emulate acts of war which have been seen through their own eyes, rather than in films and comic books, and they have no fear of the weapons and materials of war. A Christian Lebanese acquaintance, hearing about this book, told us about an incident during her last trip home about five years ago. She had been eating in an expensive, still popular restaurant in the Christian part of Beirut. Suddenly there was a dull bang and the windows of the restaurant burst inwards. A bomb had gone off immediately outside. A number of small boys, about 10–12 years old, were pursued and detained for causing the explosion. They were from one of the more violent areas of the city, had found a bomb which had been planted against Israeli invaders and had decided to have some fun with it.

It was meant to be just a game. But such games turn rapidly into reality. Many children do not play for long pretending to be their militia-men heroes. 'On the front line, Palestinian boys as young as nine are already veterans of the war. Armed with automatic rifles and grenades they are paid at least £35 a month as full time fighters' (Sadler, *Guardian*, 3 April 1987).

Circumstances may make it logical to become a fighter, for children who have no other way to turn. War means not only loss of life, limbs and 'childhood' but also, in many cases, loss of family.

> Raslan, like any other boy, went out for his mother one afternoon to buy a loaf of bread.
> As he walked into the bakery a raid started. He huddled underneath the counter till the bombers had passed then ran home to find his home destroyed and every member of his family dead (*Sunday Mirror*, 29 November 1985).

But, in some ways, Raslan had an advantage, he had a family to lose and was old enough to remember what he had lost. For others, even this is denied.

> Hamze . . . is only four . . . He doesn't answer questions about school and play, not seeming to consider them important, but will talk, if that is the word for it, about his family.
> 'Where is your daddy?'
> 'Kidnapped.'
> 'And where is your mummy?'
> 'Kidnapped.'
> . . . Hamze was burnt — down both arms and on the side of his head — when men who kidnapped his mother poured petrol over the little boy clinging to her and set it alight (*Sunday Mirror*, 29 November 1985).

In besieged camps, and in the more violent areas of the country, normality seems to have been suspended and children are simply exposed to, and abused by, the worst excesses of adult behaviour, and then neglected when they suffer from its effects. A Dutch nurse recounts seeing five children killing and eating a rat in a besieged camp where two babies had just died after being born prematurely to undernourished mothers. But even such unsavoury food was in short supply during the siege of the camps — at its height in 1987. The journalists who followed Brent Sadler in to see Pauline Cutting reported:

> Mohammed Hamoudi, 15, who escaped from Bourj al Barajneh on Friday said, 'I left because I want my six-year-old sister to eat what's left of my share of the cooked dog. I can manage to get food outside.'
> Another child who escaped the camp is Fadi Saker, 12, he crawled through the Amal lines on Thursday night. After living with his seven brothers and sisters, on the remains of a slaughtered donkey, he was found in Beirut, chewing on a handful of grass. 'We ate lots of cats, dogs, rats, donkeys and mules. Now there's a shortage.' (*Sunday Times*, 15 February 1987).

Even health facilities are not immune. A psychiatric hospital which had been a model of its kind, with 300 staff serving 800 patients and high standards of treatment during the days when Beirut was the sophisticated jewel of the Near East, was hit by bombs on no less than five occasions. By 1982 only 15 staff remained to care for the remaining 300 child and adult patients. As a result, 20 children were discovered uncared for on the second floor. They had lain without food in their own urine and excrement for days (*Woman's Own*, 23 October 1982). All these anecdotes are drawn from newspaper reports, which are always open to accusations of exaggeration and sensationalism, and yet the few professional accounts we have available of children's lives in today's Lebanon, many from doctors like Amal Shamma' and Pauline Cutting, simply echo the stories of brutalization.

Lebanon is neither the first nor the only example of child abuse and neglect through organized adult violence. The first studies of the effects of armed conflict on children took place in combat areas during the Second World War and within concentration camps. It was found that children who face armed violence on a daily basis lose, or never develop, a trust in other people and also develop profound sensations of helplessness (Freud and Burlingham 1943, a & b). In Lebanon, these results have been replicated. A study of children aged three to nine years demonstrated that mothers report increased anxiety and fear and the obsession with war toys reported by Amal Shamma' (Abu-Nasr 1985). Of course, the mothers themselves are under acute stress, because of the bombing raids, kidnappings and general military harassment, and this is bound to affect the children's feelings of security (Punamäki 1982). It is thus not surprising when teachers report that children place an overwhelming emphasis on The War in conversation, in drawing and in play: it occupies 90 per cent of their observed behaviour. Moreover, children are rebellious, possessive and defiant (Abu-Nasr 1985, quoted in UNICEF 1986).

The physical, psychological and moral effects of The War on children are not the only burdens they have to bear. Far less obvious are the social and economic consequences. This is the only one of our case studies that has not concentrated to a very large extent on education and maternal and child health. Although these facilities are not absent in Lebanon what is remarkable about the situation there is the extent to which The War has disrupted and deformed services for children. It is not possible to make an analogy with Mozambique here, because the standard of facilities before the conflict in these countries was so different. Lebanon was, to a very large extent, on a par with many European countries in these respects before 1975. The devastation caused by prolonged civil war, and its effects on children who, Palestinians apart, might otherwise have expected a reasonable standard of living, is correspondingly greater and gives a chilling reminder to any Western country of the fragility, in the face of warfare, of the services we owe to the most vulnerable among us.

The social and economic consequences of war for children in Lebanon, and especially Beirut, is subtly involved in other effects. War affects any economy, disturbing progress and development and often causing milestones of progress to be lost. Poverty, unemployment and inflation are the ugly bedfellows of the

God of War. Because of The War, thousands of families have lost their homes and there is a housing crisis; whole agricultural regions have been devastated and industrial areas destroyed. Thus the means of economic survival are wiped out, along with the landmarks of the environment with which people would normally identify. The schools and hospitals which remain undamaged find it hard to function because of the surrounding conflict and because they lack finance for salaries and equipment. Public services are almost non-existent because of lack of funds and the danger to staff. Under these circumstances, no government could make and implement medical, educational, housing or economic policies. Meanwhile, foreign aid agencies can operate only minimal programmes because of the danger to personnel.

When resources built by human effort are destroyed, it is always possible that they can be reconstructed. Far more serious is the destruction of nature's irreplaceable resources. Meanwhile, human resources themselves are depleted not only by death and maiming, but also because people who are not directly involved in the conflict lose the motivation to think and act creatively and give in to despair and despondency. Meanwhile those who fight, and those who lose people they love in the slaughter, are often consumed by anger and bitterness, which become the inheritance of subsequent generations.

The step from victim to participant is as rapid as rifle fire. Children do not take long to change from fantasy games to joining the militia, and it has been shown that their ideas of morality, their judgements about life and death and killing change, regardless of whether the militia they join is Christian, Muslim, Druze or Palestinian. In this respect, all children are the same and the rate of change is the same (Abu-Nasr et al 1978). Amal Shamma' has found that very few of the children she has spoken to are participating in the war for ideological reasons, they just want to fire a gun.

> You do have children who are very interested in death and dying, and that is the most horrifying aspect of all of this. I feel that sometimes I am more horrified by the killing than the children are and that they can tolerate much more than I can (Quoted in Bankouski and Carballo 1987 p. 102).

If children are socialized into thinking of violence as an acceptable way of solving problems, they are not likely to change suddenly when The War ends or when they become adults. The implication of this is not just that they will have shorter fuses as adults and be more prone to hit out in response to frustrations and anger in their own lives, it also means that they may be likely to support institutionalized violence and heavy governmental military spending. 'The cycle of militarism leading to poverty, despair and further militarism would have been firmly established' (Shamma' 1987 p. 89).

It is this psycho-social effect that UNICEF ignores when it talks of making children a Zone of Peace (UNICEF 1986; 1987). Immunization simply produces more young healthy soldiers. Children are not simply bodies to be filled with medicines and vaccines, they are seeing, hearing, thinking people, and there are no vaccines yet known to medical science that produce antibodies to anger and violence. Let us leave the final word to Lars Gustafsson, the

Rädda Barnen official with whom we began, because he points out that pain, illness and poverty are not the main damage that war inflicts on children. They are victims of a crueller harm, wrecked by their own perception: 'To realise as a small child that the parents have no chance of protecting the family if a group of armed men appear means that the child's faith in the good will of adults breaks down at an early age' (Gustafsson 1987 p. 20).

Because of the extraordinary degree of civilian involvement in hostilities, the situation in Lebanon is far worse than that experienced by the majority of children in the Second World War. Beirut is now showing very high numbers of street children, child prostitutes, militia-boys and child drug abusers (Gustafsson 1987 p. 22; Shamma' 1987). Children are at the centre of a triangle of chaos. The War is chaos in itself: incomprehensible to a child, not least because in Lebanon few adults have any comprehension of the situation either. Families are in chaos as they disintegrate in the face of dislocation, unemployment and bereavement. Society is in chaos, with schools, hospitals and shops barely functioning. Under these circumstances, says Gustafsson, children who show such symptoms as fear or aggression are relatively healthy, for they are at least communicating some of their own internal chaos. It is children who have no symptoms who are the most damaged, for they have been overwhelmed by chaos, they cannot communicate: 'The soul of the child is silent' (Gustafsson 1987 p. 23).

Capital: Bangkok
Area: 198,455 sq. miles
Population: 52,300,000
Urban population: 20% (1985)
Population annual growth rate: 2.1% (1980–85)
GNP per capita US$: 800 (1985)
Rate of inflation: 3.2% (1980–85)
Population below absolute poverty level { urban: 15% (1977–85) { rural: 34%
Population with access to drinking water: 66%
Life expectancy: 64

Thailand
(U5MR = 53   IMR = 41)

Births: 1,290,000
Infants with low birthweight: 12% (1982–85)
Population 0–4: 6,300,000
Population 5–16: 13,500,000
Total population under 16: 19,800,000
Deaths 0–4: 68,000
Children 0–5 suffering from malnutrition:
    mid-moderate: 27%
    severe: n.a. } (1980–86)
One year olds fully immunised { TB: 83% DPT: 62% polio: 62% measles: 39% } (1985–86)
ORS per 100 episodes of diarrhoea: 34 (1985)
Primary school enrolment ratio male/female: 93/93 (gross) (1983–86)
Grade One enrolment completing primary school: 64% (1980–86)
Secondary school enrolment ratio male/female: 35/35 (1983–86)

(all figures 1986 unless otherwise stated)

Thailand

> Once upon a time there was a fairyland Orient that caught the imagination of the Western World and spread an exotic spell. It was a strange and fascinating land of ancient cultures and ascetic traditions, of poverty and exciting riches, glorious temples and smiling, contented people. The spell, it seemed, was broken when airport runways, modern hotels and highways mixed with temples, klongs, floating markets and forgotten beaches. Far from it, Thailand still represents all the mystery and exoticism of the East. (Kuoni *WORLDWIDE* brochure 1988 p. 28)

The King and I was one of the hit musicals of our childhood. The film made Yul Brynner famous and added further lustre to the career of Deborah Kerr. While songs like 'Shall we dance?' and 'I whistle a happy tune' have remained part of the general light music repertoire, another hit of the day has been largely forgotten. This is the purely instrumental 'March of the Siamese children'. Despite its present relative obscurity, it sums up a whole generation's attitudes to Thailand for, while most of the melodies associated with the film are absolutely Western and could fit any other musical comedy of the period, the March, which in reality owes more to Sousa than to Thailand, used cymbals and other percussion instruments to produce an Eastern effect. It was also used in the film to mark the moment at which East met West.

But perhaps you are too young to have seen the film. The story is drawn from the actual memoires of Anna Leonowens, an Englishwoman who was governess to the children of the autocratic King Mongkut of Siam in the 1860s. The musical romanticizes the relationship between East and West in terms of an unfulfilled and impossible love affair between the King and the widowed Anna. It uses the 'March of the Siamese children' to herald the appearance of Anna's new pupils before their father the King and the new governess, a moment which Anna herself described thus:

> At a signal from the king, the priests chanted a hymn from the 'P'ra-jana Para-mita' [Accomplishment of Reason or Transcendental Wisdom]; and then a burst of music announced the entrance of the princes and princesses, my future pupils. They advanced in the order of their ages (Leonowens 1954 p. 67).

The musical is adapted from the novel version of Anna's memoires, *The King and I* by Margaret Landon, and makes much of the King's 'puzzlement' at the contradictions between East and West. It is based in the never-never fairyland Orient of tourist brochures, and even the children used in the film were Eurasians, with 'Westernized' oriental features. The fairy tale means that Thailand now takes the place recently vacated by India, Nepal and Peru as the source of mystic experience for young people. Students and package holidaymakers alike seem to be reaching out for contact with an untouched, exotic society, to contrast with the humdrum stress of modernity.

Thailand is not entirely untouched by industrial capitalism and its institutions. Anna's arrival was part of the modernization of Thai political, social and economic institutions along Western lines, which began in the mid-nineteenth century under Mongkut (Rama IV, 1851–68) and his son Chulalongkorn (Rama V, 1868–1910). Thai monarchy remained absolute, until a bloodless coup in 1932 heralded Western-type constitutional monarchy. But Thailand has always been independent of direct European colonial domination, a fact that brings great pride to its people and adds to their acute historical consciousness. Unlike African nations and those of Latin America, there is no need to search the history books for an authentic culture with which to combat cultural imperialism. In Thailand the confrontation between East and West is still direct and to a large extent unmediated.

Over the past three decades, Thai emergence from an almost exclusively rural, agricultural and traditional past, in a process of state-sponsored capitalism, has been rapid but based on a weak structural basis and with traumatic effects on both rural and urban life. Despite this rapidity, the roots of modern Thai experience can be found in the past and there is an inherent conflict of images between the reverence for tradition and the compulsion to modernize.

The king, the royal family and the nobility remain at the pinnacle of a hierarchy of political, military and economic elites. But Thai society rests on the base of the rural peasantry, which is the bulk of the population. This pyramid structure is held together by patron–client relationships that are the dynamic ties of political and economic life. The pervading religion is Buddhism, which includes the existence of spirits that act in ways affecting the lives of human beings.

The country is divided geographically into wet rice-growing river plains and the mountainous regions of the north and north-east. Central Thailand has long been considered the rice bowl of Asia, and the population is concentrated on the fertile plains. On the north-eastern plateau, poor soil and climate have led to pressure on arable land. In the extreme south, a largely Muslim population lives in an area of plantation agriculture, while one crop in the north is the opium poppy. The population is predominantly young and includes non-Thai refugees from Laos and Kampuchea — who live mostly in huge refugee camps near the borders — as well as minority 'hill peoples' like the Karen. It is a very varied fairyland.

The rapid growth of the Bangkok metropolitan area was unplanned, and has put enormous strains on an inadequate infrastructure. By 1978, slum sectors housed an estimated 25 per cent of the Thai population. Water supply, sewerage and pollution were identified as major problems. But there are also large differences between the amenities available in rural and urban areas. Medically trained personnel are found predominantly in Bangkok and other towns. In the capital itself, despite apparent modernity and prosperity, most of the inhabitants lack basic services, and there are sizeable problems of prostitution, drug-trafficking and drug abuse.

All the tourist brochures refer to the floating markets and klongs (canals) of Bangkok, as part of the general romance of the Orient. Bangkok is built on the estuary of the Chao Phya River, which forms a busy waterway criss-crossed by many boats and ferries. Large cargo vessels unload at Klong Toey Port and Royal Thailand continues to use the waterway for impressive river processions. Ironically, shanty towns and slums mostly lack a clean water supply, so the children who live there begin life in very unhygienic conditions, dependent in many cases on water brought in municipal trucks. Even where the municipality has laid water pipes into the slums, many families have to rely on standpipes because they cannot afford pipes to their houses. At least one Bangkok resident in ten lives in one of the nearly 300 shanty towns or slums. The largest, Klong Toey, is situated behind the harbour in the south-east of the city and is home to over 50,000 people, half of whom are under 15. Despite the lack of piped water, the slum is built on marshy ground which becomes waterlogged and flooded, even in the dry seasons, so that catwalks have to be negotiated between houses. As in shanty towns the world over, the houses are built from impermanent materials, usually second-hand and scavenged.

Prateep Ungsongtham was born in Klong Toey 36 years ago and remembers selling sweets in the streets even before she was old enough to start school at seven. She left at 10 years old and worked at various jobs, saving enough money to return to school five years later. After training as a teacher, she returned to teach in Klong Toey where she found that many children did not attend school because of 'poverty, lack of opportunity and indifference', or because they lacked birth certificates and could not enrol. Health is a major problem, made worse by poor nutrition and lack of clean water and sewerage.

> The smell of the swamp is all pervasive; stagnant and full of garbage and all sewage . . . the water rises to the ground floor level of the houses during the monsoon period and then recedes slightly during the dry season (Ungsongtham 1980 pp.28–9).

Tourists who do not see or smell this side of the mystical orient might naively imagine that such environments breed all kinds of vice and crime — for the age-old image of the slum sees it as an undifferentiated and disorganized existence from which a criminal mob threatens respectable urban dwellers. But Prateep Ungsongtham records the relatively tranquil existence of the people who live in these inhuman conditions. Far from being dens of iniquity and promiscuity, she reports that Klong Toey has community pride and a low crime rate.

> A visitor to the Klong Toey slum would probably be repelled by the smell of garbage and swampy water but would perhaps be pleasurably surprised by the neatness of most of the interiors of the houses. The floorboards are usually neat and shiny . . . and their few belongings are well in order with the clothes washed, folded and put away. (Ungsongtham 1980 p. 32)

These families demonstrate a strength we have observed in other settings, which belies the myth of disorganization. What is remarkable is that families stick together more often than not under these impossible and uncertain circumstances, and that most children do survive (although far too many die), and most get some kind of education (although too little and often of irrelevant content). Such an existence may seem intolerable from the perspective of our comfortable lives. When we get hysterical and angry about an electric power failure, we forget that other families exist permanently without such conveniences. If we think of their situation at all, we project our inability to cope on to them.

Few Western tourists are aware of the families in Third World cities that live in and off rubbish dumps. There are four garbage tips serving Bangkok. Indian journalist Sumanta Banerjee describes one at Sukhumvit in the south-east of the city. It used to be high but the authorities decided it was an eyesore for tourists and the middle classes, so it has been lowered and is now kept at a discreet height. About 70 per cent of the daily rubbish-collectors are children, mostly boys aged 6–15. The children usually live with their parents in shanty dwellings on the edge of the dump. Their economic role of recycling waste is important to the metropolitan economy, rather than peripheral. They collect plastic bags, bottles and paper which they sell to middlemen who process them and sell them back to shops and commercial establishments. Banerjee writes:

> Living conditions . . . are worse than those in the Klong Toey area. The atmosphere is always heavy with the stink of rotten vegetables and even of carcasses. There is no regular water supply, and people have to pay one baht for a bucket of water. The children who grow up there without enough or adequate food are small for their age. Stunted growth is a common sight in the area.
>
> Drinking and gambling, which are common among their parents have a disturbing effect on the children who sometimes take to drink from quite an early age and are often found gambling.
>
> . . . Tiep is a six year old girl who has already become an expert garbage picker. With a cap on her head, a hooped pole in her hand and a plastic sack tied to her belt, she can hardly be distinguished from the boys who accompany her every day on the garbage heap (Banerjee 1980 p. 48).

Tiep is a far cry from the tourist image of Thailand: 'Smiles are always on the faces of its beautiful people', states the Wings 'FARAWAYS HOLIDAYS' brochure 1987–88 (p. 60).

Tourism for the non-leisured classes of the West began in a small way with the tours and excursions arranged by Thomas Cook in 1841, which opened up the possibilities of travel for those who had no time to waste on making arrangements and hanging around in foreign ports for boats whose schedules were not known. Cook's prearranged organization enabled people from commerce and industry to travel further afield than had previously been possible for those with limited free time. But mass tourism did not begin until after the Second World War, through a combination of working people with cash to spend and the familiarity of those who had already travelled as members of the armed forces. It has also led to the development of tourist resorts, which exist solely for the diversion and entertainment of visitors in search of sun, fun and exotic excitement.

Thailand has emerged as one of the most popular of recent exotic venues, now rivalling Indian temples, Nepalese mountains and Peruvian Incaic remains as the mystic 'Nirvana' of youth on the one hand, with Bangkok on the other hand, as a rival to Manila or Colombo as the sex capital of the world. Tourism thrives on the manipulation of national images for the purposes of national growth and, according to the Thai Tourist Authority, 'Asia's most exotic destination offers the visitor many unique and unforgettable experiences'.

Despite the fact that the Tourist Organisation of Thailand booklet, *Dos and Don'ts in Thailand*, states that 'Public displays of affection between men and women are frowned upon' (p. 13), the Deputy Prime Minister of Thailand was quoted as telling provincial authorities that they should bear with '. . . some forms of entertainment that some of you might consider disgusting and shameful because they are forms of sexual entertainment . . . [to] consider the jobs that will be created for the people' (in Perpignan 1981 p. 543).

Although hidden, this aspect of Thai tourism is discernible in many 1988 holiday brochures. The coastal resort of Pattaya is described as having 'more than its fair share of girlie bars' (Kuoni 1988 p. 30). One catalogue, which states that the resort caters for the 'single male' (their quotation marks), also states that, 'Pattaya's night life offers you discotheques, nightclubs and bars, some with a definite male "appeal"' (Thomson 1988 p. 32).

But the strange and exotic also has other aspects. 'The smile . . . has its own language and is just one of the elaborate social customs that make Thailand so exotically foreign' (Wings 1987–88 p. 60). Thailand is indicated as a suitable resort for honeymooners, although an unlikely suggestion for romance is a River Kwai trip. On Wednesday morning after breakfast, 'you take an hour long journey on "Death Railway"' (Thomson 1988 p. 85). And few tours miss out the 'primitive' hill peoples. One 'Discover Thailand' itinerary includes a visit to 'the original hill tribes around Chiang Rai' on Day 13 (Thomson p. 86).

The island of Phuket has recently been promoted by the government as a Tourist Centre for the south; according to the brochures, it is the sort of resort which would attract us, if only we had £750–1,300 each to spend on a 12–19 day holiday:

About an hour's flight south of Bangkok lies the beautiful island of Phuket. High green mountain ridges fold down to secluded coves of fine white sand and everywhere you'll find a profusion of flowers and fruit, pineapple, mangoes, rambutans and oranges bursting with colour and delicate tastes.

Most hotels are tucked into their own corner of the island but there is one resort at Patong where a single narrow road passes through the village, flanked by a superb beach and boasting a small stretch of cafes and restaurants (Thomson p. 90).

A survey made by the Venereal Disease Clinic of the Provincial Health Bureau in 1984 found 36 brothels in this 'beautiful retreat' (*Human Rights in Thailand Report* Vol. 8, No. 1 pp. 22 and 25). Prostitution is reported to be big business, with customers paying $1 a time and girls serving 5–10 customers a night. Like most prostitutes in Thailand, the girls seem to be drawn largely from rural areas, from which they migrate aged between 14 and 15. Early in 1984, five prostitutes in Phuket were burned to death in a fire that eventually spread to 14 brothels in the tightly packed red-light district. The recruitment process, by which one of the 15-year-old girls wounded in the fire arrived in Phuket, was established in the course of enquiries into the tragedy:

> [She was] a native of the northeastern province of Loei. She had been lured to prostitution for a short period of time in the city district of another northeastern province of Udornthani, from where she was sold out to Mr Koleng at the price of 8,000 baht [£228]. In exchange for this she had to work, or so she was told, to obtain 20,000 baht [£571] to redeem herself. She had been informed that she would get 10 baht for one customer entertained [28p]. (*HRTR* p. 25)

One of the girls who died in the fire had been recruited from her parents in the relatively prosperous Chiengmai Province two months earlier.

> Her mother said that 'Mr Koleng and friends' . . . told the villagers that they were looking for a number of young girls for a special, unspecified, kind of work in Phuket. They very credulously let their daughter go with the visitors since there was a native of Chiengmai accompanying them. Mr Koleng gave her and the other two or three girls' parents an advance sum of 6,000 baht. Slightly after that she got a letter saying that she had no more future whatsoever, since she had been beaten and forced by Mr Koleng to prostitute herself. The only way out was to redeem her with a refund of 6,000 baht . . . [but] the mother had used up the money. (*HRTR* p. 25)

In the light of this, what are we to make of the contradiction between the statement of the Thai Minister in 1980, which we quoted above, and the protest made by the Thai delegate to the UNICEF Executive Board debate on policy for children in especially difficult circumstances, about an article published under UNICEF auspices containing references to the problem of child prostitution in Thailand? The Board's official minutes record the delegate stating that his government 'was not aware of any such situation. The article was unrealistic and gave a totally distorted view of his country.' As Nigel Cantwell comments in a 1986 issue of *International Children's Rights Monitor*, if the Thai authorities really are unaware of child prostitution in their country then they 'must somehow have missed the whole battery of information distributed in particular since the International Year of the Child (1979)' (Vol. 3, No. 2 p. 14).

What is quite clear is that more and more foreign tourists are enjoying the sun of the new 'pleasure periphery' of the Third World, many of whom confuse exotica with erotica and mistakenly believe that local customs condone behaviour that would be condemned in their home towns. Although such countries as Thailand welcome tourism and the foreign currency it brings, it is a mixed blessing. It brings in less income than expected, because of the trickle-out effect caused by the fact that most of the tourist hotels and facilities are owned by foreign financial interests. Only a small part of the local population is better off; tourists make demands on local scarce resources and raise the price of goods to a level at which the poor cannot buy them. Tourism brings growth without development and meanwhile reduces local traditions and customs to the level of a dumb show of stagnating rather than living cultures. This can have only an adverse effect on the children growing up in a host country, not just those who are directly exploited in sex tourism, for these are the tip of the iceberg. Their degradation stands as a symbol of the cultural exploitation that hedonistic mass tourism represents. If all tourists see of Third World children is 7-year-old flower girls, 10-year-old newsboys and 15-year-old prostitutes, then they unwittingly contribute to the gulf between worlds, that abyss which now threatens the future of all human beings.

The industry has grown from 50,000 tourists a year in the late 1960s, to more than two million in 1984, when it was the country's largest single foreign exchange earner. Prostitution is integral to the Thai economy and tied labour is the rule rather than the exception in the sex industry. What is usually coyly referred to as the 'special services sector' refers to a wholesale commercialization of sex, including masseurs and hostess bars, reflected in the ratio of two male to every female tourist.

The widespread sale of daughters of rural families into the special services sector is an indicator of the status of women in Thai society. Female subordination at the village level is related to ideas of female pollution and to the importance of monks in the political hierarchy. Women are seen as temptresses who are a threat to religious asceticism. But, although female sexual energy is seen as repugnant, the expression of male virility is important. The sex industry thus feeds off local gender models as well as off the fantasies of foreign tourists. Moreover, the social structures of poverty-stricken villages depend on remittances from female earners in urban areas and, given the repression of Thai rural life, some women see the masseuse parlour as a form of liberation, even though prostitutes are regarded as the lowest level of existence.

Table 8
Thailand: migrants by age and sex

Age Group	Male	Female	Total
0–9	3,704	3,849	7,553
10–19	13,543	26,465	40,008
20+	21,534	24,531	45,483

Source: National Statistics Office of Thailand 1982. *The Survey of Migration in Bangkok Metropolis*, Office of the Prime Minister, Bangkok, p. 4.

Table 8 shows that 66 per cent of rural–urban migrants in the 10–19 age group are female. Furthermore, the same Thai survey of migration indicates that 67 per cent of these girls migrate for employment-related reasons and not simply to accompany family members. Only 55 per cent of boys in this age group do this. Of children under 10, as many as 10 per cent migrate for employment, although the majority do move with their families. Even in this age group more girls than boys migrate to seek work, yet the position is reversed when it comes to seeking education. Migrant girls from rural areas reach urban areas, especially Bangkok, in large numbers every year. Most are young and have barely achieved four years of elementary education. Most come from the north and north-east of the country.

North-east Thailand, occupying about one-third of the area of the country, lies on a flat limestone plateau of poorly irrigated, thin soil. Only some parts are suitable for the cultivation of wet rice, when the rainfall is sufficient, which it frequently is not. Families also forage in the forest areas, which are rapidly dwindling due to lumber production, and seek cash through casual labour, which is rarely available. Ironically, in an area of scarce rainfall, occasional floods alternate with periods of drought. It is a desperately poor area. Villages are reported to appear virtually deserted at times because of seasonal migration by adults and young people to cities and sugar plantations. Smallholders sell their own crops at ridiculously low prices because, like peasants the world over, they are desperate to pay off persistent and pressing debts. This means that they remain in debt and still have insufficient rice to eat or seed to plant for the next year. Starvation is seldom far away.

In Somhoang Village, there were 56 households containing 320 inhabitants. In 1985, they harvested 230,400 kg of rice, but this dropped dramatically to 5,800 kg in the following year and no rice at all was planted in 1987. The villagers incurred a total of 241,650 bahts debt (£6,904): a debt of more than £21 per head, man, woman and child. Each household owed an average of about £123 — in a country with a per capita annual income of about £400, this is an impossible sum to repay, particularly in a rural area where cash is difficult to come by. A quarter of the population migrated to Bangkok in search of work. In neighbouring Khawao Khoak, the picture was much the same: the people have accumulated debts of £17 per head, or £90 per household (Thai NGO Consortium on Rural Development, 1987).

Young rural migrants usually become involved with urban recruitment agencies. Legal job placement agencies abound in Bangkok; there are about 121 in the city, most near the bus and railway stations, but many more are illegal. Some recruiters go directly to the villages:

> Sayan and Mayuri are cousins. They said that one day when they were alone at home their families away in the fields, a woman, aged about 30, came to the house and asked them if they wanted to work in Bangkok. She offered them jobs as housemaids with 500 baht (US$20) monthly salary.
>
> The two of them were very happy with what the lady offered them and left their families without informing their parents. Upon arrival at the bus terminal in Bangkok, another broker took them to a house in Sukhumvit, an

area in the central part of Bangkok.

The house they were working in, turned out to be a small dormitory with 10 rooms to rent. Their duty was to clean up these 10 rooms, 10 bathrooms and lavatories every day (*Child Workers in Asia*, Vol. 3, No. 4 p. 13).

After two months, during which they had received no pay whatsoever, Sayan and Mayuri 'escaped' and went back to their parents. Others are not so lucky. Brokers are not legally supposed to charge more than a minimum fee for commission but, in practice, they often make one-year contracts with the children or their parents and subtract a substantial amount as commission, even though the wages are set far below minimum legal rates. Children are held captive by being told that the money has already been paid to their parents, knowing that their parents will have spent it and be unable to redeem them, or they are simply hidden from their parents, so that no money ever passes from the broker either to child or to parent (*Child Workers in Asia*, Vol. 3, No. 4 p. 11).

The prime time for child migration in Thailand is during March and April, at the end of the harvest season. The Centre of Concern for Child Labour estimates that 300 children a day arrive at Hua Lampong railway station in Bangkok. Some are brought by agents, others are 'met' by freelance agents who approach the children directly when they arrive off the train, often at 5 a.m.

As researchers in 1987 commented, 'The unsuspecting visitor to Bangkok would most probably be unaware of the scale of unlawful abuse taking place behind the scenes' (Gough and Pitman 1987 p. 1). In greater Bangkok, children work in food and tobacco manufacturing, textile and shoe, wood and furniture, rubber products, mineral products, machinery. Their wages in all industries are 36.3 per cent of adult male and 54.6 per cent of adult female rates. Sometimes, as in the manufacture of electrical goods, their wages are only one-quarter of the average adult wage (Thitsa 1980 p. 26).

Employers do not use child workers simply in order to pay less for the job than the adult wage. Children are also a more quiescent workforce; they can be fed less if they reside in the workshop, as many of the child migrants do, and can be kept working in worse conditions than adults would tolerate without rebellion. The Centre of Concern for Child Labour Annual Report 1985 shows a photograph of a skeletally thin girl called Naree, aged 13, who had been a worker in a straw manufacturing company, measuring and packing straws and cleaning. She worked a seven day week, from 6 a.m. to midnight, enduring constant hunger. Her employer paid £71 to the broker for her services for a year, but her parents received only £14 of this and had to pay just over £3 to claim her back from the factory.

Police sometimes raid the sweatshops and factories. On one occasion, the Centre of Concern for Child Labour asked for assistance for 51 children employed in a factory making mosquito nets, working similar hours to Naree. They had to eat and sleep in the area where they worked, were forbidden to leave the factory and could not even speak to each other during working hours. For making mistakes they were punished by being hit over the head with scissors. They received 3,000 baht annually (£85): just £1.65 a week or 1.3p an hour! As a result of confinement and malnutrition, many children rescued from these kinds of conditions are found to suffer from lack of muscle and bone development, to have become deformed and to be unable to walk when rescued. Some have been found chained. Others suffer accidents and even death from working on unguarded machinery. Often boredom, exhaustion and inability to concentrate, due to hunger and homesickness, are contributory factors in such accidents.

Thailand shares with much of south-east Asia some of the best documented examples of child labour in sweatshops, which often produce luxury goods for sale in the West. Estimates of illegal activity always vary, but to say that there are at least 5,000 unregulated 'factories' in Thailand would probably not be an exaggeration. Although Thai law forbids the employment of children under 12, reports like those we have already given provide ample evidence that the law is being flouted.

But how should we analyse this? In terms of the vicious exploitation of minors by Thai and Chinese factory owners? In terms of the indifference of the Thai government? In terms of the poverty that drives twentieth-century Siamese children to march from the rural areas to work in these appalling conditions? Clearly all these factors should be taken into consideration. But the whole picture insists that some international factors are taken into consideration also. And it is not enough simply to point to a generalized exploitation of the South by the North, or to the need for 'development and growth' in countries like Thailand. We analyse it on the one hand with respect to the new global division of labour, which is related to the growth of transnational companies, and on the other hand to the lack of international solidarity of organized labour.

A case in point is the 1984 Granada television documentary, *Rags to Riches*, which gained publicity for reporter Ed Harriman and, with footage from concealed, hand-held cameras, showed Thai children working in sweatshops to produce textile goods, which, the programme asserted, were then sold in major high-street retailers in the United Kingdom and other parts of Europe. It led to a short-lived campaign against certain retailers, who were forced to justify purchasing clothing from European wholesalers that obtain goods from Bangkok suppliers. It also led to a campaign by United Kingdom textile trade unions to ban the import of Thai goods made with sweatshop labour, which sell at prices lower than similar British-made goods in a process which means that many skilled British workers are unemployed. As Ed Harriman himself wrote in a subsequent *New Statesman* article,

> Poor, illiterate, uneducated farm girls from Thailand's impoverished North and Northeast are the employees of choice. They work hard, ask few questions, and don't complain. In effect, buying in Bangkok enables British firms to circumvent over 150 years of British social legislation (Harriman 10 February 1984).

Development experts warned that to ban imports would do more harm than good, because this employment, bad as it is, is the only income between these young people and starvation, a point also made by the Thai government which emphasized that a backward country cannot afford to be too particular about labour laws. Feminists jumped on the bandwagon and asserted that a ban would simply drive all the girls in sweatshops into prostitution, ignoring both boys in sweatshops and boy prostitutes. Once the argument had reached this point, it ceased to be news, having effectively been neutralized by the feminist red herring (Fyfe 1985).

To us the issues seem more wide-ranging. The first, although not the most important, is that the Thai government position is somewhat damaged by the inequalities of distribution of wealth in that country. With an average annual growth rate of 2.6 per cent in the 1980s, a fairer share-out should be possible, even if the basis of growth is unstable. Moreover, in terms of human capital, no government can afford to allow large numbers of the future generation to be mistreated in this way. More important is what the type of case tells us about the depth and breadth of global capitalism. Transnational capitalism entails not just international markets but also international production, as capital seeks the lowest production costs for labour-intensive industries. Industry thus moves to countries where labour is unregulated, disorganized and unprotected. Profit-maximizing is global and efficient. The only way in which labour can combat this is to loosen its hold on purely parochial concerns. The protest by the British textile unions about the use of Thai labour in this case was almost cynically opportunistic. But, as we have already pointed out, trade unions have always worked to the benefit of their adult male members rather than for women and children. This type of protest simply mirrors the history of child labour reform in the First World, by excluding persons (be they child or adult as long as they are foreign) who are undercutting the price of British labour because they are in no position to do anything else. Instead of pressing narrow nationalistic concerns and urging retailers and customers to 'buy British and keep British work*men* in employment', a true labour movement would have sought some way to help the organization and protection of labour in Thailand — might even have contacted the Centre of Concern for Child Labour in Thailand and found some way to help. Instead, trade union arguments actually became skewed around a British story about the use of sweated child labour (of Asian origin) in Leicester textile production, and became implicitly racist to boot. No story we have come across so far has more effectively illustrated the complexity and selfishness, as well as the intimacy, of the link between First and Third worlds. There is little point in pitying the skinny, Third World children in sweatshops unless we admit that they and the products of their labour are, in fact, part of our world.

Capital: Beijing
Area: 3,691,502 sq. miles
Population: 1,072,200,000
Urban population: 21% (1985)
Population annual growth rate:
  1.2% (1980–85)
GNP per capita US$: 310
  (1985)
Rate of inflation: 2.4% (1980–85)
**Population below absolute
  poverty level** { urban: n.a.
                    { rural: n.a.
**Population with access
  to drinking water:** n.a.
Life expectancy: 69

China
(U5MR = 47   IMR = 34)

Births: 19,914,000
Infants with low birthweight: 6% (1982–85)
Population 0–4: 94,000,000
Population 5–16: 240,600,000
Total population under 16: 334,600,000
Deaths 0–4: 942,000
Children suffering from malnutrition:
        mid-moderate: n.a.
              severe: n.a.

**One year olds
  fully immunised** { TB: 70%   (12 months for 23
                    { DPT: 62%   provinces, 18
                    { polio: 68%   months for 5
                    { measles: 63% provinces,
                                    until 1986)

ORS per 100 episodes of diarrhoea: n.a.
Primary school enrolment ratio male/female: 132/114
  (gross) (1983–86)
**Grade One enrolment completing primary
  school:** 66% (1980–86)
Secondary school enrolment ratio male/female:
  45/32 (1983–86)

(all figures 1986 unless otherwise stated)

China

Everyone who has ever written about China must have left something out. This vast country confounds all attempts to create a fully comprehensive picture. How can one include every detail of all matters covering 55 ethnic minorities which make up a total of 56 million of the more than one billion people with Chinese nationality? It is all too easy to fall into the trap of concentrating on the 60 million or so Han Chinese. As we are writing these words, United Kingdom newspapers contain daily reports of unrest in Xizang (Tibet) where Han Chinese form only a small minority. Colleagues who have been on a brief field trip to the Turkish groups of the Xinjiang-Uygur Autonomous Region have provided us with anecdotal accounts but, like the limited information we have about Mongols or the Zhuang, this does not tell us much about children. Yet all the ethnic divisions are cut across by one of the most important in any society, that which separates child from adult, and what is important about China for our purposes is that, like Cuba, it tried to reformulate the role of children in society.

China has a unique and rich history. Children are legendary characters in many ancient folk-tales, alongside animals, warriors and demons. Some of them are the equivalent of our own characters, like Cinderella. In the version recorded by Tuan Ch'engshih, and written down sometime in the ninth century AD, Yeh Hsien (Cinderella) has a stepmother and stepsister rather than two ugly stepsisters, she goes to a festival rather than a ball, but it is still the slipper that gives her true identity away. She climbs the social ladder rather higher in China than in Europe, because she marries a king instead of a prince. In another story, an eleven-year-old boy, Kiti, becomes a cricket in order to win money for his much loved parents at insect contests. In a modern folk-story, Fa Mu Lan is a girl who takes her father's place in battle and grows up to be a warrior woman.

Until very recently, China had a highly conservative family life. Family was the centre point of social and economic existence, although the ideal of an extended family of three generations under one roof was achieved only by rich families with the resources to sustain such a large number of members (Croll 1987 Ch. 1). Whatever the size of the household, the younger generations had to be obedient to older generations, just as females were subordinate to males. Arranged marriages often started with child betrothals, and girls were also sold out of the poorer families, even as late as the 1920s. After marriage, women were required to move into the husband's home. This is why, as we pointed out when we discussed the Declaration of the Rights of the Child, the birth of a daughter was only a 'small happiness' compared to the birth of a son. According to a Chinese proverb, 'When you raise girls, you are raising children for strangers' (Hong Kingston 1987 p. 48). Children have always had a cultural value as the source of future welfare security for their parents in old age. This is part of a different attitude to dependency. In all societies the productive workers in their prime have overall responsibility for the young, the old and the weak, 'but in the West, the moral emphasis is on the importance of caring for children, and in China, the moral emphasis is on the importance of caring for the old. Child care is a means to an end, a form of long range self-interest' (Heins Potter 1987 p. 37).

In the past 40 years, Chinese society has radically changed some of the traditions which had developed slowly over more than 40 centuries of recorded history. Some of the present changes began in the nineteenth century, others have their roots in the Nationalist period but, since the People's Republic of China was established in 1949, despite the sometimes drastic changes of ideology and policy from the Great Leap Forward, to the Cultural Revolution and present market orientation, Chinese childhood and family have been subjected to extraordinary changes. Even so, some characteristics of the past remain: the strength of family solidarity, respect for parents and an acute sense of the importance of morality are the foundations from the past on which the history of future generations is being built.

What is different is the relationship between the family and the state or, for our purposes, the state and children. It is as if the patriarchal authority by which the family was ruled in traditional society has been replaced by a kind of 'public patriarchy', with state supervision of all areas of family life (Stacey 1983 pp. 227, 229). China represents the most thoroughgoing intervention by any government into private behaviour. This is because new ways of thought and new ways of living had to be found to replace the central role which family had in pre-communist China. Loyalty to the family had to be changed to loyalty to the New China (Adams and Winston 1980 p. 212). But this did not entail a change from individualism to collectivism, for the previous three-generational family unit and the family clan were 'tied to a system of collective obligations and rewards' which left 'little protection for the individual against collective demands' (p. 213).

The Marriage Law of 1950 was designed to destroy the feudal family in China, replacing it with a new democratic family which was to be the basic unit of socialist development. According to its tenets, a new set of intra-familial relationships was designed to exemplify the equality of the New China: spouses should be companions and parent/child relationships should be reciprocal. Since 1949, the government has tried to formulate a working official policy on family relations. The policy is intended to advocate egalitarianism within the family, thus breaking down the old patriarchal forms. The fundamental ideas are that equality between males and females within the family should be combined with egalitarianism as far as is possible through the age structure. This means tempering the authority elders had over younger generations, shown for example in official scorn of corporal punishment as a means of disciplining and controlling children. According to the new Marriage Law of the People's Republic of China of 1 January 1981, men and women have equal property rights, and children may adopt the family name of either their mother or their father. Children's rights are reflected in the stated obligation of parents to rear and educate their children. This is balanced by the duty of children to support and assist their parents. When parents fail, their dependent children have the right to demand that their parents pay for their care and, when adult children fail to perform the duty of supporting their elderly or sick parents, they too have a reciprocal right. Moreover, grandchildren who have the capacity to bear the relevant costs have a duty to support and assist their paternal and, in some cases, maternal grandparents. Thus the new law reflects some of the old priorities.

State patriarchy puts a strain on individuals who have to balance these family obligations against the requirements to put their primary loyalty at the service of the collective good. Individuals are left with decisions and compromises which may be difficult to live with. BBC television producer Howard Reid recorded this when he went to make a film in China about women's rights:

> One of the things which influenced me to make the film, very early on, was meeting a university professor who worked long hours; she had to spend evenings correcting papers, preparing lectures and just trying to assemble her thoughts, and as her child was getting more active and demanding, she found it impossible to do this.
> At eight months she decided to send him to grandparents to live and she said to me with such emotion: 'On the day I was sending him away I wished I had never heard of women's lib. I desperately didn't want to leave him.' (In Neustatter 1987)

Such private sacrifices have undoubtedly contributed to considerable improvements in the quality of life in the community as a whole. In 1949, the Chinese state was in a situation of underdevelopment, exacerbated by years of civil strife and war with Japan. There had long been acute food shortages, with periodic famines. Agriculture was heavily dependent on labour-intensive and under-productive peasant farming which had been made worse by the exploitative landholding classes. Child mortality was high and the expectation of life one of the lowest in the world. Industrial development lagged well behind both the West and the Soviet Union.

In order to feed its huge and often starving population and to develop a secure economic base, China had to both limit population growth and use the labour of every available productive member of society. Thus two major concerns of the new People's Republic were the integration of women into the workforce, and population control. As in Cuba, the solution to the first has been an attempt to provide comprehensive child-care facilities. This began in the early 1950s, with networks of nurseries run by neighbourhood organizations, factories, schools, shops and co-operatives. During the Great Leap Forward (1958–60), while collectivization of agriculture proceeded at an unprecedented rate, further attempts were made to socialize all forms of domestic labour, including child care, in order to release women for production. This was combined with a recommendation that pre-school facilities should provide a better educational environment than could be found in homes. Nursery hours were tailored to local production schedules and child-care facilities were ideally supposed to be located close to the mother's workplace (Croll 1978 pp. 247, 268–9). All these measures were designed to encourage women to participate in the work of national growth. Nevertheless, day-care facilities in China have been more successful in urban than in rural areas and it has always been difficult to find people to work in nurseries. It is reported that, in rural areas where seedtime and harvest bring only seasonal demand for child care, nurseries are staffed by untrained personnel, usually women who are too old or too weak to work in the fields (Adams and Winston 1980; Croll 1983 p. 309).

Although early childhood education has not had an even record of success, the People's Republic has enviable achievements in reducing child mortality. Within the first three decades, many doctors were trained in Western methods. Enormous numbers of paramedics and traditional practitioners were re-trained to bring their methods into line with those of modern practitioners. The numbers of nurses and hospital beds relative to the population now available are in line with most middle-income countries, even though the Chinese per capita income remains relatively low. A decline in infant mortality has brought it to a level that can be compared with other middle-income countries, although there are urban, rural and regional variations that conceal higher figures. Despite the fact that the medical system has been nationalized, many of its services are available only by paying fees, and insurance programmes are not universal, most being concentrated in urban areas. Rural people have to organize their own insurance programmes if they want to be covered at all.

Despite the number of Western-style doctors, China has concentrated on preventive rather than curative medicine, placing emphasis on innoculation campaigns and public sanitation. Major immunization drives against infectious diseases have been carried out through schools, work places and neighbourhoods. These have reduced the threat of large-scale epidemics, which had particularly serious consequences for child victims. The elimination of vermin and insect breeding places has been periodically used to reduce diseases such as malaria. With the elimination of major epidemics, children have a far greater chance of surviving to adulthood.

Family planning is seen as a child health matter. There have been three main phases of family structure. Before 1949 the joint family ideal sought both continuity and security for the old by seeking to produce as many children as the economic situation of a domestic group could bear. Between 1950 and the late 1970s two to three children per couple was advocated and the 1980s has seen attempts to limit couples to one child only (Croll 1987 p. 3). Family size policy has always run up against the contradiction between the traditional value of children for families and the need to limit the number of births in order to lower infant and child mortality figures, which is summed up in the slogan: 'One pregnancy, one live birth; one live birth, one healthy child' (quoted in Croll 1987 p. 13). Population control was one of the most pressing and most delicate problems facing the new communist government in 1949, and one response has been the public-patriarchy supervision of sexual relationships. Manuals about 'normal' sexual activity, for instance, suggest that this should be limited to once a fortnight, and late marriage and birth control are encouraged, not only through education but also through material incentives. Early attempts to check population growth began in the 1950s, but were halted by the idea that Malthusian theories about population growth are essentially bourgeois. Resumption of population policies in the 1960s was likewise halted by the Cultural Revolution. But, after the death of Mao Zedong in 1976, a comprehensive campaign to limit births began, using such methods as Birth Control Committees, media campaigns, material sanctions on excessive family growth and incentives to sterilization.

The New Marriage Law of 1981 has been called an anti-natalist document (Stacey 1983 p. 274). The age for marriage was raised to 22 for men and 20 for women, contraception is obligatory and family size limited to one child, although two could be permissible in rural areas, and ethnic groups were not limited in the same way. A system of rewards and sanctions was instituted to implement the new law (Stacey 1983 p. 276). Nevertheless, these measures were relaxed fairly rapidly because they were clearly leading to problems, not least for children. Parents who were limited to a single child have been observed to be breaching collective ideals by placing too great an emphasis upon the child's individual personality and material welfare. It is alleged that an only child is more dependent and self-centred than others who have siblings with whom they have to compete for parental affection and privileges within the family. Senior government officials define the moral education of 'spoiled children' as a policy priority (Wyer 1987). Parents and grandparents expect too much and bribe the child upon whom all their future hopes depend, and the government has felt obliged to institute Parent Training classes (Stacey 1983 and Lin 1987).

Perhaps more serious is that it has become clear that the one-child policy can have severe repercussions for welfare in general. China does not have the resources for a comprehensive welfare system and relies on the family to care for the old, the sick and the disabled. The generation raised in one-child families will result in a generation of adults not only with no aunts, uncles or cousins to help in child care and family welfare, but also with a heavy burden of care for elderly parents. It has been called the 4-2-1 Problem: four grandparents and two parents to each child.

Inter-generational relationships have clearly undergone some changes. Although the obligation to care for the elderly still rests with the family, the old have less control over families than they had in the past. This allows scope for greater freedom of choice and individuality amongst younger family members, even though state patriarchy replaces that of the family. Nevertheless, respect still characterizes inter-generational relationships and may be encouraged by the necessities of modern life. The process begins in early infancy when children are fondled and held a good deal but rarely given any mental stimulation because they are considered incapable of learning much before they reach two or three years old. After 56 days of paid maternity leave, most mothers return to work. Large work places and many neighbourhoods offer crêches and kindergartens; children are often left with grandparents, or the better-off may hire a child-minder. The consequence may be distance between the generations.

Although young children are treated with affection, this decreases considerably as they reach school age. Then they are expected to be 'responsible' and to begin to help around the home. At about the same stage in their lives, parents, especially fathers, become far more stern and distant toward them. Paternal discipline is strict and a child of five or six years old is supposed to restrain all aggressive behaviour.

By the time they are ten, children are expected to take on major duties in the home, especially those, such as shopping and preparation of meals, which help their working parents. As they get a little older they remain respectful within the family but become independent outside. Children of this age often come in for state criticism for their unruly behaviour in public. Yet when they are at home, children often discuss problems with their parents — an important behavioural dichotomy that emerged during the Cultural Revolution. By day young people were Red Guards, openly involved in acts of public violence and vandalism, often arguing heatedly with state officials; by night they were dutiful family members.

Although a revolutionary socialist government took power in 1949, the values of traditional China have never been entirely surrendered to progressive substitutes. China has a profound moral tradition in which the main virtues are hard work, bravery, respect and responsibility for others. Accordingly, these virtues have been integrated into Chinese education. Children learn to love their country, people, labour, science and public property. Chinese educational research thus explores the moral development of children almost as closely as academic progress.

We were reminded of this at a Conference in Norway in June 1987. Lin Chong De, a child psychologist from the University of Beijing, presented a paper, called 'Moral Development in a Changing World: A Chinese Perspective'. The audience was largely from Western or capitalist-oriented countries and his eagerly-anticipated paper was greeted with stunned silence. We were unprepared for statements like: 'many teachers blindly pursue the propelling of children and adolescents into higher education, to the neglect of ideological and moral training' (Lin 1987 p. 4) or 'all persons working in cultural fields, film and TV production, newspapers and magazines, should consciously try their best to provide children and adolescents with nourishment for the mind, and eradicate bad ideological influences' (p. 5), or for discussion of 'Work-Study schools . . . for morally unhealthy children and adolescents' (p. 7), with principles like '[the] purpose of moral education is to form good habits' (p. 9). According to our consumer concepts, culture has to do with entertainment rather than ideology, and we have no discourse that discusses moral health, because we have debased discussion of morality to the level of prohibitions regarding personal sexuality and legal bundles called ethical guidelines. It was difficult for Westerners to understand the paper because it had a totally different concept of the place of the child in society. We think of childhood as a preparation for adult individual futures, whereas Chinese childhood is regarded as the preparation for a new future for society.

Chinese education shares with that of Cuba the explicit conception of childhood as a time of preparation for work within the national economy. Even during early education, children are encouraged to perform some productive work as part of the learning process. This may be linked to the work of a local factory, for instance, and factory workers visit the schools to explain to the children their part in the production process and to praise their efforts. In all senses, Chinese childhood encourages responsibility from an early age, children being given the task of re-educating parents who show feudal or bourgeois tendencies (Adams and Winston 1980 p. 213).

A stumbling block in the process is the uneven development of the education system. Educational standards suffered from early attempts to achieve universal education in the face of poor resources. Rapid growth meant that teachers who would not normally have met requirements were recruited into the system, which contributed to a negative view of education amongst the Chinese. Teachers in urban areas have been accused of intellectual elitism, especially when stories of excess discipline of working-class children were circulated. In rural areas there are few incentives to attain high grades since achievement means little when peasant children are expected to become agriculturists like their parents. Peasant youth have an extremely restricted range of opportunities available to them compared with urban youth. Since government regulations strictly control rural to urban migration there is little choice but to remain on the land.

Notwithstanding these weaknesses, education in the People's Republic has been relatively successful. Attainment levels have increased; most children have access to education, and problems associated with social and class barriers have in general been overcome. To quote Article 46 in Chapter Two of the Constitution of the People's Republic of China, under the Fundamental Rights and Duties of Citizens:

> Citizens of the People's Republic of China have the duty as well as the right to receive education.
> The state promotes the all-round moral, intellectual and physical development of children and young people.

Capital: Havana
Area: 44,218 sq. miles
Population: 10,100,000
Urban population: 72% (1985)
Population annual growth rate:
  0.8% (1980–85)
GNP per capita US$: n.a.
Rate of inflation: n.a.
Population below absolute
  poverty level { urban: n.a.
                  { rural: n.a.
Population with access
  to drinking water: n.a.
Life expectancy: 74

Births: 181,000
Infants with low birthweight: 9% (1982–85)
Population 0–4: 800,000
Population 5–16: 2,000,000
Total population under 16: 2,800,000
Deaths 0–4: 3,000
Children suffering from malnutrition:
        mid-moderate: n.a.
        severe: n.a.

One year olds   { TB: 98%
fully immunised   { DPT: 91%
                    { polio: 88%   } (1985–86)
                    { (2 doses only)
                    { measles: 85%

ORS per 100 episodes of diarrhoea: n.a.

Primary school enrolment ratio male/female:
  108/101 (gross) 94/94 (net) (1983–86)

Grade One enrolment completing primary
  school: 86% (1980–86)

Secondary school enrolment ratio male/female:
  82/88 (1983–86)

Cuba
(U5MR = 19   IMR = 15)

(all figures 1986 unless otherwise stated)

Cuba

We work for children, because children know how to love, because children are the hope of the world. (José Martí)

In our four Latin American case studies Cuba is the odd one out. In fact, of all 12 studies it falls into a category of its own. Nearly all the things one does with demography show it to be a reasonably uncrowded country. There are under 230 people to each square mile as against 580 in the United Kingdom. Urban and rural populations were fairly equal at the time of the Revolution — about 55 per cent lived in cities, although this has altered to show an urban population of 72 per cent in 1985. Even so, the relationship between urban and rural life is more intimate than in most Western states.

Pre-revolutionary Cuba was very like many poor Latin American countries today. There was a wide gap between rich and poor, a repressive government and almost no social welfare provision. Family life for all classes was dominated by *machismo*, which demands honour and power from men and purity from women. Children were subject to fathers and women to men. Many children had to work, and Havana in particular had a street-child problem similar in scale to the *gamines* of Bogotá. Even in the capital, schooling was beyond the reach of most families and, in rural areas, secondary education was non-existent. Malnutrition and infant mortality rates were high.

Infant mortality is now low, life expectancy high and adult literacy very high. The annual rate of growth is low enough for the state to cope with increasing population. If one wanted to use a revolutionary state as a model for possible Third World developments then Cuba is almost certainly the one to use. That does not make it a perfect environment for children, but it is many times better than prevalent conditions in many Western nations let alone those that are just trying to find their way.

When Fulgencio Batista resigned the Presidency on 31 December 1958, a new age began for Cuba. Fidel Castro's rebels ceased to be rebels and became the legitimate leaders of their nation. The armed struggle had been the forerunner of changes that were to take place, the real Revolution. There have been, in many respects, no greater beneficiaries of the revolution than children and youth. We often hear about Cubans as military advisers in countries such as Angola and Mozambique, but other Cuban experts also contribute their skills and experience to constructing nurseries, schools and hospitals in foreign lands.

Cuban society was not defined as explicitly socialist by its leaders until 1961. It shares with China an overt expression of childhood as a time for the socialization of young people into work and citizenship, which contrasts strongly with the emphasis capitalism places on childhood as a time for play and lack of cares. The socialization of production tends to increase rather than decrease individual obligations at all ages. The individual is responsible for the economy and national growth. In the early days of societal change, a particular duty to make the change take place is vested in the next generation: 'the prime movers and beneficiaries of the new society' (Leiner 1974 p. 3).

Cuban revolutionary leaders considered education to be the best channel through which to change social values and abolish elitism. Fidel Castro made this clear in a speech in 1967, when he announced that,

> Our children will learn the meaning of work from the youngest age. Even if they are six and only in the first grade at school, they will learn how to grow lettuce. In addition, they will learn how to water a plant or tend a flower bed so as to make their surroundings more pleasant. They will do what they can, but the important thing is that as soon as they are old enough to reason, material goods are produced ... In this way, they will acquire a noble concept of work. (Quoted in Matthews, 1975)

In early childhood education, children begin to learn the fundamentals of the new Cuban ideal of collective, brotherly love rather than family solidarity. The idea of 'Cuban Man', which was particularly current in the 1960s, promoted in the media as well as through schools, provides a new model of citizenship. It is 'a fundamentally humanistic, altruistic concept of the human being, which combines classical Marxism, collective consciousness, and the view that people are perfectible beings' (Leiner 1974 p. 16). Schooling is designed to be group-centred, so that children are not singled out for exceptional qualities, and even the playpens for toddlers are designed to accommodate a dozen infants. This did not require a fundamental change of attitudes. Pre-revolutionary child care often placed children in groups with grandmothers or aunts, out of economic necessity, and individualism has not taken the place of family solidarity in any Latin American country. What is new is that children are brought into directed and structured learning situations from a very early age; and the message is clear and consistent. At later stages in their educational life they will be taught in a system that combines work and study, manual and mental labour, often in a 50–50 mixture and frequently in a residential setting.

Between 1958 and 1968 the number of schools doubled and enrolment figures rose accordingly (see Table 9).

Peak enrolment figures of 1,664,634 in 1971 are explained by the number of adults who benefited from literacy programmes, but there are still nearly a million and a half children in compulsory elementary education, and over 80,000 teachers. The 15:1 teacher:pupil ratio which this represents is more than creditable. Compulsory education ends at age 11, but secondary school

Table 9
Teachers and school enrolment in Cuba

	Primary pupils	Primary schools	Teachers
1959	717,417	7,567	17,355
1969	1,460,754	14,807	48,994

attendance is well over 50 per cent and it is planned to extend compulsory education to 18, bridging the gap that now exists between education and military service.

Throughout the 1970s, new schools were given high priority in building programmes. This meant that all children have easy access to education, even though the quality is variable and the emphasis on ideological problems too overt for Western taste. The educational content reflects the government's Marxist–Leninist interpretation of history. Schoolwork must be educational, productive and socially useful. The end result is intended to make every student live according to a three-part commitment to '*estudio, trabajo y fusil*' (study, work, and a rifle).

Such an education does instil a sense of duty to the continuation of the Revolution, and protects present and future generations against growing into an adult world where a reversion to pre-revolutionary conditions could occur. Militancy, discipline, high technical and cultural awareness and skills firmly anchor political loyalties. As a child grows to adulthood, levels of skill and knowledge-acquisition reveal differences in potential. Theoretically, it should make no difference whether a child is white or black, male or female, urban or rural, because all opportunities develop from the potential within the growing individual. It does appear, though, that there are differences in achievement according to race, gender and place of origin, but these are not as marked as in the Western world. Although the state tries to provide the best possible local schools, older children who live in isolated areas can go to central schools where the state houses, feeds and clothes them, with the idea of placing all students on an equal basis. In the city, children at elementary schools are provided with a midday meal and milk with the same object.

Government minister Armado Hart summed up the object of socialist education as 'the ideological, scientific and technical formation of whole generations capable of actively constructing socialism and communism' (quoted in Suchlicki 1972 p. 14). The style of expression conjures up in us a mischievous image of young Hart in short trousers, sitting on Lenin's knee, being told that was why he had to go to school. But, in practice, there are results. A bare three decades after the Batista regime was overthrown, Cuba's foreign policy is able to benefit from its education system. Cuban missions to Third World countries consist of doctors, nurses, engineers, building personnel, technicians and teachers as well as diplomatic, political and military experts. Fidel Castro has claimed that Cuban doctors working in the Third

World exceed those of the World Health Organization.

Revolutions have a common characteristic of bringing out the puritanism in their leaders. This may have been a problem during the early years of the Revolution but, since the 1970s, education has become broadly co-educational, except where the characteristics of the teaching area inhibit or forbid it. Sex education is integrated into the curriculum in such a way that it needs no separate or special courses. The idea is that questions arising about sexuality or sexual relations be answered with sufficient information to tell the child or youth the truth when he or she asks questions in school or at home. The dissipation of ignorance and prejudices is approached through the integration of sex education into the broad programme of subjects.

Infants have good kindergarten and nursery provision where necessary, many of them being kept in *circulos infantiles* while their mothers work. Because work outside the home benefits the economy, it is encouraged and even the youngest children enjoy the socialization offered by pre-school groups. Day nurseries are available to all children from the 45th day after birth and, at the age of five, pre-school national schools are available to prepare children for compulsory education, which begins after their next birthday. The day care and education systems combined are major items in a fairly comprehensive state welfare provision.

At the time of the Revolution, Cuba was not as poor as many other developing nations, therefore medical services were already quite reasonable. The revolutionary government increased the number of hospitals and health centres. By 1984 there were 60,673 hospital beds and 20,545 physicians, health services are free. Nevertheless, infant mortality rates went up from a pre-revolutionary 33.7 in 1958 to 44.7 in 1967. It has been assessed that this was due to economic deterioration rather than lack of medical personnel or facilities. By the early 1980s this indicator had shown great improvement, reaching 17.4 per 1,000 at one stage. The life expectancy of a person who survives childhood is 74. In 1978, Cuba, according to the Overseas Development Council in the USA, had the third highest Physical Quality of Life (PQLI) in Latin America.

Unlike their Latin American 'cousins', Cubans have the benefit of a State Social Security System that gives employees benefits for sickness, accidents, maternity, disability, retirement and unemployment. Since most people have work most of the time there will be few people not entitled to benefits. Therefore the phenomenon of children as bread-winners for disabled parents or co-earners to support impoverished families should not exist. Since health services are free the problems experienced by poor children in Brazil or Peru do not generally occur. No child needs to miss education or to go hungry. The budget allocation in 1985 earmarked about US$2,000 million for health and education services. This is partly possible because economic strategies have resulted in growth rates that compare favourably with those of other Latin American countries. But it is the structural changes that have accompanied economic policy that are responsible for the overall improvement in the situation of children (Brundenius 1981 p. 91). Hunger is virtually eliminated and the infant mortality rate places Cuba alongside the wealthiest countries in the world. The government's commitment to the protection of the poor and of children is reflected in the fact that, in the face of world recession in the 1980s, it has chosen to maintain expenditure on health and education at pre-recession rates, while reducing other public-sector spending (Gutierres Muniz et al, 1984 p. 258).

Because Cuba has not suffered from the sort of destabilizing influences that have crippled socialist endeavours in Mozambique and Somalia, it has thus far been able to maintain a policy of providing welfare services for all citizens. Cuban children are therefore particularly advantaged by history. The state the revolutionaries took over was not poor. Demographic surveys of the 1950s show that, because of a moderately small population and a substantial level of modernization, fertility levels and mortality were already comparable with many advanced countries. What happened was that the revolution stopped Cuba from developing the desperate inequalities of its Latin American neighbours.

Although the rate of urbanization has changed from a reasonably even balance between city and countryside to a predominantly urban-based population, the slums and shanty-towns typical of developing countries have not grown up. This is partly because of a planning policy which places public amenities in communities which we would scarcely regard as urban. There is no specific elite, although differences of income and life style do equate with education, profession and income. The government has made immense improvements in the quality of life in rural areas, changed some aspects of women's roles and made birth control easily accessible.

The socialization of young Cubans has been designed to draw them away from whatever stereotypical views may have been handed down by previous generations. Their education tells them that all Cubans have equal rights irrespective of race, class, gender or wealth. A poem by a Cuban child in a book compiled by Chris Searle illustrates this:

> My house is not my house
> If there's someone without a house
> Alongside my house.
>
> The thing is that my house
> Can't be my house
> If it's not also the house
> Of whoever has no house.
>
> (In Searle 1983, p. 32)

The uniqueness of this poem lies in the fact that if homelessness occurs in Cuba it is certainly not comparable with that of other developing nations. The unselfish expression of a child's words speak out for the world rather than Cuba, the 'whoever' has no house is highly likely to be in Nicaragua or Mozambique or wherever the author's imagination chooses to travel.

Afterword

One of the advantages of word processors is that authors type their own manuscripts. This not only saves hard cash but also means that authors are really the first readers of their own books. In the case of this book it has given us an appreciation of the repetitions of style and of themes that we have incorporated unknowingly. Some are clearly irritating and these we have tried to correct. Others have been a revelation. For instance, we did not realize while we were writing that this book would be an anti-war statement. Yet, as we read it we realize that, if nothing else, we have demonstrated Eglantyne Jebb's assertion that 'all wars are waged against children'. We do not apologize for this. It just turned out that way; the evidence is clear and persistent.

Other repetitive features are the use of certain words. While we were typing we realized that particular terms are repeated and initially we imagined that this was a stylistic error, caused by our limited vocabulary. But, when we tried to make changes, we found it impossible and began to look for reasons. The words we persistently repeated are simple. We find that we use 'even' a lot, not as an adjective meaning 'smooth' but in phrases like 'even children as young as six'. This is clearly a sign of our own, Western, age-specific expectations. We do not expect children of eight to be in employment or children of 12 to be in armies. How correct this is is a matter for discussion. Perhaps we are being ethnocentric, or maybe we are being ageist. Like other human beings, children should have a choice in these matters. The important thing is that they *should have a choice*. The evidence we have presented makes us wonder how often they actually do.

A further repetition we noticed is that we frequently use the words 'suffer' and 'suffering'. We could have changed this to misery of course, because suffer has another meaning and another resonance, as in the phrase 'Suffer (allow) the little children to come unto me'. There are two ideas we think we need to unpack here. The first is that the term brings us back once again to the need for children to have enabling rights, to the respect for their autonomy which allows them to voice their own opinions and experiences. Secondly, we fear that we may have been emphasizing suffering too much. It has been a very depressing book to write, which is paradoxical because nothing pleases either of us more than spending time with children, both in our home country and in the developing world. We can remember few experiences more exhilarating than our drive into the jungle from Lima in 1983. We were with the Save the Children Fund Field Director in Peru at that time, and he had invited two boys from the Ashaninka village, where SCF was building a clinic, to spend a week or so in Lima, on the premise that it would be good for the future of their remote community if two of the next generation had some experience of the capital. They had thoroughly enjoyed themselves and chattered constantly, as the Nissan Patrol drove over the high Andean pass towards La Merced and the jungle, about the things they had seen. Although they were talking in Ashaninka, which none of us understood, their spontaneous hilarity and hoots of laughter, as they commented on things as strange as horses, set the whole car load of adults off into fits of companionable mirth. Later, we were also impressed by their skill as they helped us to light fires to heat food and water, in conditions for which no Brownie pack or Woodcraft Folk experience had prepared us.

It is also problematic to describe as suffering the lives of the shanty-town families we know. Yes they do 'suffer' from worries and illnesses and bereavements which are not our lot. They have also been quick to appreciate our own family problems, with a sort of sympathy most of our Western friends seem not to know, which heals the pain of bereavements and disappointments. By using the words suffering and suffer so frequently, we think we may have been guilty of an injustice, by implying passivity instead of action and indulging in the very pornography of misery we criticize. If we have failed to tread surely the fine line between the romanticism of poverty and wallowing in it, we apologize. We are as subject as anyone else to cultural straitjackets.

We did not set out to sum up the world in 12 short case studies, nor do we feel there is any particular political message in our words. We chose the same order as UNICEF to rank our studies. That is to say, from the highest under-five mortality rate (U5MR) to the lowest in order. Sierra Leone, Somalia and Mozambique are what UNICEF calls very high U5MR countries: there are more than 170 deaths per 1,000 children. Cuba alone is in the group of low U5MR countries. Nevertheless that does not itself support any argument that socialism is better than capitalism. Sierra Leone cannot be seen as a capitalist country; Mozambique has a legitimate socialist government, although in a state of civil war — a divided and poverty-stricken country. We chose countries that cover a range of pre-capitalist, early to advanced capitalist, and different types of centrally planned economies. This does not correlate exactly with the order according to U5MR. It could be argued that India and Nicaragua should be exchanged and that Thailand, for instance, is misplaced.

Although we have described Third World countries, we do not exclude countries like our own from the analysis. Not so many generations ago, the life expectancy here was about the same as in Sierra Leone today. At a recent social history seminar, we heard one student say that it was 'hardly worth living' in England in the conditions prevailing a century ago, when our grandmothers were born. The student saw the misery from a woman's point of view. From early teens to an early death a woman bore children; some survived infancy and childhood, many did not. When she was not bearing children, her life was a drudgery of work within and for the family. She may have died in pregnancy, at birth or because of it, or a life of hard work may have broken her strength and will to survive. Men, we add, had no bed of roses; as today, their spouses frequently outlived them. Long, hard years of low-paid labour made sure of that.

That view takes social history at face value. It is a narrow perspective that tells us very little about conditions for all members of society. Children worked from the earliest ages; families depended on every member contributing to their common survival. There was no education, therefore little literacy; no health and welfare provision; no drugs or vaccines; sanitation was poor; just about every possible thing we can think of must have been unfavourable. The comparison with any country today should end there, because it raises ethical questions. How dare we allow Sierra Leone, or any other country, to have worse conditions of life than our own? How can we account for a life expectancy of 36 years and for the death of almost 300 in every 1,000 children, when we expect to live more than twice as long and when we feel that eleven in every 1,000 children dying is eleven too many? We now live in a society where four generations of a family are very likely to be alive, five is becoming more common and six is not unheard of. A 36-year-old may still receive many of the privileges and protections of childhood from doting parents and grandparents. In Sierra Leone it is unlikely that the average person will be a grandparent for very long.

One of the chief distinctions between First and Third worlds is the proportion of people in different age groups. Our Peruvian friends often comment when they first arrive in Europe that there must be many families without children, because they see so few children and so many elderly people on buses and trains. For our part we never cease to be amazed by the teeming hordes of schoolchildren on buses and streets as school hours begin and end in Lima. The world population was reckoned to have reached five billion on 11 July 1987. That five-billionth child, wherever it was born, will be 13 years old in the year 2,000 — if it survives. We often hear that there is a population problem, and this is sometimes translated into anti-natalist policies. But the problem really is one of redistribution and re-education in the use of resources. The problem is that there is no global planning capacity which can cope with this number of new citizens. If there were, and if technology and resources were properly harnessed and harvested, this could be a beautiful world for as many as 20 billion people. In the sad mess we have made of this planet, the greatest number of children, the greatest strains on resources and the greatest suffering are all in what has been made into the Third World.

The first part of the book considered the ten principles of the United Nations Declaration of the Rights of the Child. Our country studies show how far most childhoods stray from this ideal. Life itself is not always too short, but childhood always is. Yet it holds the key to the future and thus we owe it to all children to make them aware of what basic human rights are. They cannot speak out against violations of rights they do not know they have. They also cannot speak out if we do not listen. Where do children stand in the international arena in which the new Convention is discussed? The answer is simple: they are left outside, marginalized, while elder stateswomen and men decide their future. Little attention is paid to their points of view, less to their perceived needs, which are also decided by elders.

Writing the case studies was the hardest part of this book, indeed the most difficult piece of writing we have ever done. This was not only because we had to work our way through so much distressing and frustrating material, and to work through our own anger at the same time. It was also hard because children are so invisible, which is a paradox because their images are so visible. In the case of Mozambique, for example, it would not have been difficult to assemble a huge photographic collection of Mozambican children, who remain extraordinarily photogenic even in extreme misery. These photographs adorn (this is the only possible word) articles on the economy, the guerrilla fighting and the famine. Nameless, speechless children stare out through the camera lenses of newspaper reporters (for whom they often gain prizes), unable to tell their story. They are usually only referred to in the text through the caption; for example 'A young refugee in Mozambique's Quelimane province faces an uncertain future' (Brittain 1988). The toddler concerned, wrapped shyly in his hooded sweater, was actually only facing the cameraman, of course.

Official statistics tell us little more. Children are accounted for by their deaths, illnesses and school attendance. Hard facts about children are hard to come by in many countries, which accounts for the different lengths of our case studies. On a worldwide basis, there is a great deal more information about children under five and over 15 than about any other age group. Between five and 15 they disappear into schools (perhaps), but of their lives we know very little. In First and Third World countries their statistical presence is contained in family statistics, usually separated by gender but seldom by any meaningful age characteristics. The most usual age-groups provided are 0–1, 2–5, 5–10, 10–15/19, which are simply not fine enough to catch the delicate nuances of growing up. Larger age intervals may work for statistics about adults, but to mix 10-year-olds and 15-year-olds in this way is to go against one's observation of the physical, social, emotional, sexual and political differences separating them. It is actually 10–12-year-olds who are the least visible in statistics. The most puzzling group of the next generation, those who are now reaching puberty and who will reach full adulthood at the turn of the century, is the group about whom we know least in any country.

In family statistics, the tendency is to use either the household or the mother as the statistical unit. Thus it is possible to tell how many families have a mother as household head and how many families have four, five or six children. But no one knows how many children live in one-parent families, or how many children live with more than five siblings. If the child were made a unit of statistics, which could be achieved using figures already available, we should know more about the way in which childhoods are experienced (Sgritti 1987).

Few researchers bother to collect children's words as opposed to the images which exist in photography or in the researcher's mind. The best we have is usually anecdotal and this was where we often experienced the greatest difficulty collecting material. Although accounts of individual children do appear in various sources, closer research often reveals the same anecdote endlessly repeated, usually in work published well after the child concerned would have been expected to reach adulthood (see Ennew 1986 (a)). Moreover, the image presented, besides being a product of the reporter rather than the child, seldom provides children with opinions. Does no one ever listen to children? Does no one ever ask them what they think and give them time to reply properly? It is, in fact, more relevant that the Mozambican toddler is looking at a strange man pointing a camera than at a posited uncertain future. Why are words so often put in their mouths?

Our observation of child-oriented aid programmes over the past decade led us to the conclusion that the bigger and more powerful an organization, the less likely will a child's point of view be represented within it. United Nations agencies are perhaps the least sensitive of all, with some of the large charities following close behind. That is not to say that everyone in those organizations is insensitive to children themselves. In the field there are many faithful and dedicated people who give everything they have to give to children. But in New York, Geneva, Rome, Vienna and London, highly paid executives are using children as pawns in games that are played out between competing agencies. Competition is inevitable when several large groups are bidding for relatively little money, but what a pity it is that, once money is found, it does not all flow evenly through the system. On the contrary, there are many grassroots organizations that are also competing for funds. Their priority is to find money for their work. Although the age of the aristocratic or wealthy philanthropist is over, this is where their ilk can be found today. They are seldom now wealthy, independent people, but they are no less devoted to their work. They are the most sensitive to children's needs. That is where children are always visible, unlike the situation 'at the top' where glossy photographs of starving children are hung out on sterile, white reception area walls.

The invisibility of children, the way in which their interests are subsumed under those of different groups, is clear in two recent Oxfam publications. It is not deliberate, and results from the desire most aid agencies now show to be sensitive to women's issues. Oxfam published two special reports on Mozambique in 1987, both of which we used in our country study. The first, written by Julian Quan, gives a very competent and well researched account of the general situation and has a special section on women, but no such treatment is accorded to children. Indeed they are referred to as 'kids' on page 16 (imagine the furore if Quan had referred to women as 'chicks'). But more serious than this is the picture of a small *girl* carrying a water bucket on her head, on page 23, which is captioned '*Women* spend several hours each day fetching the family water supply' (our emphasis).

The second publication is a photographic report called *Chicualacuala: Life on the Front Line* in which sensitivity to women's issues is carried to extreme lengths at the expense of children of both sexes. Pages 22 and 23 deal with the topic of food. Women are described as having to do all the tasks of food preparation and production even though, of three photographs used, only one shows women preparing food. The other two show children engaged in these tasks, and it is perfectly clear that some of these children are boys. Moreover, the text complains: 'As more schools are built and more children attend classes there are fewer helping hands at home — and it is women who will have to take on still more of the work' (p. 23). This contradicts our own data from Jamaica and Peru, which indicate that children take a heavy share of household tasks on top of a hard day at school and often earning in the street as well. Some mothers even appear particularly lazy and exploitative of their captive slaves. As yet nobody has made that into an 'issue'.

We do not want to give the impression that all organizations are insensitive; nothing could be more untrue. Some are genuinely concerned to put children first, and are not fiercely competitive or bureaucratized; their salaries at all levels are low and they are careful not to mix issues. We only wish they could all be this way.

The rights and needs of human beings are political in every sense, but we ought to decide how far this politicization should be allowed to extend. Certainly not into the agencies themselves. Children have been political pawns far too long: used whenever they were needed. Slogans for recruitment to war using children, such as Jack Cornwell or Khomeini's martyrs, are an obvious example. But newspapers also use headlines and pictures of children to draw attention to articles in which they are not mentioned. The emotive use of possible dangers to or benefits for children are exploited by political parties of all persuasions to gain votes. Even in the more benign situation of the World Food Conference the image of 'the child' (whoever heard of 'the adult'?) is manipulated, albeit for good reason. The United Nations convened the last meeting in Rome in 1974. World food production and stocks were low and prices were climbing to new heights. Henry Kissinger vowed that 'within a decade, no child will go to bed hungry, . . . no family will fear for its next day's bread.' Something went wrong. Today, in 1988, UNICEF tell us that 40,000 children still die daily from hunger or hunger-related illness. We know that the European Economic Community and the United States are producing in excess of their needs and that global redistribution of those stocks will be suggested. Rhetorically all possible solutions can be proposed; in practice children still go to bed hungry.

In her latest book, the economist Susan George expounds the view that solutions to hunger and the effective expansion of development projects will come from within the Third World nations. She believes small farmers have that potential (George 1988). Many of the people working those farms are children. If, as she wishes, those farmers gain access to research, fair prices, marketing and credit, how do they use them without education? If their children were taught how to use them, then possibly the next generation of small farmers would be far better off than their parents. If, as she also advocates, they were given more political power in their own societies, perhaps the need for crusades by outsiders like ourselves would no longer be necessary. We are probably unrealistic to hope that we are like Dorothy, standing at the beginning of the Yellow Brick Road — one day it may all seem like a bad dream we had last night.

In 1989, a decade after the International Year of the Child, the Convention on the Rights of the Child is due to be presented to the world at the General Assembly of the United Nations. First of all we have to see who endorses it, who signs it and finally who ratifies it. It will then need to be implemented by national authorities. We will then see who turns the articles of the Convention into practice. Our hopes are not high, but each improvement is a step forward, and the Convention may help many children take several. What is important about it is that it implies that children should have the right to articulate their views. If a full interpretation of Article 7 includes the right to express those views to the United Nations, then perhaps we will eventually see a child stand up in front of the General Assembly and say 'We children . . .'

Children have never been given their own place in the theories human beings have developed to explain the mysteries of their existence. Children are absorbed into countless '-isms' and '-ologies', are hidden factors in a few '-ics' and can be found lost in the 'fogs' of a number of '-ions'. The '-osophies' and '-ographies' seem generally to have passed them over.

Who has ever heard of '*childism*'? The idea of ageism exists because of our attitude toward the elderly or persons older than ourselves, sometimes, for their attitude to younger persons, who tend to be adults rather than children. With very few exceptions, racism is geared to adult situations. Sexism largely overlooks children's problems. Feminism has adopted children to its own, although it is backward in answering the difficult question about when a boy becomes a man.

And '*childology*'? Psychology looks at them and decides what they are and what is wrong with them, rather than what is right with them. Sociology occasionally separates them as numbers when empirical demands have to be met. Ideology forgets them. Doxology too. Theology seems more concerned about the 'Virgin Birth' and a sentimental celebration of childhood innocence.

Nor are there any '*childics*'. Paediatrics do belong to children, but only to their bodies. Economics ignore them. Politics take us full circle to '-isms' because it matters little whether we look at conservatism, liberalism or socialism, fascism, communism or anarchism, no one gives children a voice.

'*Childion*' is such a foreign looking word we could never expect it to exist. The same religion that makes display of the saying 'Suffer the little children to come unto me' is often party to their greatest suffering. But it would be hard to say what religion has a better record, certainly not one that demands children to be martyrs in a holy war. Fiction has done somewhat better but, unfortunately, it does little to improve real lives.

Apart from sounding like a medical instrument, '*childosophy*' does not exist. Philosophy and theosophy are ways of knowing which do not know children.

It almost seems irreverent that there are no '*childographies*', considering so many things have been bent into that framework already. There is no geography of childhood. They are a boon to photography, not infrequently in the form of pornography. Biography and autobiography sometimes include quite graphic illustrations, but not as often as they should since everyone owes adulthood to having had a childhood.

If children are present they are not necessarily seen, and very rarely heard. But why invent '-isms', '-ologies' or anything else for children when so far these theories seem to do adults so little good? As soon as an '-ism' exists the whole process takes on abnormal proportions. Since we are all human beings we should cast aside these devices. What remains to be said is that of all '-isms' we think that optimism should be foremost and if any '-ologies' are to mean anything at all then it should be the apologies we owe children for generations of neglect.

Epilogue

We dedicated this book to Carla, who was then eight years old. Her mother tells us that when the news reached her in hospital in Munich, her face lit up at the idea of a 'whole book for me about all the children in the world'. She knew she was dying and a few days later she joined many other eight-year-olds whose lives needlessly ended in childhood. She is our personal symbol of the real tragedy. Had she been born in Europe rather than in Peru, she would probably have had more ready access to both diagnosis and treatment. But she lost precious time because she was a Third World child. Until just before she died, friends of her family all over Europe, made through her mother's devotion to the welfare of slum children in Lima, had been desperately trying to raise the funds for a bone marrow transplant operation, which she never became strong enough to have. At least she and her parents and brother Miguel were given some hope and her journey in search of life half-way across the world brought home to her German doctor the need to teach his colleagues in Latin America the techniques of treating childhood leukaemia, which now save the lives of up to 60 per cent of sufferers in developed countries.

This eight-year-old, who grew too tall and too thin because of her therapy, and blithely hid the loss of her dark curls under a red woollen hat, is also a symbol of something else for us. She was positive in her approach to her illness and to the unpleasant radiation and chemical treatments she had to endure. She developed a philosophical approach to cultural and linguistic differences and also remarked how lucky it was that she had always liked to sit and read or draw, because this made the tedium of treatment more bearable for her. In this Carla showed how important it is not to pity and look down on children, even when they are deserving of compassion and help. First or Third World, they are individuals with stories to hear and wisdom to learn from, before we have the temerity to discipline, patronize, control and punish them.

Appendix

United Nations Draft Convention on the Rights of the Child

Declaration of the Rights of Mozambican Children

United Nations Draft Convention on the Rights of the Child

(text of the Convention adopted to 1988)

1978	–	The Government of Poland submits a proposed text to the Commission on Human Rights for a UN Convention on the Rights of the Child (E/CN.4/1349) with a view to its adoption in 1979, the International Year of the Child.
1979	–	At the request of the UN General Assembly an open-ended working group is set up in Geneva by the Commission on Human Rights to draft a convention using the Polish text as the basic working document. The working group meets for the first time.
1981	–	The Polish Government revises its original proposal and this becomes the working document for the group (A/C.3/36/6).
1979–1987	–	The group meets for one week per year (generally in the week preceding the opening of the UN Commission on Human Rights in Geneva, i.e., end of January).
1985	–	The Polish Government submits a text modifying the proposed articles which remain to be adopted (A/C.3/40/3).
1988	–	The group meets for two weeks and the first reading of the Convention is completed.
Nov–Dec 1988	–	The working group finalizes the second reading of the text.
1989	–	The 10th Anniversary of the International Year of the Child.

1989 — The 30th Anniversary of the UN Declaration of the Rights of the Child.

It is hoped that 1989 will also be the year in which the Convention on the Rights of the Child will be adopted by the United Nations General Assembly.

The Role of Non-Governmental Organizations

1983	–	An informal ad hoc group composed of International Non-Governmental Organizations (INGOs) is established to prepare joint INGO proposals and submit them to the UN working group.
1983–1987	–	INGOs meet twice a year to prepare their participation in the UN working group and submit joint proposals.

*   *   *   *   *

March 1988 — The Preamble and 51 Articles have been adopted, many of which have their origins in NGO proposals.

*   *   *   *   *

ARTICLES ADOPTED
1979 – 1988

*Preamble

Art. 1	– Definition of a child
*Art. 1 bis	– Right to Life, Child's Survival and Development
Art. 2	– Right to Name and Nationality
Art. 3	– Best Interests of Child; primary consideration
Art. 4	– Non-discrimination
Art. 5	– Implementation by States of Rights Recognized
*Art. 5 bis	– Parental Direction and Guidance
Art. 6	– Parental Care/Non-separation from Parents
Art. 6 bis	– Family Reunification/Contact with Parents
Art. 6 ter	– Illicit Transfer and Non-return of Children
Art. 7	– Child's Right to Express Opinions
*Art. 7a	– Freedom of Expression and Information
Art. 7 bis	– Freedom of Thought, Conscience and Religion
*Art. 7 ter	– Freedom of Association and Freedom of Peaceful Assembly
*Art. 7 quater	– Privacy, Honour, Reputation
Art. 8	– Parent/Guardian Responsibility in Upbringing
Art. 8 bis	– Protection from Abuse (by the family or by legal guardians)
Art. 9	– Access to Information
Art. 9 bis	– Preservation of Identity
Art. 10	– Substitute Care
Art. 11	– Adoption
Art. 11 bis	– Refugee Child
Art. 12	– Disabled Child
*Art. 12 bis	– Health and Access to Medical Services
Art. 12 ter	– Periodic Review of Care, Protection and Medical Treatment
Art. 13	– Social Security
*Art. 14	– Standard of Living
Art. 15	– Education
Art. 16	– Objectives of Education
Art. 16 bis	– Children belonging to Minorities or Indigenous Populations
Art. 17	– Play, Leisure, Participation in Cultural and Artistic Life
Art. 18	– Protection from Economic Exploitation
Art. 18 bis	– Protection from Narcotic and Psychotropic Substances
Art. 18 ter	– Protection from Sexual Exploitation
Art. 18 quater	– Prevention of Abduction, Sale or Traffic in Children
Art. 18 quinto	– Protection from All Other Forms of Exploitation
*Art. 18 sixt	– Physical and Psychological Recovery and Social Re-integration of Victims of Exploitation and Torture
Art. 19	– Treatment in Penal Matters
*Art. 20	– Armed Conflicts

Text of the Draft Convention of the Rights of the Child Adopted by the Working Group

PREAMBLE

The States Parties to the Convention,

Considering that in accordance with the principles proclaimed in the Charter of the United Nations, recognition of the inherent dignity and of the equal and inalienable rights of all members of the human family is the foundation of freedom, justice and peace in the world,

Bearing in mind that the peoples of the United Nations have, in the Charter, reaffirmed their faith in fundamental human rights and in the dignity and worth of the human person, and have determined to promote social progress and better standards of life in larger freedom,

Recognizing that the United Nations has, in the Universal Declaration of Human Rights and in the International Covenants on Human Rights, proclaimed and agreed that everyone is entitled to all the rights and freedoms set forth therein, without distinction of any kind, such as race, colour, sex, language, religion, political or other opinion, national or social origin, property, birth or other status,

Recalling that, in the Universal Declaration of Human Rights, the United Nations has proclaimed that childhood is entitled to special care and assistance,

Convinced that the family, as the basic unit of society and the natural environment for the growth and well-being of all its members and particularly children, should be afforded the necessary protection and assistance so that it can fully assume its responsibilities within the community,

Recognizing that, as indicated in the Declaration of the Rights of the Child adopted in 1959, the child, due to the needs of his physical and mental development, requires particular care and assistance with regard to health, physical, mental, moral and social development, and requires legal protection in conditions of freedom, dignity and security,

Recognizing that the child, for the full and harmonious development of his personality, should grow up in a family environment, in an atmosphere of happiness, love and understanding,

Recognizing that in all countries in the world there are children living in exceptionally difficult conditions, and that such children need special consideration,*

Bearing in mind that the need for extending particular care to the child has been stated in the Geneva Declaration on the Rights of the Child of 1924 and in the Declaration of the Rights of the Child adopted by the United Nations in 1959 and recognized in the Universal Declaration of Human Rights, in the International Covenant on Civil and Political Rights (in particular in articles 23 and 24) in the International Covenant on Economic, Social and Cultural Rights (in particular in its article 10) and in the statutes of specialized agencies and international organizations concerned with the welfare of children,

Considering that the child should be fully prepared to live an individual life in society, and brought up in the spirit of the ideals proclaimed in the Charter of the United Nations, and in particular in the spirit of peace, dignity, tolerance, freedom and brotherhood,

Have agreed as follows:

Article 1

According to the present Convention a child is every human being to the age of 18 years unless, under the law of his State, he has attained his age of majority earlier.

Article 1 bis*

1. The States' Parties to the present Convention recognize that every child has the inherent right to life.

2. States' Parties shall ensure to the maximum extent possible the survival and development of the child.

Article 2

1. The child shall have the right from his birth to a name and to acquire a nationality.

2. The States' Parties to the present Convention shall ensure that their legislation recognizes the principle according to which a child shall acquire the nationality of the State in the territory of which he has been born if, at the time of the child's birth, he is not granted nationality by any other State in accordance with its laws.

Article 3

1. In all actions concerning children, whether undertaken by public or private social welfare institutions, courts of law, or administrative authorities, the best interests of the child shall be a primary consideration.

2. In all judicial or administrative proceedings affecting a child that is capable of forming his own views, an opportunity shall be provided for the views of the child to be heard, either directly or indirectly through a representative, as a party to the proceedings, and those views shall be taken into consideration by the competent authorities, in a manner consistent with the procedures followed in the State Party for the application of its legislation.

3. The States' Parties to the present Convention undertake to ensure the child such protection and care as is necessary for his well-being, taking into account the rights and duties of his parents, legal guardians, or other individuals legally responsible for him, and, to this end, shall take all appropriate legislative and administrative measures.

4. The States' Parties to the present Convention shall ensure competent supervision of officials and personnel of institutions directly responsible for the care of children.

Article 4

1. The States's Parties to the present Convention shall respect and extend all the rights set forth in this Convention to each child in their territories without distinction of any kind, irrespective of the child's or his parent's or legal guardian's race, colour, sex, language, religion, political or other opinion, national or social origin, family status, ethnic origin, cultural beliefs or practices, property, educational attainment, birth, or any other basis whatever.

2. States' Parties to the present Convention shall take all appropriate measures to ensure that the child is protected against all forms of discrimination or punishment on the basis of the status, activities, expressed opinions, or beliefs of the child's parents, legal guardians, or other family members.

Article 5

The States' Parties to the present Convention shall undertake all appropriate administrative and legislative measures, in accordance with their available resources, and, where needed, within the framework of international co-operation, for the implementation of the rights recognized in this Convention.

Article 5 bis*

The States' Parties to the present Convention shall respect the responsibilities, rights, and duties of parents or, where applicable, legal guardians or other individuals legally responsible for the child, to provide, in a manner consistent with the evolving capacities of the child, appropriate direction and guidance in the exercise by the child of the rights recognized in the present Convention.

Article 6

1.   The States' Parties to the present Convention recognize that the child should enjoy parental care and should have his place of residence determined by his parent(s), except as provided herein.

2.   States' Parties shall ensure that a child shall not be separated from his parents against their will, except when competent authorities subject to judicial review determine, in accordance with applicable law and procedures, that such separation is necessary for the best interests of the child. Such a determination may be necessary in a particular case such as one involving abuse or neglect of the child by the parents, or one where the parents are living separately and a decision must be made as to the child's place of residence. Such determinations shall not be made until all interested parties have been given an opportunity to participate in the proceedings and to make their views known. Such views shall be taken into account by the competent authorities in making their determination.

3.   A child who is separated from one or both parents has the right to maintain personal relations and direct contacts with both parents on a regular basis, save in exceptional circumstances.

4.   Where such separation results from any action initiated by a State party, such as the detention, imprisonment, exile, deportation or death (including death arising from any cause while the person is in the custody of the State) of one or both parents or of the child, that State Party shall, upon request, provide the parents, the child or, if appropriate, another member of the family with essential information concerning the whereabouts of the absent member(s) of the family unless the provision of the information would be detrimental to the well-being of the child. States' Parties shall further ensure that the submission of such a request shall of itself entail no adverse consequences for the person(s) concerned.

Article 6 bis

1.   In accordance with the obligation of States' Parties under Article 6, paragraph 2, applications by a child or his parents to enter or leave a State Party for the purpose of family reunification shall be dealt with by States' Parties in a positive, humane and expeditious manner. States' Parties shall further ensure that the submission of such a request shall entail no adverse consequences for the applicants and for the members of their family.

2.   A child whose parents reside in different States shall have the right to maintain on a regular basis, save in exceptional circumstances, personal relations and direct contacts with both parents. Towards that end and in accordance with the obligation of States' Parties under Article 6, paragraph 2, States' Parties shall respect the right of the child and his parents to leave any country, including their own, and to enter their own country. The right to leave any country shall be subject only to such restrictions as are prescribed by law and which are necessary to protect the national security, public order (*ordre public*), public health or morals or the rights and freedoms of others and are consistent with the other rights recognized in the present Convention.

Article 6 ter

1.   The States' Parties to the present Convention shall take appropriate measures to combat the illicit transfer and non-return of children abroad.

2.   To this end, the States' Parties shall promote the conclusion of bilateral or multilateral agreements or accession to existing agreements, as well as the introduction of periodic consultations between the competent national authorities.

Article 7

The States' Parties to the present Convention shall assure to the child who is capable of forming his own views the right to express his opinion freely in all matters, the wishes of the child being given due weight in accordance with his age and maturity.

Article 7a*

1. The child shall have the right to freedom of expression; this right shall include freedom to seek, receive and impart information and ideas of all kinds, regardless of frontiers, either orally, in writing or in print, in the form of art, or through any other media of the child's choice.

2. The exercise of this right may be subject to certain restrictions, but these shall only be such as are provided by law and are necessary:

   (a) for respect of the rights and reputations of others; or

   (b) for the protection of national security or of public order (*ordre public*), or of public health or morals.

Article 7 bis

1. The States' Parties to the present Convention shall respect the right of the child to freedom of thought, conscience and religion.

2. This right shall include in particular the freedom to have or to adopt a religion or whatsoever belief of his choice and freedom, either individually or in community with others and in public or private, to manifest his religion or belief, subject only to such limitations as are prescribed by law and are necessary to protect public safety, order, health and morals, and the right to have access to education in the matter of religion or belief.

3. The States' Parties shall respect the rights and duties of the parents and, where applicable, legal guardians, to provide direction to the child in the exercise of his right in a manner consistent with the evolving capacities of the child.

4. The States' Parties shall equally respect the liberty of the child and his parents and, where applicable, legal guardians, to ensure the religious and moral education of the child in conformity with convictions of their choice.

Article 7 ter*

1. The States' Parties to the present Convention recognize the rights of the child to freedom of association and to freedom of peaceful assembly.

2. No restrictions may be placed on the exercise of these rights other than those imposed in conformity with the law and which are necessary in a democratic society in the interests of national security or public safety, public order (*ordre public*), the protection of public health or morals or the protection of the rights and freedoms of others.

Article 7 quater*

1. The States' Parties to the present Convention recognize the right of the child not to be subjected to arbitrary or unlawful interference with his or her privacy, family, home or correspondence, nor to unlawful attacks on his or her honour and reputation.

2. The child has the right to the protection of the law against such interference or attacks.

Article 8

1. Parents or, as the case may be, guardians, have the primary responsibility for the upbringing and development of the child. The best interests of the child will be their basic concern. States' Parties shall use their best efforts to ensure recognition of the principle that

both parents have common and similar responsibilities for the upbringing and development of the child.

2.   For the purpose of guaranteeing and promoting the rights set forth in this Convention, the States' Parties to the present Convention shall render appropriate assistance to parents and guardians in the performance of the child-rearing responsibilities and shall ensure the development of institutions for the care of children.

3.   States' Parties shall take all appropriate measures to ensure that children of working parents have the right to benefit from child care services and facilities for which they are eligible.

4.   The institutions, services and facilities referred to in paragraphs 2 and 3 of this article shall conform with the standards established by competent authorities particularly in the areas of safety, health, and in the number and suitability of their staff.

Article 8 bis

1.   The States' Parties to the present Convention shall take all appropriate legislative, administrative, social and educational measures to protect the child from all forms of physical or mental injury or abuse, neglect or negligent treatment, maltreatment or exploitation including sexual abuse, while in the care of parent(s), legal guardian(s) or any other person who has the care of the child.

2.   Such protective measures should, as appropriate, include effective procedures for the establishment of social programmes to provide necessary support for the child and for those who have the care of the child, as well as for other forms of prevention and for identification, reporting, referral, investigation, treatment, and follow-up of instances of child maltreatment described heretofore, and, as appropriate, for judicial involvement.

Article 9

The States' Parties to the present Convention recognize the important function performed by the mass media and shall ensure that the child has access to information and material from a diversity of national and international sources, including those aimed at the promoting of his social, spiritual and moral well-being and physical and mental health. To this end, the State's Parties shall:

(a) Encourage the mass media agencies to disseminate information and material of social and cultural benefit to the child and in accordance with the spirit of article 16;

(b) Encourage international co-operation in the production, exchange and dissemination of such information and material from a diversity of cultural, national and international sources;

(c) Encourage the production and dissemination of children's books;

(d) Encourage the mass media agencies to have particular regard to the linguistic needs of the child who belongs to a minority group or an indigenous population;

(e) Encourage the development of appropriate guidelines for the protection of the child from information and material potentially injurious to his well-being bearing in mind the provisions of article 8.

Article 9 bis

1.   The States' Parties to the present Convention undertake to respect the right of the child to preserve his or her identity (nationality, name, family relations as recognized by law) without unlawful interference.

2.   Where a child is illegally deprived of some or all of the elements of his or her identity, the States' Parties shall provide appropriate assistance and protection, with a view to speedily re-establishing his or her identity.

Article 10

1. A child permanently or temporarily deprived of his family environment for any reason shall be entitled to special protection and assistance provided by the State.

2. The States' Parties to the present Convention shall ensure that a child who is parentless, or who is temporarily or permanently deprived of his family environment, or who in his best interests cannot be brought up or be allowed to remain in that environment shall be provided with alternative family care which could include, *inter alia*, adoption, foster placement, or placement in suitable institutions for the care of children. When considering alternative family care for the child and the best interests of the child, due regard shall be paid to the desirability of continuity in a child's upbringing and to the child's ethnic, religious or linguistic background.

Article 11

1. The States' Parties to the present Convention shall undertake measures, where appropriate, to facilitate the process of adoption of the child. Adoption of a child shall be authorized only by competent authorities who determine, in accordance with applicable law and procedures and on the basis of all pertinent and reliable information, that the adoption is permissible in view of the child's status concerning parents, relatives and guardians and that, if required, the appropriate persons concerned have given their informed consent to the adoption on the basis of such counselling as may be necessary.

2. The States' Parties to the present Convention shall take all appropriate measures to secure the best interests of the child who is the subject of intercountry adoption. States' Parties shall ensure that placements are made by authorized agencies or appropriate persons under the adequate supervision of competent authorities, providing the same safeguards and standards that are applied in exclusively domestic adoptions. The competent authorities shall make every possible effort to ensure the legal validity of the adoption in the countries involved. States' Parties shall endeavour, where appropriate, to promote these objectives by entering into bilateral or multilateral agreements.

Article 11 bis

The States' Parties to the present Convention shall take appropriate measures to ensure that a child who is seeking refugee status or who is considered a refugee in accordance with applicable international or domestic law and procedures shall, whether unaccompanied or accompanied by his parents, legal guardians or close relatives, receive appropriate protection and humanitarian assistance in the enjoyment of applicable rights set forth in this Convention and other international human rights or humanitarian instruments to which the said States are Parties. In view of the important functions performed in refugee protection and assistance matters by the United Nations and other competent intergovernmental and non-governmental organizations, the States' Parties to the present Convention shall provide appropriate co-operation in any efforts by these organizations to protect and assist such a child and to trace the parents or other close relatives of an unaccompanied refugee child in order to obtain information necessary for reunification with his family. In cases where no parents, legal guardians or close relatives can be found, the child shall be accorded the same protection as any other child permanently or temporarily deprived of his family environment for any reason, as set forth in the present Convention.

Article 12

1. The States' Parties to the present Convention recognize that a mentally or physically disabled child should enjoy a full and decent life in conditions which ensure his dignity, promote his self-reliance, and facilitate his active participation in the community.

2. The States' Parties to the present Convention recognize the right of the disabled child to special care and shall encourage and ensure the extension, subject to available resources, to the eligible child and those responsible for his care, of assistance for which application is made

and which is appropriate to the child's condition and to the circumstances of the parents or others caring for the child.

3. Recognizing the special needs of a disabled child, assistance extended in accordance with paragraph 2 shall be provided free of charge, whenever possible, taking into account the financial resources of the parents or others caring for the child, and shall be designed to ensure that the disabled child has effective access to and receives education, training, health care services, rehabilitation services, preparation for employment and recreation opportunities in a manner conducive to the child's achieving the fullest possible social integration and individual development, including his cultural and spiritual development.

2. States' Parties shall promote in the spirit of international co-operation the exchange of appropriate information in the field of preventive health care and of medical, psychological and functional treatment of disabled children, including dissemination of and access to information concerning methods of rehabilitation education and vocational services, with the aim of enabling States' Parties to improve their capabilities and skills and to widen their experience in these areas. In this regard, particular account shall be taken of the needs of developing countries.

Article 12 bis

1. The States' Parties to the present Convention recognize the right of the child to the enjoyment of the highest attainable standard of health and to medical and rehabilitation facilities. The States' Parties shall strive to ensure that no child is deprived for financial reasons of his right of access to such health care services.

2. The States' Parties to the present Convention shall pursue full implementation of this right and in particular, shall take appropriate measures to:

(a) diminish infant and child mortality,

(b) ensure the provision of necessary medical assistance and health care to all children with emphasis on the development of primary health care,

(c) combat disease and malnutrition within the framework of primary health care, through the application of readily available technology and through the provision of adequate nutritious foods and clean drinking water,*

(d) ensure appropriate health care for expectant mothers,*

(e) ensure that all segments of society, in particular parents and children, are informed, and supported in the use, of basic knowledge of child health and nutrition, the advantages of breast-feeding, hygiene and environmental sanitation and the prevention of accidents,*

(f) develop preventive health care and family planning education and services.

3. The States' Parties to the present Convention shall seek to take all effective and appropriate measures with a view to abolishing traditional practices prejudicial to the health of children.

4. States' Parties to the present Convention undertake to promote and encourage international co-operation with a view to achieving progressively the full realization of the right recognized in this article. In this regard particular account shall be taken of the needs of developing countries.

Article 12 ter

States' Parties to the present Convention recognize the right of a child who has been placed by the competent authorities for the purposes of care, protection, or treatment of his or her physical or mental health, to a periodic review of the treatment provided to the child and all other circumstances relevant to his or her placement.

Article 13

1.   The States' Parties to the present Convention shall, in a manner appropriate to national conditions, recognize for every child the right to benefit from social security and shall take the necessary measures to achieve the full realization of this right.

2.   The benefits should, where appropriate, be granted taking into account the national resources available and the resources and the circumstances of the child and persons having responsibility for the maintenance of the child as well as any other consideration relevant to an application for benefits made by or on behalf of the child.

Article 14

1.   The States' Parties to the present Convention recognize the right of every child to a standard of living adequate for the child's physical, mental, spiritual, moral and social development.

2.   The parent(s) or others responsible for the child have the primary responsibility to secure, within their abilities and financial capacities, the conditions of living necessary for the child's development.

3.   The States' Parties to the present Convention, in accordance with national conditions and within their means, shall take appropriate measures to assist parents and others responsible for the child to implement this right and shall in case of need provide material assistance and support programmes, particularly with regard to nutrition, clothing and housing.

4.   States' Parties to the present Convention shall take all appropriate measures to secure the recovery of maintenance for the child from the parents or other persons having financial responsibility for the child, both within the State Party and from abroad. In particular, where the person having financial responsibility for the child lives in a different state from the child, States' Parties shall promote the accession to international agreements or the conclusion of such agreements as well as the making of other appropriate arrangements.*

Article 15

1.   The States' Parties to the present Convention recognize the right of the child to education and, with a view to achieving the full realization of this right on the basis of equal opportunity, they shall, in particular:

(a)   make primary education free and compulsory as early as possible,

(b)   encourage the development of different forms of secondary education systems, both general and vocational, to make them available and accessible to all children, and take appropriate measures such as the introduction of free education and offering financial assistance in case of need,

(c)   make higher education equally accessible to all on the basis of capacity by every appropriate means.

2.   States' Parties shall take all appropriate measures to ensure that school discipline is administered in a manner reflective of the child's human dignity.

3.   The States' Parties to the present Convention shall respect the rights and duties of the parents and, where applicable, legal guardians to provide direction to the child in the exercise of his right to education in a manner consistent with the evolving capacities of the child.

4.   States' Parties to the present Convention shall promote and encourage international co-operation in matters relating to education, in particular with a view to contributing to the elimination of ignorance and illiteracy throughout the world and facilitating access to scientific and technical knowledge and modern teaching methods. In this regard, particular account shall be taken of the needs of developing countries.

Article 16

1. The States' Parties to the present Convention agree that the education of the child shall be directed to:

(a) The promotion of the development of the child's personality, talents and mental and physical abilities to their fullest potential and the fostering of respect for all human rights and fundamental freedoms.

(b) The preparation of the child for responsible life in a free society, in the spirit of understanding, peace, tolerance and friendship among all peoples, ethnic and religious groups.

(c) The development of respect for the natural environment and for the principles of the Charter of the United Nations.

(d) The development of respect for the child's own cultural identity and values, for the national values of the country in which the child is living, for civilizations different from its own, and for human rights and fundamental freedoms.

2. No part of paragraph 1 of this article shall be construed so as to interfere with the liberty of individuals and bodies to establish and direct educational institutions, subject always to the observance of the principles set forth in paragraph 1 and to the requirement that the education given in such institutions shall conform to such minimum standards as may be laid down by the State.

Article 16 bis

In those States in which ethnic, religious or linguistic minorities or indigenous populations exist, a child belonging to such minorities or populations shall not be denied the right, in community with other members of its group, to enjoy its own culture, to profess and practise its own religion, or to use its own language.

Article 17

1. States' Parties to the present Convention recognize the right of the child to rest and leisure, to engage in play and recreational activities appropriate to the age of the child and to participate freely in cultural life and the arts.

2. The States' Parties to the present Convention shall respect and promote the right of the child to fully participate in cultural and artistic life and shall encourage the provision of appropriate and equal opportunities for cultural, artistic, recreational and leisure activity.

Article 18

1. The States' Parties to the present Convention recognize the right of the child to be protected from economic exploitation and from performing any work that is likely to be hazardous or to interfere with the child's education, or to be harmful to the child's health or physical, mental, spiritual, moral or social development.

2. The States' Parties to the present Convention shall take legislative and administrative measures to ensure the implementation of this article. To this end, and having regard to the relevant provisions of other international instruments, the States' Parties shall in particular:

(a) provide for a minimum age or minimum ages for admission to employment;

(b) provide for appropriate regulation of the hours and conditions of employment; and

(c) provide for appropriate penalties or other sanctions to ensure the effective enforcement of this article.

Article 18 bis

The States' Parties to the present Convention shall take all appropriate measures, including legislative, social and educational measures, to protect children from the illegal use of narcotic and psychotropic substances as defined in the relevant international treaties, and to prevent the use of children in the illegal production and trafficking of such substances.

Article 18 ter

The States' Parties to the present Convention undertake to protect the child from all forms of sexual exploitation and sexual abuse. For these purposes the States' Parties shall in particular take all appropriate national, bilateral and multilateral measures to prevent:

(a) the inducement or coercion of a child to engage in any unlawful sexual activity;

(b) the exploitative use of children in prostitution or other unlawful sexual practices;

(c) the exploitative use of children in pornographic performances and materials.

Article 18 quater

The States' Parties to the present Convention shall take all appropriate national, bilateral and multilateral measures to prevent the abduction, the sale of or traffic in children for any purpose or in any form.

Article 18 quinto

The States' Parties to the present Convention shall protect the child against all other forms of exploitation prejudicial to any aspects of the child's welfare.

Article 18 sixt*

The States' Parties to the present Convention shall take all appropriate measures to ensure the physical and psychological recovery and social re-integration of a child victim of: any form of neglect, exploitation or abuse; torture or any other form of cruel, inhuman or degrading treatment or punishment. Such recovery and re-integration shall take place in an environment which fosters the health, self-respect and dignity of the child.

Article 19

1. States' Parties to the present Convention recognize the right of children who are accused or recognized as having infringed the penal law to be treated in a manner which is consistent with promoting their sense of dignity and worth and intensifying their respect for the human rights and fundamental freedoms of others, and which takes into account their age and the desirability of promoting their rehabilitation.

2. To this end, and having regard to the relevant provisions of international instruments, the States' Parties to the present Convention shall, in particular, ensure that:

(a) no child is arbitrarily detained or imprisoned or subjected to torture, cruel, inhuman or degrading treatment or punishment;

(b) capital punishment or life imprisonment without possibility of release is not imposed for crimes committed by persons below 18 years of age;

(c) children accused of infringing the penal law:

   (i) are presumed innocent until proven guilty according to law;

   (ii) are informed promptly of the charges against them and, as of the time of being accused, have legal or other appropriate assistance in the preparation and presentation of their defence;

   (iii) have the matter determined according to law in a fair hearing within a reasonable period of time by an independent and impartial tribunal; and

   (iv) if found guilty are entitled to have their conviction and sentence reviewed by a higher tribunal according to law.

3. An essential aim of treatment of children found guilty of infringing the penal law shall be their reformation and social rehabilitation. A variety of dispositions, including programmes of education and vocational training and alternatives to institutional care shall be available to ensure that children are dealt with in a manner appropriate and proportionate both to their circumstances and the offence.

4. All children deprived of their liberty shall be treated with humanity and respect for the inherent dignity of the human person, and shall in particular:

(a) be brought as speedily as possible for adjudication;

(b) be separated from adults accused or convicted of having committed an offence unless it is considered in the child's best interest not to do so, or it is unnecessary for the protection of the child; and

(c) have the right to maintain contact with their family through correspondence and visits, save in exceptional circumstances.

Article 20

1. The States' Parties to the present Convention undertake to respect and to ensure respect for rules of international humanitarian law applicable to them in armed conflicts which are relevant to the child.

2. States' Parties to the present Convention shall take all feasible measures to ensure that no child takes a direct part in hostilities and they shall refrain in particular from recruiting any child who has not attained the age of 15 years into their armed forces. In recruiting among those persons who have attained the age of 15 years but who have not attained the age of 18 years, the States' Parties to the present Convention shall endeavour to give priority to those who are oldest.**

3. In accordance with their obligations under international humanitarian law to protect the civilian population in armed conflicts, States' Parties to this Convention shall take all feasible measures to ensure protection and care of children who are affected by an armed conflict.

Article 21

Nothing in this Convention shall affect any provisions that are more conducive to the realization of the rights of the child and that may be contained in:

(a) The law of a State Party; or

(b) Any other international convention, treaty or agreement in force for that State.

Article 21 bis

The States' Parties to the present Convention undertake to make the principles and provisions of the Convention widely known, by appropriate and active means, to adults and children alike.

Article 22*

1. For the purpose of examining the progress made by States' Parties in achieving the realization of the obligations undertaken in the present Convention, there shall be established a Committee on the Rights of the Child, which shall carry out the function hereinafter provided.

2. The Committee shall consist of 10 experts of high moral standing and recognized competence in the field covered by this Convention. The members of the Committee shall be elected by the States' Parties from among their nationals and shall serve in their personal capacity, consideration being given to equitable geographical distribution as well as to the principal legal systems.

3. The members of the Committee shall be elected by secret ballot from a list of persons

nominated by States' Parties. Each State Party may nominate one person from among its own nationals.

4.   The initial election to the Committee shall be held no later than six months after the date of the entry into force of the present Convention and thereafter every second year. At least four months before the date of each election, the Secretary-General of the United Nations shall address a letter to the States' Parties inviting them to submit their nominations within two months. The Secretary-General shall subsequently prepare a list in alphabetical order of all persons thus nominated, indicating the States' Parties which have nominated them, and shall submit it to the States' Parties to the present Convention.

5.   The elections shall be held at meetings of the States' Parties convened by the Secretary-General at United Nations Headquarters. At those meetings, for which two-thirds of the States' Parties shall constitute a quorum, the persons elected to the Committee shall be those who obtain the largest number of votes and an absolute majority of the votes of the representatives of States' Parties present and voting.

6.   The members of the Committee shall be elected for a term of four years. They shall be eligible for re-election if renominated. The term of 5 of the members elected at the first election shall expire at the end of two years; immediately after the first election the names of these 5 members shall be chosen by lot by the Chairman of the meeting.

7.   If a member of the Committee dies or resigns or for any other cause can no longer perform the duties of the Committee, the State Party which nominated the member shall appoint another expert from among its nationals to serve for the remainder of the term, subject to the approval of the Committee.

8.   The Committee shall establish its own rules of procedure.

9.   The Committee shall elect its officers for a period of two years.

10.   The meetings of the Committee shall normally be held at the United Nations Headquarters or at any other convenient place as determined by the Committee. The Committee shall normally meet annually. The duration of the meetings of the Committee shall be determined, and reviewed, if necessary, by a meeting of the States' Parties to the present Convention, subject to the approval of the General Assembly.

10 bis.   The Secretary-General of the United Nations shall provide the necessary staff and facilities for the effective performance of the functions of the Committee under the present Convention.

11.   [With the approval of the General Assembly, the members of the Committee established under the present Convention shall receive emoluments from the United Nations resources on such terms and conditions as the Assembly may decide.]

or

[States' Parties shall be responsible for the expenses of the members of the Committee while they are in performance of Committee duties.]

[12.   The States' Parties shall be responsible for expenses incurred in connection with the holding of meetings of the States' Parties and of the Committee, including reimbursement to the United Nations for any expenses, such as the cost of staff and facilities, incurred by the United Nations pursuant to Paragraph 10 of this Article.]

*Article 23**

1.   States' Parties to the present Convention undertake to submit to the Committee, through the Secretary-General of the United Nations, reports on the measures they have adopted which give effect to the rights recognized herein and on the progress made on the enjoyment of those rights:

(a) within two years of the entry into force of the Convention for the State Party concerned;

(b) thereafter every five years.

2.   Reports made under this Article shall indicate factors and difficulties, if any, affecting the degree of fulfilment of the obligations under the present Convention. Reports shall also contain sufficient information to provide the Committee with a comprehensive understanding of the implementation of the Convention in that country.

3.   A State Party which has submitted a comprehensive initial report to the Committee need not in its subsequent reports submitted in accordance with Paragraph 1(b) repeat basic information previously provided.

4.   The Committee may request from the State Parties further information relevant to the implementation of the Convention.

5.   The Committee shall submit to the General Assembly of the United Nations through the Economic and Social Council, every two years, reports on its activities.

6.   The States' Parties shall make their reports widely available to the public in their own countries.

Article 24*

In order to foster the effective implementation of the Convention and to encourage international co-operation in the field covered by the Convention:

(a)   The specialized agencies and UNICEF shall be entitled to be represented at the consideration of the implementation of such provisions of the present Convention as fall within the scope of their mandate. The Committee may invite the specialized agencies, UNICEF and other competent bodies as it may consider appropriate to provide expert advice on the implementation of the Convention in areas falling within the scope of their respective mandates. The Committee may invite the specialized agencies and UNICEF to submit reports on the implementation of the Convention in areas falling within the scope of their activities.

(b)   The Committee shall transmit, as it may consider appropriate, to the specialized agencies, UNICEF and other competent bodies, any reports from States' Parties that contain a request, or indicate a need, for technical advice or assistance along with the Committee's observations and suggestions, if any, on these requests or indications.

(c)   The Committee may recommend to the General Assembly to request the Secretary-General to undertake on its behalf studies on specific issues relating to the rights of the child.

(d)   The Committee may make suggestions and general recommendations based on information received pursuant to Articles 23 and 24 of this Convention. Such suggestions and general recommendations shall be transmitted to any State Party concerned and reported to the General Assembly, together with comments, if any, from States' Parties.

Article 25*

1.   The present Convention shall be open for signature by all States.

2.   The Secretary-General of the United Nations is designated as the depository of the present Convention.

3.   The present Convention is subject to ratification. Instruments of ratification shall be deposited with the Secretary-General of the United Nations.

4.   The present Convention shall be open to accession by all States. Accession shall be effected by the deposit of an instrument of accession with the Secretary-General of the United Nations.

Article 26*

1.   Any State Party to the present Convention may propose an amendment and file it with the

Secretary-General of the United Nations. The Secretary-General shall thereupon communicate the proposed amendment to the States' Parties to the present Convention with a request that they indicate whether they favour a conference of States' Parties for the purpose of considering and voting upon the proposals. In the event that within four months from the date of such communication at least one-third of the States' Parties favour such a conference, the Secretary-General shall convene the conference under the auspices of the United Nations. Any amendment adopted by a majority of the States' Parties present and voting at the conference shall be submitted to the General Assembly of the United Nations for approval.

2.   An amendment adopted in accordance with paragraph (1) of this Article shall enter into force when it has been approved by the General Assembly of the United Nations and accepted by a two-thirds majority of the States' Parties to this Convention.

3.   When an amendment enters into force, it shall be binding on those States' Parties which have accepted it, other States' Parties still being bound by the provisions of this Convention and any earlier amendments which they have accepted.

*Article 27**

1.   The present Convention shall enter into force on the thirtieth day after the date of deposit with the Secretary-General of the United Nations of the twentieth instrument of ratification or accession.

2.   For each State ratifying the present Convention or acceding to it after the deposit of the twentieth instrument of ratification or accession, the Convention shall enter into force on the thirtieth day after the date of the deposit of its own instrument of ratification or accession.

*Article 28**

1.   The Secretary-General of the United Nations shall receive and circulate to all States the text of reservations made by States at the time of ratification or accession.

2.   A reservation incompatible with the object and purpose of the present Convention shall not be permitted.

3.   Reservations may be withdrawn at any time by notification to this effect addressed to the Secretary-General of the United Nations, who shall then inform all States thereof. Such notification shall take effect on the date on which it is received.

*Article 29**

A State Party may denounce this Convention by written notification to the Secretary-General of the United Nations. Denunciation becomes effective one year after the date of receipt of the notification by the Secretary-General.

*Article 30**

The Secretary-General of the United Nations shall inform all States' Members of the United Nations and all States which have signed this Convention or acceded to it of the following:

   (a) Signatures, ratifications and accessions;

   (b) The date of entry into force of this Convention and the date of the entry into force of any amendments;

   (c) Denunciations.

*Article 31**

1.   This Convention, of which the Arabic, Chinese, English, French, Russian and Spanish

texts are equally authentic, shall be deposited with the Secretary-General of the United Nations.

2.   The Secretary-General of the United Nations shall transmit certified copies of this Convention to all States.

* Article, paragraph or sub-paragraph adopted by the Working Group in 1988.

** Last sentence adopted by the Working Group in 1988.

Declaration of the Rights of Mozambican Children

First – You, the children, are the ones who will carry on the Revolution. You are the hope of the future that shines in your smiles when you are happy. You are the guarantees of our socialist nation. Socialism means justice, means every citizen having the same rights and duties. What is written here is that every child has the same rights.

Second – You have the right to grow up in a climate of peace and security, surrounded by love and understanding.

Third – You have the right to live in a family. You have the right to a name, so that your parents, brothers and sisters and friends can call you and so that you can be known wherever you are. If you do not have your own family, you have the right to live in a family that loves you like their own child.

Fourth – In order to grow up strong and healthy, you have the right to be fed, sheltered, clothed and educated by your family.

You have the right to play and to practise sports, so that your body develops full of health and energy.

Fifth – You have the right to receive an education so that you will become a citizen of tomorrow. You have the right to know about the world in which you are living and how to transform it, to know the history and culture of your people, to learn to master science and technology. Your school should teach you to understand the world in a scientific and revolutionary way, and to know and love your country and all the peoples of the world.

Sixth – You have the right to an education so that when you are grown up you can fulfil your duty of serving the people. You have the right to be educated to respect work, to respect the people's property, and to participate in production.

Seventh –The kindergartens, where you learn and play with children of your age, and the schools, are mainly for you.

We will steadily increase their number so that they can have room for every child in the country.

Eighth – You have the right to protection of your health, to live in a healthy environment, to have a good diet, to be taught how to defend yourself against illness.

When you are ill you have the right to be treated with the best of medical care, and with tenderness and affection.

Ninth – You have the right not to be submitted to initiation rites, premature marriage or brideprice. They are against the principles of our Revolution.

You have the right not to be employed or engaged in activities that harm your health, your education, your physical development or your brain.

Tenth – You have the right to have the mistakes you make explained so that you understand and do not repeat them. You have the right not to be subjected to violence and ill treatment.

Eleventh – In dangerous situations, you have the right to be among the first to receive help and protection.

Twelfth – So that you can begin to take part in the Revolution, and so that you can learn to live in an organized way and get to know other children like yourselves, you have the right to take part in the Organization of Mozambican Pioneers.

Bibliography

Published Sources

Abu Nasr, J., et al, (1987) *Moral Judgement of Lebanese Children After the Lebanese War*. Beirut University College: Institute for Women's Studies.

Adams, C. T. and Winston, K. T., (1980) *Mothers at Work: Public Policies in the United States, Sweden and China*. New York: Longman.

Ali Baig, T., (1987) 'A Child's Right to be Human', *The Right to be Human*. New Delhi: India International Centre.

Ariès, P., (1973) *Centuries of Childhood: A Social History of Family Life*. New York: Alfred Knopf.

Bagnell, K., (1980) *The Little Immigrants*. Canada: Macmillan.

Banerjee, S., (1980) *Child Labour in Thailand*. London: Anti-Slavery Society.

Bankowski, Z. and Carballo, M., (eds), (1986) *Battered Children and Child Abuse*, Proceedings of the XIXth CIOMS Round Table Conference, Berne, Switzerland. Switzerland: CIOMS and WHO.

Barrig, M., (1982) *Convivir: La Pareja en la Pobreza*. Lima, Peru: Mosca Azul.

Baskar, J.P., (1985) *In Search of Refuge: A Brief Case Study of Sri Lanka Tamil Refugees*. Dindigul, India: Peace Trust.

Bledsoe, C. and Robey, K. M., (1986) 'Arabic Literacy and Secrecy Among the Mende of Sierra Leone', *MAN* (NS), No. 21, pp. 202–26.

Boudhiba, A., (1982) *Exploitation of Child Labour: Final Report of the Special Rapporteur of the UN Sub-Commission on Prevention of Discrimination and Protection of Minorities*. Geneva: United Nations.

Boyden, J. and Hudson, A., (1986) *Children: Rights and Responsibilities*. Minority Rights Group Report No. 69. London: Minority Rights Group.

Bray, I., (1987) *Chicualacuala: Life on the Front Line*, Oxford: Oxfam.

Brittain, V., (1979) *Testament of Youth*. UK: Fontana.

Brittain, V., (1988) 'Front Line State of Emergency', *The Guardian*, 4.3.88, London.

Brown, A., (1979) *Colour, Class and Politics in Jamaica*. New Brunswick, New Jersey: Transaction Books.

Brundenius, (1981) *Economic Growth, Basic Needs and Income Distribution in Revolutionary Cuba*. Sweden: Research Policy Institute, University of Lund.

Burger, J., (1987) *Report from the Frontier: The State of the World's Indigenous Peoples*. London: Zed Books.

Burra, N., (1986) 'Child Labour in India: Poverty, Exploitation and Vested Interest', *Social Action* Vol 36, July–September 1986, pp. 241–63.

Camus, A., (1955) *The Myth of Sisyphus*, trans. by J. O'Brien. London: Hamish Hamilton.

Clark, E., (1957) *My Mother who Fathered Me*. London: George Allen & Unwin.
Cliff, J. Kanji, N. and Muller, M., (1986) 'Mozambique Health Holding the Line', *Review of African Political Economy*. London.
Croll, E., (1978) *Feminism and Socialism in China*. London: Routledge & Kegan Paul.
—— (1983) *The Family Rice Bowl*. London: Zed Press.
—— (1987) 'Introduction: Fertility Norms and Family Size in China', in Croll, E. Davin, D. and Kane, P. (eds) *China's One-Child Family Policy*. London: Macmillan.
Curlin, G. T. Chen, L. C. and Hussein, S. B., (1976) 'Demographic crisis: the impact of the Bangladesh' in *Population Studies* No. 30, pp. 80–105.
Cutting, P., (1988) *Children of the Siege*. London: Pan Books.
Dickens, C., (1838) *Oliver Twist*. London: Odhams Press.
—— (1853) *Bleak House*. London: Odhams Press.
Dring, S., (1986–87) 'Images of Love and War', *Children First*. Issue 2, Winter 1986/87. London: UNICEF–UK.
Elson, D., (1982) 'The Differentiation of Children's Labour in the Capitalist Labour Market', *Development and Change* Vol. 13, No. 4, pp. 488–99.
Encuesta Nacional de Fecundidad Lima, Peru: (1979) Government of Peru, Oficina Nacional de Estadisticas y Censos.
Ennew, J. and Young, P., (1982) *Child Labour in Jamaica*. London: Quartermaine Press for the Anti-Slavery Society.
Ennew, J., 'Mujercita y Mamacita: Girls Growing Up in Lima', (1986) *Bulletin of Latin American Research* Vol. 5, No. 2, pp. 49–66.
—— *The Sexual Exploitation of Children*, (1986). Cambridge: Polity Press.
Espínola, B., Glauser, B., Ortiz, R-M., Ortiz de Carrizosa, S., (1987) *En La Calle: Menores trabajdores de la calle en Asunción. Un Libro para Acción*. Asunción, Paraguay: Published by the authors.
Figueroa, J., (1971) *Society, Schools and Progress in the West Indies*. Pergamon Press.
Fitzgibbon, L., (1982) *The Betrayal of the Somalis*. London: Rex Collings.
Fraser, M., (1974) *Children in Conflict*. London: Penguin.
Freire, P., (1972) *The Pedagogy of the Oppressed*. London: Penguin.
—— (1973) *Education: the Practice of Freedom*. London: Writers and Readers Cooperative.
Freud, A. and Buckingham, D., (1943) *Young Children in Wartime*. London: Allen & Unwin.
Fyfe, A., (1985) *All Work and No Play: Child Labour Today*. London: TUC.
George, S., (1988) *A Fate Worse than Debt*. London: Penguin.
Gorky, M., (1966) *My Childhood*. Harmondsworth: Penguin.
Greene, G., (1936) *Journey Without Maps*. London: Pan.
Gustafsson, L. H., (1987) 'The STOP sign — a model for intervention to assist children in war', in *Children in Emergencies*. Geneva, Switzerland: Rädda Barnen.
Gutierres Muniz, J. Camarós Fabián, J. Cobas Manriquez, J. and Hertenberg, R., (1984) 'The recent worldwide economic crisis and the welfare of children: the case of Cuba' in Jolly, R., and Andrea Cornia, G., (eds) The Impact of World Recession on Children, *World Development* Vol. 12, No. 3, Special Issue on Children.
Hammerman, S. and Tishman, F., (1983) 'Disabled Children: Third World within the Third World', *Development* 1. Rome, Italy.

Hanlon, J., (1984) *Mozambique: the revolution under fire*. London: Zed Books.

Harriman, E., (1984) 'Modern slavery', *New Statesman* 10.2.84.

Haughton, J., (1979) *A Commonsense Look at Education in Jamaica Today*. Kingston, Jamaica: NUDT.

Heins Potter, S., (1987) 'Birth planning in rural China: a cultural account', in Scheper-Hughes, N., (ed.) *Child Survival Today*. Dordrecht: D Reidel.

Henriques, F., (1953) *Family and Colour in Jamaica*. McGibbon & Kee.

Hong Kingston, M., (1977) *The Woman Warrior*. London: Picador.

Horowitz, M. J. & Solomon, G. H., (1975) 'A prediction of delayed stress response syndromes in Viet Nam veterans', *Journal of Social Issues*, Vol. 31, pp. 181–95.

Hoyles, M., (ed.) (1976) *Changing Childhood*. London: Writers and Readers Publishing Cooperative.

ICDS, (1984) *Integrated Child Development Services in India*, New Delhi: UNICEF.

Jaffrey, M., (1985) *A Taste of India*. London: Pavilion.

Jenkins, T., (1985) 'Front Runner', *The Guardian* 12.1.85.

Jupp, M., (1987) *Children Under Apartheid*, New York: Defence for Children International–USA.

Juyal, B. N., (1987) 'Child labour in the carpet industry', *Child Workers in Asia* Vol. 3 Nos. 2 & 3.

Laitlin, D. D., (1977) *Politics, Language and Thought: The Somali Experience*, Chicago: University of Chicago Press.

Laye, C., (1954) *The Dark Child: The Autobiography of an African Boy*, New York: Farrar, Straus & Giroux.

Lee, L., (1959) *Cider with Rosie*, Harmondsworth, Penguin.

Leiner, M., (1974 (1978)) *Children are the Revolution: Day Care in Cuba*, Harmondsworth: Penguin.

Lewis, I. M., (1980) *A Modern History of Somalia: Nation and State in the Horn of Africa* (Revised Edition), London: Longman.

Lewis, O., (1964) *Children of Sanchez*, Harmondsworth: Penguin.

McCallin, M., (1987) 'The spiritual and non-material needs of refugee children, towards a communal strategy', *Children Worldwide* Vol. 14, No. 2. Geneva: ICCB.

MacCormack, C. P., (1979) 'Sande: The public face of a secret society', in Jules-Rosette, B., (ed.) *The New Religions of Africa*. Norwood, New Jersey: Ablex.

——— (1982) 'Health, fertility and birth in Majamba District, Sierra Leone', in MacCormack, C. P. (ed.) *The Ethnography of Fertility and Birth*. London: Academic Press.

McLachlan, F., (1986) 'Children in Prison', in Reynolds, P., and Burman, S., (eds) *Growing Up in a Divided Society*. Johannesberg: Ravan Press, in association with the Centre for Cross-Cultural Research on Women, Queen Elizabeth House, Oxford.

Massey, D., (1987) *Nicaragua*. Open University Press.

Matthews, H. L., (1975) *Revolution in Cuba*, New York: Charles Scribner's Sons.

Maybury-Lewis, D., (1967) *Akwe-Shavante Society*. Oxford:

Mead, M., (1955) 'Theoretical Setting 1954', in Mead, M. and Wolfstein, M., (eds) *Childhood in Contemporary Culture*. Phoenix Books, University of Chicago Press.

Mendel, G., (1972) 'Introduction'. In *Rights and Responsibilities of Youth* compiled by the United Nations Educational Studies and Documents, Number 6. Paris: UNESCO, 1972.

Mendelievich, E., (ed.) (1979) *Children at Work*, Geneva: International Labour Office.

Meyer, P., (1983) *The Child and the State*. Cambridge: CUP.

Meza Cuarda, A., (1983) 'Problemática de la salud en el desarollo del niño', in La Semilla (ed.) *El Niño en el Perú: Presente y Futuro*. Lima, Peru: Centro de Estudios, Communicaciones y Promoción Social.

Miller, E., (1976) 'Education and society', *Savacou* No. 5, Kingston, Jamaica.

Ministry of Education (Jamaica), (1978) *Annual Report 1977-78*, Kingston, Jamaica:

Molyneux, M., (1985) 'Mobilization without emancipation? Women's interests, the State and revolution in Nicaragua', *Feminist Studies*, Vol. II, No. 2.

Moynihan, D. P., (1965) *The Negro Family: the Case for National Action*, USA: Office of Policy Planning and Research, US Department of Labor.

Naidu, U. S., and Kapadia, K. R., (eds), (1985) *Child Labour and Health: Problems and Prospects*, Bombay: Tata Institute of Social Sciences.

Namazi, M. B., (1986) 'Children as Zones of Peace', in *Children in Emergencies*, Geneva, Switzerland: Rädda Barnen.

National Planning Agency (Jamaica), (1978) *Five Year Development Plan 1978-82* (Main Document), Kingston, Jamaica:

Neustatter, A., (1987) 'Paying a high price for liberation', *Guardian* 22.12.87.

Nyrop, R. F., (ed.), (1983) *Brazil: A Country Study*, Washington, D.C.: The American University.

Pastore, J., (1982) *Inequality and Social Mobility in Brazil*, (trans. by R. M. Oxley). Madison: University of Wisconsin Press.

Perpignan, Sr. M-S., (1981) 'Prostitution tourism', in World Council of Churches *Women in a Changing World: Prostitution and Tourism* No. 11, December.

Phillips, A., (1973) *Adolescence in Jamaica*. Jamaica Publishing House.

Punamäki, R-J., (1982) 'Children in the shadow of war', *Current Research on Peace and Violence*, Vol. 1. Finland: Tampere Peace Research Unit.

Quan, J., (1987) *Mozambique: A Cry for Peace*, Oxford: Oxfam.

Race Relations Survey. South African Institute of Race Relations, Johannesburg, 1985 cited in Jupp 1987, p. 21.

Roden, C., (1968) *A Book of Middle Eastern Food*, Harmondsworth: Penguin.

Rosaldo, M. Z., (1980) *Knowledge and Passion: Ilongot Notions of Self and Social Life*, Cambridge: Cambridge University Press.

Rushdie, S., (1988) 'Midnight's Real Children', *The Guardian* 25.3.88, p. 25.

Sahlins, M., (1974) *Stone Age Economics*, London: Tavistock.

Salazar Bondy, S., (1973) *Lima La Horrible*. Lima, Peru: Biblioteca Peruana.

Searle, C., (1982) *Sunflower of Hope. Poems from the Mozambican Revolution*. London: Allison & Busby.

—— (1983) *Wheel Around the World*. London: Macdonald.

Shamma', A., (1987) 'Children in War: Implications for the Health Worker in the Eighties', in Bankowski, Z. and Carballo, M., (eds), *Battered Children and Child Abuse* Proceedings of the XIXth CIOMS Round Table Conference, Berne, Switzerland. Switzerland: CIOMS & WHO.

Sieghart, P., (1985) *The Lawful Rights of Mankind*, Oxford: Oxford University Press.

Smith, A., (1970) *The Wealth of Nations*, Harmondsworth: Penguin.

Stacey, J., (1983) *Patriarchy and Socialist Revolution in China*. University of California Press.

Suchlicki, J., (ed.), (1972) *Cuba, Castro and Revolution*, Coral Gables, Florida: University of Miami Press.

Thitsa, K., (1980) *Providence and Prostitution – Image and Reality for Women in Buddhist Thailand*, London: Change International.

Tomashevski, K., (1987) 'Family Reunification: Right, privilege or utopia?' *International Children's Rights Monitor*. Geneva, Switzerland: DCI.

Ungsongtham, P., (1980) *Development of Education and Welfare Programmes for Children in Klong Toey Slum, Bangkok, Thailand*, (2nd Edition). Bangkok, Thailand: Duang Prateep Foundation.

UNICEF, *The State of the World's Children 1984*, Oxford: OUP.

—— (1986) 'UNICEF at 40' *UNICEF News* Issue 123. New York: UNICEF.

—— (1986 (b)) *The State of the World's Children 1986*, Oxford: OUP.

—— (1987) *Children on the Front Line: The Impact of Apartheid, Destabilisation and Warfare on Children in Southern and South Africa*, New York and Geneva: UNICEF.

—— (1987) *Children on the Front Line*, Information Sheet No. 4. London: UNICEF–UK.

—— (1988) *The State of the World's Children 1988*, Oxford: OUP.

Wilson, G., (1976) 'The White Flame', *World's Children*, September.

World Bank, (1982) *Tribal peoples and economic development: human ecological considerations*, May 1982. Washington, D.C.:

Wyer, J., (1986) 'Child Labour in Brazilian Agriculture' *Critique of Anthropology* Vol. 6, No. 2.

Unpublished Sources

Barnes de Carlotto, E., Statement on behalf of the organization Grandmothers of the Plaza de Mayo, to a special meeting of Amnesty International, London, 27 November 1987.

Barundy, J., 'The therapeutic value of solidarity and hope', in ICCB Report of the Proceedings of a Planning Meeting to discuss the design of training programmes in mental health issues for non-professional staff in refugee camps, and intervention programmes for refugee children to alleviate the effects of the refugee experience, Refugee Studies Programme, Oxford, 1987.

Berry, J., 'Acculturation and mental health: theoretical and methodological issues' in ICCB Report of the Proceedings of a Planning Meeting to discuss the design of training programmes in mental health issues for non-professional staff in refugee camps, and intervention programmes for refugee children to alleviate the effects of the refugee experience, Refugee Studies Programme, Oxford, 1987.

Bindman, G., 'Preliminary report on South Africa' (International Commission of Jurists) in *The Review* No. 38, 1984, London. Background Document B7 for International Conference on Children, Repression and the Law in Apartheid South Africa, Harare, 24–27 September 1987.

Bledsoe, C., 'The Politics of Polygyny in Mende Education and Child Fosterage Transactions'. Unpublished paper, Northwestern University, 1987.

Bolton, C. and Bolton, R., 'El Trabajo de Niños en la Sociedad Andina'. Paper presented at Congreso de Investigación Acerca de la Mujer en la Región Andina, 7–10 June, 1982, Lima, Peru.

Boyden, J., Children in Development: Policy and Programming for Especially Disadvantaged Children in Lima, Peru. Report for UNICEF (New York) and OXFAM, 1986.

Burra, N., A Report on Child Labour in the Gem Polishing Industry of Jaipur, Rajasthan, India. Prepared for UNICEF, New Delhi, 1987.

Chikane, F., The Political Context of the War Against Children. Conference Statement C8, International Conference on Children, Repression and the Law in Apartheid South Africa, Harare, 24–27 September 1987.

CIIR, Xaafadda, Suuqa Iyo Jidka, 'A study of disadvantaged areas and groups in Muqdisho, Somalia'. Prepared by BOCD (Catholic Institute of International Relations) and the Municipality of Mugudisho, Mogadishu, Somalia, 1987.

Ennew, J., Young Hustlers: Work and Childhood in Jamaica. Unpublished Report for the Anti-Slavery Society, 1982.

—— *Juvenile Street Workers in Lima, Peru.* Report for the Overseas Development Administration, U.K., 1985.

—— Children as Commodities, Paper for Child Care and Development Group Seminar, University of Cambridge, 1986(a).

Fryers, T., 'Prevalence Studies of Severe Mental Retardation'. Paper presented to the Asian Conference on Mental Retardation, Bangalore, India, May 1981.

Gouveia, A. J., Youth Employment and Schooling in Brazil. Unpublished MSS, University of São Paulo, Dept. of Social Sciences, 1983.

Gough, H. and Pitman, J., 1987 Cambridge University Thailand Project, Streetwise International, Cambridge.

Inter American Parliamentary Group on Population and Development. *Bulletin* No. 2, 1984.

Jewkes, R., The Case for South Africa's Expulsion from International Psychiatry. United Nations Centre Against Apartheid, New York, 1984.

Langa, P., South African Security Laws versus the Child. Background Document B9 to International Conference on Children, Repression and the Law in Apartheid South Africa, Harare, 24–27 September 1987.

Lin Chong-De, 'Moral Development in a changing world: A Chinese perspective'. Paper presented to conference 'Growing into a Modern World', Trondheim, Norway, 1–13 June 1987.

Morrow, V., A look at the Hand-made Carpet Industry, with particular reference to India and Kashmir. Unpublished report for Streetwise International, Cambridge, UK 1987.

Nassar, C., Psychological Effects of the War on Lebanese Children of Various Social Groups. Unpublished PhD Thesis, Sorbonne, Paris, 1985.

Paul, A., Child Development in India. Paper presented to conference 'Growing into a Modern World', Trondheim, Norway, 10–13 June 1987.

Seeley, J., *Poverty in Lusaka. Preliminary Report.* Unpublished report for the Overseas Development Administration, UK, 1988.

Sgritta, G. B., Notes on some limits of conventional social research on childhood. Paper presented to conference 'Childhood as a Social Phenomenon: Implications for future social policy', Selbu, 13–17 June 1987.

Sgritta, G. B., and Saporitti, A., 1987 *Myth and Reality of The Discovery of Childhood: the Case of Official Statistics.* Unpublished Paper, University of Rome, La Sapinza, Department of Demography, 1 August 1989.

Sharma, A., Intervention in Child Development: An Indian Perspective. Text of paper presented to conference 'Growing into a Modern World', Norway, 10–13 June 1987. (Published abridged in Proceedings of Conference).

Tambo, O., Conference Statement C2. International Conference on Children, Repression and the Law in Apartheid South Africa, Harare, 24–27 September 1987.

Taçon, P., *My child Minus One*. Report for UNICEF South America. July 1981.

Thai NGO Consortium on Rural Development. Severe Droughts in the Northeast. Bangkok, Thailand, 1987.

Thompson, M., An investigation into the validity of predictions for high school success. MA Thesis, University of the West Indies, Kingston, Jamaica, 1969.

Vittachi, T., Text of address to commemorate the 40th Anniversary of the Founding of UNICEF, London, 10 December 1986.

UNICEF, Regional Programme for Latin America and the Caribbean: Ongoing Project Information, Brazil, Colombia, Mexico. UNICEF, Bogotá, Colombia, 1983–84.

—— Abandoned and Street Children: Summary of Regional Programme. UNICEF, Bogotá, Colombia, 1984–85.

—— *Children in Situations of Armed Conflict*. E/ICEF/1986/CRP.2, 10 March 1986. UNICEF Executive Board 1986 Session.

Yacoub, G., *Psychological Disturbances in Lebanese Children During and After the War*. Educational Council for Research and Development, Beirut, 1978.

Newspaper and Magazine Stories

Amnesty International Publications, London.

Central America, London.

Child Workers in Asia Newsletter, Bangkok, Thailand.

Children First!, London: UNICEF-UK.

Development, Journal of the Society for International Development, Rome, Italy.

Economic and Political Weekly, Bombay, India.

Guardian, London: Guardian Newspapers Ltd.

The Hindu, Bangalore, Karnataka.

Human Rights in Thailand Report, Bangkok, Thailand.

Independent, London: Newspaper Publishing plc.

Indian Express, Hyderabad.

Indian Express, New Delhi.

International Children's Rights Monitor, Geneva: DCI.

Observer Magazine, London: Observer Ltd.

Philippines Human Rights Update, Manila, Philippines.

Refugees, Geneva: UNHCR.

Sunday Mirror, London: Mirror Group.

Sunday Times, London: News Group Newspapers Ltd.

The Times of India, New Delhi.

Woman's Own, London: IPC Woman's Weeklies Group.

Advertising Brochures

Kuoni, *Worldwide* brochure, Leicester, UK, 1988.

Thomas Cook, *Thailand: Kingdom of Gold*, London, 1987–88.

Thomson, *Worldwide*, The Artisan Press, England, 1987–88.

Wings, *Faraway Holidays* brochure, Welwyn, England, 1987–88.

Index